More Praise for Ma

"Using process metaphysics as a theological framework, Monica Coleman offers a challenging constructive womanist theology. It is an important postmodern theological statement that speaks to religious pluralism and the realities of black women's lives."

—*James H. Cone, Union Theological Seminary, New York*

"This book is classic Monica Coleman—interdisciplinary, interreligious, professional and personal, cutting-edge and linked to traditions. She crafts a womanist theology interwoven with postmodern and process theologies, rooted in the Christian gospel, yet also drawing on Yoruba religion. And then we are graced with the way-out-of-no-way resulting in a vision for a communal theology."

—*Dwight N. Hopkins, University of Chicago Divinity School*

innovations
African American religious thought

Katie Geneva Cannon and Anthony B. Pinn, editors

Innovations publishes creative and innovative works in African American religious thought and experience. The series highlights creatively progressive projects in Womanist and Black theology and ethics. It also encourages interdisciplinary discourse that expands understanding of African American religion and religious experience as well as the manner in which African Americans have envisioned and articulated their religiosity.

Titles in the series—

Making a Way Out of No Way

A Womanist Theology

Monica A. Coleman

Fortress Press

Minneapolis

MAKING A WAY OUT OF NO WAY
A Womanist Theology

Cover art: *Dancing* by Elizabeth Catlett (2003). Lithograph, 23.5" x 31.5". © Elizabeth Catlett/Licensed by VAGA, New York, NY. Image courtesy of Sragow Gallery, NYC.
Cover design: Ivy Palmer Skrade
Book design: Jeremy Keller

Library of Congress Cataloging-in-Publication Data
Coleman, Monica A., 1974-
   Making a way out of no way : a womanist theology / Monica A.
      p. cm. — (Innovations : African American religious thought)
   Includes bibliographical references and index.
   ISBN 978-0-8006-6293-6 (alk. paper)
1. Womanist theology. I. Title.
   BT83.9.C65 2008
   230.082—dc22
                                        2008011151

Contents

Foreword

From early essays regarding the shortcomings of black theological discourse and work on the constructive task of presenting black women's thought and life as academic resource, womanist scholarship has grown over the years. The initial struggle to have the liberative nature of religious faith and the academic merit of black women's contributions to this transformative process has expanded and is now recognized for its tremendous importance through conferences, curricula, books, articles, and a growing number of womanists working across academic disciplines. We recognize that African American women are generating some of the most creative and vital study of African American religious thought and life; and we are delighted that this series contributes to the presentation of some of these scholars.

Monica A. Coleman is one of the new voices in womanist theology. Trained in process studies, but with a commitment to the intellectual significance of African American experience, Coleman has given attention to the development of a womanist postmodern theology that speaks to faith and social responsibility in complex and creative ways. *Making a Way Out of No Way* is her most substantive presentation of this theology. It weaves together a variety of theoretical and methodological tools, including those underutilized in black religious studies such as process thought. This book is both academic and personal, speaking to collective realities and interior concerns but in a way that is mindful of the nuances of individual encounters and perspectives. There is in *Making a Way Out of No Way* an impressive blending of general, insightful concerns with Coleman's personal narrative as well as serious stories and wise living of other women. In this regard this text articulates lessons culled from the work of a variety of womanists who push for a sensitive balance between the individual and the collective as a way of maintaining the integrity of personal identity as related to but not consumed by communal associations. Embedded in this book is an important question: How does one do womanist theology, and what does it mean to do this theology within the context of difference that marks the community and experiences of black women? This is not the first time Coleman has responded to this question, but this book certainly represents her most intellectually mature response. It fits well into the canon of womanist discourse, serving to further advance its creativity, challenge, and methodological/theoretical systems.

Coleman seeks to understand the dynamics of the postmodern world and the ways in which that world frames our sense of proper *thinking* and transformative *doing*. Taking seriously the call for wholeness drawn from the work of Alice Walker and the works that currently saturate the scholarship of womanist thinkers, Coleman's book promotes reading the religious significance of black women's lives in ways that do not flatten it out, narrow its scope, and limit its reach. Rather, she seeks to maintain the thick and at times tense nature of religious engagement within the African American community. In a word, Coleman troubles the assumption that womanist theology can be articulated only using a Christian vocabulary and grammar, arguing instead that sensitivity to religious pluralism marks the spiritual commitments in African American communities. As Coleman remarks, "In a postmodern womanist theology, I can find a language that has a rich past, resonates with spirit and memory, and evokes images particular to the experiences of black women." The book you have started to read is not only cognizant of the experiences of black women, but it is also shaped by and influenced deeply by those experiences—seeking to provide a reasonable and faith-based response to the turmoil of life.

We are pleased to have this volume in our series, and we are convinced that it marks a significant contribution to black religious studies in general and womanist scholarship in particular.

Katie Geneva Cannon
Anthony B. Pinn

Preface

"Theology is autobiography." This phrase is often invoked to illustrate that our constructive theological proposals are intensely personal. They are shaped by our personal histories, our past and current contexts, the specific issues that concern us. They are shaped by whom and what we have encountered—what we read, whom we know, those whom we engage in conversation. And yet, as I constantly remind my students at the Lutheran School of Theology at Chicago (LSTC), theology, while personal, cannot be private. It must be something that could apply to someone other than the theologian. It should be something you would recommend to others. It should be something you'd be willing to preach.

This book reflects my own faith and social commitments. When I wrestle with pain and suffering, I press God and faith communities for answers. When I experience undulating joy and friendship, I feel a deep connection with God and community. I want to ask how and why and "says who?" I'm a faithful black woman who wants to know how things work. Some kind of womanist and metaphysical work was almost inevitable for me.

I am a theologian because I believe that faith matters. I believe that what we believe about God, ourselves, and the world affects how we operate within the world. I believe theology should expand our world. This book is a womanist theology inasmuch as and because it is grounded in and tested by the religious experiences of black women. I am honored to join a conversation, hewn from tough academic rock, that asserts that black women's lives can be the center of theological activity. This book is also a constructive postmodern theology, a process theology, because I stand with religious scholars who are inspired by the philosophies of Alfred North Whitehead and Charles Hartshorne. We who embrace change, process, and becoming as the foundations of our understanding of God and the world have formed an international community impassioned by the power of this outlook.

This work also reflects my North American context. I am an educated woman of African American and Cherokee ancestry who lives in the United States. I've worked as a minister, professor, community organizer, women's advocate, freelance writer, grocery store cashier, and a couple of other things here and there. These experiences help inform this work. This book also reflects my personal taste in literature, music, and scholarship. In many ways, I've written about and used the sources I find authoritative in both my personal spirituality and my constructive theological activity. The constructive work here feels like braiding hair. I'm pulling together different strands of conversations, scholarship, stories, and experiences into a unity.

Thus, this book represents my attempt to answer some of my own questions and reflect on my own faith while also trying to hold together the experiences of many people and communities I've come to know and love. I want to honor my grandmother's tenacious black Baptist faith, which runs throughout every family gathering we have. I also want to celebrate my friends who feed candy to a concrete head with cowrie-shell eyes as part of their practice of *Ifa* or *Santería*. I want to respect the sleepless hours caused by unspeakable acts of violence and physical pain, without neglecting the exuberance felt when love is reciprocal, rhythm ignites our bodies, or everything seems to come together as we hoped and planned. I pray I have done justice to these communities and experiences.

The writing of this book has been a communal process influenced equally by those who contributed to my personal and professional development, those who encouraged me in the present, and those who believed in the direction of my research and career. I thank my parents, Pauline A. Bigby and the late Allen M. Coleman, who have always supported my education. I've written this in part so that my parents could understand what I do. While I am grieved that my father did not live to see this publication, I am inspired by the pride he took in me and my work. Thank you, Mama, for how you have fostered my critical inquiry and also inquire about what I do.

I am grateful to the following theologians for their impact on my desire to be a theologian: Sallie McFague, James H. Cone, Delores S. Williams, Marjorie Hewitt Suchocki, and David Ray Griffin. I am grateful to all the members of my dissertation committee who helped to lay the foundation for this project: Marjorie Suchocki, who gave me the rare opportunity to write about something in which I truly believe, Kathleen O'Brien Wicker, Ellen Ott Marshall, and Delores S. Williams. I am indebted to my colleague Kirsten A. S. Mebust. Her friendship and attention to every version of this manuscript—the thought processes and the written words—make her a true co-sojourner.

I also greatly appreciate my editor, Michael West, and Fortress Press for their belief in the success of this project. Carolyn Banks, David Lott and Lynette Johnson have been so good with all the important details. Thank you. I'm proud to be in a series edited by Anthony B. Pinn and Katie G. Cannon. Victor Anderson, Anthony Pinn, Dwight Hopkins, and Linda Thomas supported this project in its infancy, giving both detailed and personal support for my ideas. Karen Baker-Fletcher was available for countless conversations as I tried to find my place in the larger discourse. Carol P. Christ generously read several chapters and helped to sharpen, refine, and encourage my ideas. Henry Young and Theodore Walker Jr. are glorious companions in black process theological work. Nancy Howell at the St. Paul School of Theology teaches my work, and her students, especially Charity Godwin, have challenged me to give images of "what this looks like in real life."

I value the financial and personal support of Christine O'Brien at the Ford Foundation and the incomparable Sharon Watson Fluker at the Fund for Theological Education. Their belief in my scholarship holds me to a higher standard. I thank The Village and the *Ifa* community, and Sumayya Coleman and Ujima House, Inc., of Nashville, Tennessee, for bringing my academic learning into embodied living. I am also grateful to Kathi Martin for sharing her journey with GSN Ministries with me, that I might share it with others here. Thank you, David Smith, for your sharing as well. I am grateful to Connie L. Tuttle and Karen O'Kelley, who truly understand the need to have a "room of one's own" and offer one to me. I am appreciative of the Church School at Bethel AME Church in Ann Arbor, Michigan, for their questions and support, and for the reminder that church folk really do care about process theology. Special thanks to Jan Collins Eaglin and Ronald Brown for giving their perspective on chapter drafts. I especially appreciate the detailed and speedy work of my graduate assistant at LSTC, Robert C. Saler.

For emotional support during the years I worked on this, I thank Herbert Robinson Marbury, April Yvonne Garrett, Warren Chain, Jennie Kitch, Eyerusalem, Anthony, Nathan, and Ella.

To God be the glory.

Introduction

All simplifications of religious dogma are shipwrecked upon the rock of the problem of evil.—Alfred North Whitehead[1]

The wisdom and knowledge required to make decisions that promote survival, healing and liberation are dependent on the power of memory.—Karen Baker-Fletcher[2]

I dashed through the rain, holding a folder over my head, as my supervisor, the executive director of a small domestic violence program, fumbled with the key to the church. Together we led a weekly support group for women who were wrestling with the reality of violence inflicted against them and/or their children in their homes. No one else was using the church this evening, and we met in the small boardroom usually used for counting money after services on Sundays. Within minutes, the room filled with several other African American women, as well as one white woman, the mother of African American children. On this particular evening, a woman, let's call her Lisa, was the center of attention. I stood behind Lisa to her right, while my supervisor stood to Lisa's left. Together we were braiding down the patches of Lisa's hair so that we could fit her for a wig.

Earlier that day, Lisa's boyfriend had pulled her around the apartment by her hair, dragging her limp and battered body behind him. This left bald patches all over her scalp, as her hair had literally been ripped from her head in handfuls. Her body was sore with visible purplish brown bruises on her arms and legs and the invisible sting of carpet burns. This evening, Lisa only touched the sides of her scalp as she complained of the ache in her head.

She also feared that her children would be taken from her if they were exposed to any more violence. It was a legitimate fear. I had spent most of the afternoon talking with her social worker, who was also my good friend and colleague in church ministry. He reminded me that Lisa had chosen to stay with her boyfriend, and that this was not the first time, or even the second, that the children had witnessed this kind of violence. He talked about the eldest daughter, her pregnancy, the father she would not name (Lisa's boyfriend, he suspected), and the two younger children. His job, he repeated, was to protect the children. In our conversation, we didn't talk about how Lisa would keep the children. We talked about how I would explain the inevitable to her.

I didn't talk about Lisa's children that night. I held the right side of her head with the palm of my hand. Her entire body quivered, and this made the task of braiding all the more difficult. The other women in the group were quiet as they gently rubbed Lisa's shoulders or leg to assure her of their sympathetic presence: *Yeah, girl, we know.* Many of them did.

The executive director whispered to me, "This is why I started a program for black women. No other program in this city would know to braid Lisa's hair."

I smiled with my eyes and quickly nodded. Who else could understand that hair was not trivial for black women? We knew that Lisa would not feel strong enough or woman enough to go to work, confront her boyfriend, or be seen anywhere in public as long as her hair looked like this.

But Lisa was still crying as we were pulling tiny pieces of hair into small plaits, working around the bald spots.

In the midst of her sobbing, Lisa asked, "What did I do to deserve this? Why is God letting this happen to me? What am I supposed to do now?"

I thought about the things that I had heard in church, the things that had been said to me. "God let this happen for a reason." "All things work together for the good of those who are called according to God's purpose." "God never puts more on you than you can bear." These were all sentences and phrases that I had used to reassure myself in difficult times. These ideas had often brought me hope, purpose, and the energy to go on. But I couldn't say them. Even if I believed these words—and in that moment I wasn't sure if I did—to say them to her in this instant would be at best insensitive and at worst theologically abusive.

Lisa had experienced a radical, intimate, painful encounter with violence. And she had some questions about it. Lisa wasn't trying to shake the foundations of my theology, my director's theology, or that of the other women in the room. I don't know if Lisa cared that we were meeting in a church, or if she even knew that I was an ordained minister with plans to earn a doctorate in theology. But her question reminded me that we are all theologians—people who think about God. And theologian to theologian, she asked about the nature of evil, God's presence in the midst of evil, human participation in perpetuating evil, and human agency in the midst of evil. This is where she got stuck. This is where so many of us get stuck. Shipwrecked.

Lisa's particular shipwreck sent me into a discomforting silence. I needed something to say to Lisa. I needed a language that honored the context of her experience as an African American woman living in a southern city where black church religiosity was served up with a bowl of grits on Sunday morning. I had to honor the beautiful parts of her life—giggling at her toddling child's laughter after a small stumble; moving her hips to the rhythm that comes through the open window of a passing car; cooking her favorite meal for friends who are coming over to watch television together. I also had to recognize the difficult parts of her life—working a thirty-nine-hour-a-week job that left her tired enough to call it "work" but was one hour shy of health coverage; living in a housing project so unpredictable that taxi cabs refused to pick up or drop off after dark; and feeling emotionally dependent on a man who took her hair out by the fistful. I wanted to connect the specificity of her story with the ways that she inherited the complexities of living at the intersection of blackness, womanhood, and some category lower than "working class."

I needed something to say to Lisa. I needed a religious perspective that would not attribute her experience of violence to God, to a small man in red with a tail and pitchfork, or to a greater lesson that she would learn if she just kept "holding on." I wanted to find a way to tell Lisa that the violence was not her fault, but that she bore some responsibility for her current situation. I had to honor the fact that things were not "okay" for her and weren't going to be "okay" for a while. I needed a religious view that maintained hope for Lisa no matter how many times she left and went back and left and went back to her boyfriend. But I wanted to emphasize that Lisa's current reality was not her long-term fate; with support from my organization, the other women, our partners throughout the city and government, and a good dose of prayer, things could be different. I wanted to affirm that braiding patchwork hair was more than an act of compassion, that it might indeed be an act of salvation. I wanted to connect the specificity of her story with a worldview that acknowledges the reality of evil and loss and finds opportunities for life in each new moment without either waiting on God to make it happen or making Lisa do it all herself.

I needed a postmodern womanist theology.

Less than a week later, on the other side of town, other women approached life's challenges in a different setting. Walking across the stones and mud in the unpaved parking lot, I made my way to the nondescript front door of what was, by anyone's first glance, a dilapidated chemical factory with yellow paint chipping off the bricks. During the week, the studio and small store on the first floor are bustling with men, women, and children taking drum and dance lessons, but this Sunday morning, the halls were dark and empty. I opened the you-could-miss-it-if-you-weren't-looking-for-it concrete door in the northeast corner of the dance floor and walked up the steep staircase into the open space, well lit by sunlight streaming through the second-story windows. We were all wearing white clothing—jeans, tennis shoes, basic T-shirts, tank tops, long hand-sewn skirts, and skirts made from bolts of cotton wrapped and tied around the waist. Women with short hair wore small knitted caps, while others had their heads wrapped and covered in the same size cloth as the skirts.

The men and boys stood around the walls, while the women and girls walked clockwise in a circle to the beat of the drum played by one of the men. My friend from West African dance class, let's call her Maria, motioned for me to join in. As she approached the place where I was standing, she broke from the circle to tie a maroon sash around my waist. Donning Oya's color, we moved around in a circle, letting our bodies' natural rhythm and the training from class guide us to the beat of the drum. When the break came—*da da-da-da da da da da*—we turned the other way. One woman moved to the center of the circle. I knew her fairly well because she helped train me—she had been working in the domestic violence field for twenty years. She took the sash off of her waist and held it between her hands, moving it behind her back and above her head. She was, I assumed, doing Oya's dance.

The Sunday morning meetings were ritual worship for members of this Ifa community, but Maria invited me because the òrìṣà Oya was being honored.* Oya's winds are said to usher in a change in practice and consciousness. Whenever she appears, there is a call for growth and evolution. Maria had just moved to the city with her new husband and his son from a previous relationship, and she knew that I would soon leave my life in full-time ministry and nonprofit work in order to attend a doctoral program. "Oya," she told me, "helps us with change."

Around the circle were a recent divorcée, a college senior, another friend from dance class who had just announced her pregnancy, and several other women I knew only by face. Most of us were not members of the Ifa community, but our paths crossed through friendship, dance classes, or as parents or volunteers in the after-school program held in the same building. We smiled at each other between twists and turns.

Maria leaned in to me and said, "I don't know how this works, but it makes me feel whole."

I thought about what I knew about Ifa from my anthropology classes in college. I had studied the ways that the traditional religion of the Yoruba people in West Africa spread to the Western hemisphere through the triangular slave trade. In class, I had both read about and met priests from a religion that acknowledged a high God but devoted considerable energy to honoring the òrìṣà, who have genders, stories, and geographical and natural associations. Many Caribbean religions have relatively clear connections to Yoruba

---

* Oya is a divinity-spirit-ancestor of Yoruba-based religions

religion—Haiti's Vodun, Cuba's Santería, Brazil's Candomblé, and Trindad's Shango and Orisha worship. In the United States, many African Americans and a handful of European Americans practice what they refer to simply as "Yoruba" or "Ifa," as they intentionally reclaim and revive a traditional Yoruba religion they did not inherit from their parents or grandparents. This was the case for most of the members of this Ifa community. But no one in the circle needed a history lesson on black religion. We were too busy dancing and calling on the power of an ancestor spirit who could guide us to the next place in life.

Maria and the other women in the circle were going through changes that were part of the normal course of life. Maria wasn't suggesting that these transitions were extraordinary, nor that they were easy. She was honoring the fact that life changes were real, and honoring them in community somehow made a difference. Maria knew I was an ordained minister, but she wasn't trying to engage me in a long conversation about religion. Her statement—"I don't know how this works, but it makes me feel whole"—reminded me that, even when we don't understand it, most of us default to a functional theology—a theology that works for us at our most crucial moments. A functional theology cares little for systems and consistency; it's the rock-bottom faith we cling to at two o'clock in the morning when we can't sleep.[3] And black woman to black woman, she was talking about change, survival, and wholeness. This is what she really cared about on a daily basis. This is what concerns so many of us. Salvation.

Maria's approach to salvation left me without a response. I needed something to say to Maria. I needed something to say to myself. I needed a language that honored the commonalities of the women in the circle—single mothers, young women, college students, stay-at-home mothers, budding journalists and nonprofit community advocates. I had to honor the beautiful parts of our transitions—waking up next to the one face that will never grow old or ugly; rubbing a growing belly with a new little girl or boy within; buying a new wardrobe to go with the first full-time job. I also had to recognize the difficult parts of these transitions—going on the federal assistance she swore she would never use because she had been a stay-at-home mom for four years, but didn't have time to find a job because she refused to be hit again; trying to discipline a boy who kept repeating, "You're not my mother" every time he disobeyed; realizing that the new income would have to be split three ways for living expenses, school loans, and younger siblings back home. I wanted to connect the specificities of these stories with the ways we represented the diversity of black women's experiences across geographical origin, class, and status.

I needed something to explain this Sunday morning. I needed a religious perspective that would hold the truths of women who variously prayed at

Jummah on Fridays, preached on Sunday mornings, and danced in *egbe* on Saturdays. I wanted to find a way to talk about the one thing that some of us found in Jesus, others in submission to Allah, and still others in divination and òrìṣà worship. I had to honor that our transitions were exciting and scary at the same time, and that even the best new things involved some kind of loss. But I also wanted to emphasize that even in the most painful life changes, the past holds opportunities for something new. I needed a religious view that acknowledged the power of the cultural and personal past as instructive for living in the present and into the future. I needed a way to talk about how women who had seen tornadoes destroy their homes and businesses a few years earlier could still dance with a goddess who brought winds of change. I wanted to affirm that there was more than a release of personal tension and physical fitness in the dance, but that it might indeed be an act of salvation. I wanted to connect the specificities of this Sunday morning with a world-view that acknowledged the past as something that often holds both a strong destructive influence on the present and creative power for moving into the future.

I needed a postmodern womanist theology.

Womanist theology is a response to sexism in black theology and racism in feminist theology. When early black theologians spoke of "the black experience," they only included the experience of black men and boys. They did not address the unique oppression of black women. Feminist theologians, on the other hand, unwittingly spoke only of white women's experience, especially of middle- and upper-class white women. They did not include issues of race and economics in their critiques. Many womanists also feel that feminist theology operates in opposition to men and is anathema to the church. Womanist theologians want to maintain their connection to black men and remain faithful to the church traditions from which they come. The term *womanist* allows black women to affirm their identity as black while also owning a connection with feminism. Employing Alice Walker's definition of *womanist* in her 1983 collection of essays *In Search of Our Mother's Gardens*, womanist theology makes significant contributions to the fields of black and liberation theologies.[4]

Womanist theology examines the social construction of black womanhood in relation to the African American community and religious concepts. Womanist theological anthropologist Linda Thomas defines womanist theology as "critical reflection upon black women's place in the world that God has created; it takes seriously black women's experience as human beings who are made in the image of God; it affirms and critiques the positive and negative attributes of the church, the African American community, and the larger society."⁵ Womanist theology is known for its analysis of religion and society in light of the triple oppression of racism, sexism, and classism that characterizes the experience of many black women.

Womanist religious scholars want to unearth the hidden voices in history, scripture, and the experiences of contemporary marginalized African American women to discover fragments that can create a narrative for the present and future. Womanist theology uses a wide range of sources—traditional church doctrines, African American fiction and poetry, nineteenth-century black women leaders, poor and working-class black women in holiness churches, gospel music, spirituals, personal narratives, conjure, and syncretic black religiosity, and the experiences of black women in slavery. Womanist theologian Delores Williams writes that these traditions are "valuable resources for indicating and validating the kind of data upon which womanist theologians can reflect as they bring black women's social, religious, and cultural experience into the discourse of theology, ethics, biblical and religious studies."⁶ Ultimately, black women's experiences are the foundation for womanist theology.

Postmodernism recognizes that scientific and economic advancements have thoroughly changed the way that most people understand the world. Postmodernists agree that "modernity" is no longer the norm for human society, but rather contains errors that have destructive effects. The majority of postmodern thinkers portray modernity as either an economic worldview marking the shift from an agrarian society to the industrial age and the specialization of labor—a view easily associated with the rise of capitalism—or a scientific worldview that developed out of the mechanistic theories of Galileo, Descartes, Bacon, and Newton. With Einstein's theory of relativity and the development of quantum physics, postmodernists realized that previous scientific understandings were inaccurate and inadequate to describe what was now known about the world. The more socially conscious postmodern thinkers describe the disastrous effects of modernity and its accompanying dualism, determinism, and detachment as recognizable initially in World War I, and then in totalitarian states, Nazi genocide, World War II, and today's poverty, as well as ecological, sociological, and nuclear crises.

Postmodern theologians argue that these new perspectives change the way we think about God's role in the world. Postmodernism purports a decentralization of philosophical and theological power. Postmodern theologians realize that they cannot speak in one voice for all people, because within the discourse of modernity the "one voice" offering "universal statements" about humanity was privileged, usually white, wealthy, European or Euro-American, and male. Postmodernism has meant *openness* to meaning and authority from unexpected places—from science to the lived experiences of women and people of color.

Process theology offers a postmodern theology based on the philosophy of mathematician-philosopher Alfred North Whitehead. In process theology, everything that happens is a product of the past, what's presently possible, and what we do with those things. Whether you are a quark, an amoeba, or a person, you undergo this continual process of sorting through these three inputs: what you inherit from the world, what's possible in your context, and what you do about it. God is the one who offers the possibilities to the world, urging us to choose the paths that lead to a vision of the common good. While the principles of God's vision do not change, the way it gets played out on earth depends on what is happening in the world. God takes in, or incorporates, the events of the world into who God is. God then relates those events with God's vision for the common good, searching for the best of what has happened in order to offer those aspects back to us in our next instance of living. In short, our experiences in the world influence who we are and what we do. We then go on to influence those around us. What we do also affects God and how God relates to the world.

Womanist and process theologies are uncommon yet potent conversation partners. Discussions between process and black theologies have employed the language of compatibility, consistency, and assessment. Is a process God compatible with the God of black theology, who stands unequivocally on the side of the oppressed?[7] Can process theology effectively name and combat structural social evils, especially racism? Is the "limited power" of a process God consistent with the power exercised by the God of black theology?[8] Can black theology operate effectively without a philosophical or universal foundation? Process thinker Gene Reeves identifies points of confluence between process and black theologies.[9] Both process and black theologies express dissatisfaction with the world as it is, a desire for liberation and freedom, a privileging of empiricism, and a social/relational view of reality and the importance of God. In the broadest sense, they are both postmodern theologies that are grounded in the experiences of the world.

I believe that insights from womanist theology and process theology can give me an answer to Lisa's questions about the problem of evil and Maria's declarations about survival, healing, and salvation. In a postmodern womanist theology, I can find a language that has a rich past, resonates with spirit and memory, and evokes images particular to the experiences of black women. In a postmodern womanist theology, I can also find a view of the world that connects the pursuit of justice to a faith that does not negate the wealth of the past while living in a twenty-first-century world. A postmodern womanist theology can explain why salvation is found both among black women braiding hair in a church on a rainy night and black women dancing to a drumbeat in an old warehouse on a sunny Sunday morning. A postmodern womanist theology is able to talk about how we can make a way out of no way.

"Making a way out of no way" is a central theme in black women's struggles and God's assistance in helping them to overcome oppression. "Making a way out of no way" can serve as a summarizing concept for the ways that various womanist theologians describe God's liberation of black women. But today's context challenges a womanist theology to address the religious pluralism within the black community. In order to be relevant to contemporary society, a womanist theology needs to address this challenge within an explicitly postmodern framework.

Whitehead's understanding of evil and redemption reveals the characteristics of a relevant postmodern framework. In process theology, the world can use its freedom to diverge from God's calling and create evil in the world. Because of the interdependence of the world, evil is not an isolated event. When one of us chooses to operate in a way that is divergent from God's calling, it influences all of us. We often do this repeatedly within systems of power and influence and create greater problems—systemic evils. But evil is to be combated, and God is involved in this combat. Because of its acknowledgment of interdependence, process theology discusses ideas about God and evil that do not contradict everything else we know about the world.

But does this postmodern framework speak to the experiences of black women? Black religious scholars have critiqued process theology for its failure to focus on the experiences of the oppressed and the pursuit of social justice on earth. Indeed, womanist theology asks new questions of this postmodern framework: Does God's vision for the world include any understanding of justice? Is the philosophical language of process theology compatible with the kind of metaphorical language and emotional experiences that have served black women during their most difficult times? And can this framework account for the complexity of black religion—a synthesis of traditional African, indigenous, and Western religions? In order to serve black women, a postmodern framework needs to account for the pursuit of justice and the components of black religious experience.

One

Making a Way Out of No Way
Womanist Theologians on Salvation

I don't know how this works, but it makes me feel whole.—"Maria"

Womanist theologies maintains an unflinching commitment to reflect on the social, cultural, and religious experiences of black women. Womanist theologies are ultimately grounded in and accountable to the religious reality of black women's lives. As a form of liberation theology, womanist theologies aim for the freedom of oppressed peoples and creatures. More specifically, womanist theologies add the goals of survival, quality of life, and wholeness to black theology's goals of liberation and justice. Womanist theologians analyze the oppressive aspects of society that prevent black women from having the quality of life and wholeness that God desires for them and for all of creation.

Theological reflection on oppression and its defeat leads to a conversation about salvation. Oppressive forces are identified as death-dealing for creation and sinful from God's perspective. Efforts to overcome sin constitute various concepts of salvation. While religious concepts of salvation often focus on peace and eternal life in a realm beyond this world, black and womanist theologies maintain a focus on achieving life and liberation here in the land of the living. In this way, they are faithful to the root meaning of the word *salvation*, which literally means health and wholeness. A theological response to Maria's comment—"I don't know how it works, but it makes me feel whole"—will investigate reflections on salvation.

This chapter focuses on five womanist theologians who give sustained attention to the forces that impede black women from experiencing wholeness and quality of life. These same thinkers offer proposals for how these obstacles can be overcome and about God's role in achieving these goals within the lives of black women. Because these womanist theologians emerge from a Christian context, their reflections on salvation are connected to their understanding of Jesus in general and the relationship between black women and the figure of Jesus Christ in particular. Thus, this examination of womanist views on salvation will also involve some exploration of womanist understandings of Jesus Christ. From these womanist theological approaches to Jesus Christ and salvation, I will gather a womanist theology that describes black women's salvation in terms of a relationship with a God who "makes a way out of no way."

The concept of "making a way out of no way" articulates black women's relationships with God as they navigate the reality of their lives in the pursuit of wholeness and justice. No one womanist theologian directly points to "making a way out of no way" as a theory of salvation. Nevertheless, an examination of "making a way out of no way" reveals that this concept is a construction of salvation that brings together the different emphases of various womanists without denying their particularities. "Making a way out of no way" is a summarizing concept for black women's experiences of struggle and God's assistance in helping them to overcome oppression.

While "making a way out of no way" is a historic expression, it can still speak to the needs of today's society. Critics of black and womanist theologies assert that these theologies have failed to address the religious pluralism within the black community. Indeed, the realities of the late twentieth and early twenty-first centuries pose a couple of questions to womanist theology: How can we explain deliverance for non-Christian women of African descent? Do our understandings of God's interaction in the world change with what science and technology tell us about how the world works? In order to be relevant to contemporary society, a womanist theology needs to address these challenges within an explicitly postmodern framework.

Womanist Theologians on Salvation

Womanist theologians interpret the concept of salvation within the Christian tradition in light of the experiences of African American women.[1] Womanist theologians connect biblical witnesses of Jesus with the experiences of contemporary African American women to discuss God's transformative role in their lives. As womanist theologians discuss the particularity of black women's lives, they often focus on the suffering of black women and how it is overcome. Collectively, womanists understand salvation as a social activity of teaching and healing that leads toward survival, quality of life, and the holistic transformation of the world. Womanist concepts of Jesus Christ and salvation reveal the powerful images that comprise a postmodern womanist theology.

For womanist theologians, religious proposals must address the oppression and marginalization of African American women. Womanist constructions of salvation discuss the ways in which black women are liberated from various forms of historical and contemporary assaults against the full realization of their personhood. For this reason, womanist concepts of salvation begin with definitions of sin and descriptions of the suffering of black women. Womanists have articulated the experiences of black women in America differently, making their proposed solutions as various as the theologians themselves. Drawing from the lived religious experiences of African American women and the ways that black women have expressed their faith, womanist theologians bring both strong metaphorical language and particularity to the concept of soteriology, theories about how salvation works.

Jacquelyn Grant and Kelly Brown Douglas provide constructions of Jesus that emphasize Jesus' humanity and the ability to view Christ as a black woman. In their interpretations of Jesus, they suggest that salvation is social and this-worldly, but they do not provide overt doctrines of salvation. Delores S. Williams and JoAnne Marie Terrell give two very different reconstructions of the doctrine of salvation. Williams emphasizes the life and ministry of Jesus; she finds no redemptive meaning in the death of Christ. Her theology suggests that salvation comes from humanity's embrace of Jesus' activities of teaching, healing, and identifying with the marginalized. Terrell, on the other hand, discusses the sacrifice of Jesus on the cross to conclude that there is something sacred and powerful in the blood of both Jesus and black women. Lastly, Karen Baker-Fletcher expands upon the ideas of previous womanist theologies to include consideration of the natural world and the ancestral world in the attainment of healing and liberation.

Jacquelyn Grant

For Jacquelyn Grant, salvation must address the core problems of black women as they experience racism, sexism, and classism. Christian theological language sometimes reflects these forms of oppression. Grant never gives an explicit theory of salvation; it must be extrapolated from her writings on Jesus Christ. An investigation of Grant's writing reveals two components to her view of salvation. First, black women identify with Jesus as sufferer, embracer of the outcast and liberator. This identification is so strong that Grant describes Christ as a black woman. Second, black women can pattern their lives as disciples rather than as servants. Salvation, then, is black women's invitation to full participation in church and society.

Grant frames the discussion of black women's experiences by looking at the particular ways that black women have suffered throughout United States history. Grant's definition of the particular oppression faced by black women is derived from the work of the black feminists of the 1970s and 1980s. In the early years of the academic study of black women by black women, Frances Beale described the experiences of black women as being in "double jeopardy."[2] With this term, Beale attempted to express the context of black women's experiences as distinct from their black male and white female counterparts. Black women are negatively affected by both racism and sexism. Black feminist Theressa Hoover looked specifically at the treatment of black women in churches and concluded that black women experience "triple jeopardy"—racism, sexism, and classism.[3] Grant's review of black feminism concludes that black women consider three sources of oppression: "Black feminism grows out of Black women's tri-dimensional reality of race/sex/class. It holds that full human liberation cannot be achieved simply by the elimination of any one form of oppression."[4] This "tri-dimensional reality" becomes Grant's category of sin. It is not a sin that black women commit; rather, it is a sin of humanity, the sin committed against black women from which they must be saved.

One place to locate Grant's understanding of salvation is in her work on Jesus Christ. In *White Women's Christ, Black Women's Jesus*, Grant notes the ways that black women have understood and identified with Jesus. She argues that black women draw upon both the teachings of the Bible and God's direct revelation in their lives for their understandings of God. Black people identify with the story of the exodus, in which God delivers the Hebrews from Egyptian slavery. They understand God as a creator, sustainer, and liberator. The role of Jesus as divine co-sufferer is the most salient for Grant. "[Black women] identified with Jesus because they believed that Jesus identified with them."[5] Jesus was persecuted and forced to suffer. Likewise, black women have been persecuted and forced to suffer. During the period of American slavery, black women were systematically and legally raped, sold, and forced to watch their children being sold. Grant calls this a type of crucifixion. Black women identify with Jesus through the shared experiences of persecution and suffering.

Black women understand Jesus as one who cares about the least respected people in society. Jesus identified with the lowest in society during his own day. Examining the Synoptic Gospels of Matthew, Mark, and particularly Luke, Grant concludes that Jesus was one who welcomed the most despised of his own society; he associated with lepers, women, and tax collectors. Grant also looks at the testimonies of nineteenth-century black women—the abolitionist Sojourner Truth and Christian preacher Jarena Lee. Grant concludes that black women have understood Jesus' care for the marginalized as the same quality that welcomes and cares for past and contemporary black women. That is, Jesus is able to identify with black women because they constitute the lowest social group in contemporary society. Grant boldly states, "Christ among the least must also mean Christ in the community of black women."[6] Jesus' suffering and identification with the outcast are the touch points between Jesus and black women.

According to Grant, black women also understand Jesus as one who leads them to freedom. In particular, the resurrection of Jesus gives hope that there is liberation from oppression. Just as Jesus overcame his persecution and suffering in the resurrection from death, black women will also overcome their situations of oppression. Grant writes of the significance of the resurrection: "For as the Resurrection signified that there is more of life than the cross for Jesus Christ, for Black women it signifies that their tri-dimensional oppressive existence is not the end, but it merely represents the context in which a particular people struggle to experience hope and liberation."[7] Jesus is seen as a liberator.

Grant focuses on Jesus' humanity because black women identify with and are inspired by Jesus. Grant concludes that Jesus' maleness is not an issue, as some feminist theologians believe. Because Jesus is Savior, gender is irrelevant: "If Jesus Christ were a Savior of men then it is true the maleness of Christ would be paramount. But if Christ is Savior of all, then it is the humanity— the wholeness—of Christ which is significant."[8] Grant cares about Christ's humanity, his life and ministry, his suffering and his resurrection. The similarity of the experiences of both Jesus and black women means that Christ is not only found in the experiences of black women, but that Christ can be seen as a black woman.[9] Christ is a black woman.

Grant's understanding of salvation in a womanist context can also be derived from her critique of Christian theological language of servanthood and its feminist theological reconstruction. In her essay "The Sin of Servanthood and the Deliverance of Discipleship," Grant examines the Christian use of the term *servanthood* as a metaphor for the ideal relationship between God and humanity. She notes that both the Bible and generations of theologians have used the concept of servanthood as an appropriate description of Jesus to God and God's people, and therefore of the relationship between humanity and God, and amongst humanity. That is, Jesus has been understood as a servant of God, the fulfillment of the "suffering servant" described in the book of Isaiah, and humans, by proxy, should understand themselves as God's servants on earth. Grant finds the language of servanthood unhelpful and damaging in the context of black women's experiences in the world and in the church. Black women have often functioned as the servants of society—either unpaid in slavery or in menial jobs as domestic laborers after the end of slavery. Grant argues that the servanthood of black women is also servitude since it is accompanied by unjust financial compensation and a belief in the ontological inferiority of the servant. Not only are black women in service positions often underpaid for their work, but they are also understood as less equal, indeed less human, than those for whom they work. Thus, their servanthood is more properly called *servitude*. Grant writes, "As critical components to Christianity, the notions of 'service' and 'servanthood,' when viewed in light of human iniquities perpetrated against those who have been the 'real servants' of the society, represent contradictions."[10] Servant language, Grant argues, has not necessarily caused the structures of pain and suffering for oppressed peoples, but it has undergirded and supported it within a Christian religious context.

Grant acknowledges that the language of servanthood can have positive value in the African American community. Black women have been able to call themselves "servants of Christ" because it meant that black women were not the servants of whites. Grant notes that Martin Luther King Jr. discusses suffering as redemptive because true redemption "takes place when one experiences the redeemer even as it is in the context of oppression."[11] Black women have experienced redemption in this context and transformed the meaning of servanthood. Grant writes that "being a servant of the redeemer means joining in the struggle of the redeemer against oppression, wherever it is found."[12] Black women have embraced the language of servanthood and inverted it to rebel against their oppression.

Although black women have reinterpreted the language of servanthood, this interpretation is a survival strategy and cannot provide liberation. Grant understands servanthood as sin and rejects the language, because black women have been servants more than others, and servanthood, in this context, is sin. "The sin of servanthood is the sin of humanity that results from the sociopolitical interests of proponents of the status quo and their attempts to undergird their intended goal through psychological conditioning that comes partially with the institutionalization of oppressive language, even theological language."[13] Grant denounces the term *servanthood* completely: "For liberation to happen the psychological, political and social conditions must be created to nurture the processes. Servant language does not do this."[14] For this reason, Grant proposes a moratorium on the use of "servant language" among oppressed people and proposes the language of "discipleship" instead.

Discipleship language comes from both Jesus' inclusion of the outcast among his own disciples and the black church tradition of issuing a call for discipleship at the end of a worship service. At its best, discipleship is a call to be invited into power and participation in relationship to God and in the community of faith. The traditional model of discipleship focuses on Jesus as the leader of a select group of men. This model has supported the exclusive power of men within the black church. Yet Grant's model of discipleship is empowering because it allows black women to undermine traditional exclusive under-standings of discipleship that only include men and white people. The lan-guage of discipleship fulfills Grant's requirements of "challeng[ing] the servant mentality of oppressed peoples and the oppressive mentality of oppressors."[15]

Grant's theology of Jesus and her examination of servant language have implications for a womanist concept of salvation. Salvation is the deliverance of black women in this world. It is political, economic, and social freedom from the oppressive forces of racism, sexism, and classism. Salvation is about a positive transformation of the current society. Salvation is about improving the quality of black women's lives. For Grant, Jesus models salvation. Jesus models the ways in which a savior must identify with the oppressed and downtrodden of any particular context and not let oppression have the last word. Grant is also the first theologian to state that the savior can be seen as a black woman.

Grant's concept of discipleship can be seen as a way of achieving this sal-vation. Grant does not articulate this forthrightly, but she does see the lan-guage and model of discipleship as a way to combat the sin of servanthood. Understanding discipleship as salvation implies that salvation is an ongoing process. It is a model for life. To be a disciple, to be saved, one must follow the teachings and lessons of Jesus. Salvation is the way we relate to each other and to God. It is a sharing of power. Salvation is the insurrectionary and revo-lutionary process of challenging the status quo and demanding equality and inclusion.

Kelly Brown Douglas

Kelly Brown Douglas also investigates Jesus Christ in light of the experi-ences of black women. Like Grant, Douglas does not overtly discuss salvation. Douglas's theory of salvation lies in the lives of those who, imitating Christ, are working for the betterment of the community. Douglas defines sin as the multidimensional oppression of black women. This oppression is overcome in the struggle for black women's wholeness. From Douglas's writings, one can identify salvation in all those who strive for this wholeness.

In *The Black Christ*, Douglas identifies the sources of black women's oppression in terms similar to those used by Grant. She discusses historical understandings of the Black Christ—the religious and political assertion that the historical Jesus was a black man. Yet Douglas states that racism is not the only challenge for theologians to consider; they must also consider sexism, classism, and heterosexism. Douglas is particularly adamant about the need to examine issues of heterosexism: "[Womanist scholars] must make clear that homophobia in any form is unacceptable, and that heterosexism must be eradicated as it is a part of the same interlocking system of race, gender, and class oppression."[16] Black women's experiences of multidimensional oppression are overcome through the pursuit and achievement of wholeness.

The goal of Douglas's theology is a vision of wholeness for black women and the black community. Douglas derives this goal from part of Alice Walker's definition of womanist: one who is "committed to the survival and wholeness of an entire people."[17] Being committed to wholeness means that womanist theology addresses heterosexism both outside and inside the black community. This goal of wholeness is also achieved as womanists explore the connection between African American women and other women in the two-thirds world, and address the individual needs of black women. While Douglas wants to keep the focus of her womanist theology on the wholeness of the community, she is sure to balance this with concern for individual black women: "This [sociopolitical] analysis urges Black people, especially Black women, to confront the ways in which societal oppression has left them less than whole human beings—spiritually, emotionally, psychologically and so forth."[18] On individual and sociopolitical levels, the goal of wholeness is crucial for Douglas.

Douglas's model of achieving wholeness is informed by the life and ministry of Jesus. She focuses on the actions of Jesus: "[A womanist understanding of Jesus] starts in history with Jesus' ministry as that is recorded in the Gospels. What Jesus did becomes the basis for what it means for him to be Christ. This makes Christ more accessible to ordinary Christians."[19] Highlighting Jesus' inclusion of the least respected in society, Douglas sees Jesus as the Savior who can be seen working for the wholeness of his community. Douglas's Jesus is not just the sustainer and liberator of black theology. Jesus is also a prophet "challenging the black community to rid itself of anything that divides it against itself and to renounce any way in which it oppresses others."[20] Ultimately, Douglas affirms the blackness of Christ. Douglas's Christ is phenotypically black, as argued in the historical concept of "the Black Christ."[21] Yet Douglas is less concerned with the physical blackness of Christ: "Essentially, Christ's biological characteristics have little significance to discerning Christ's sustaining, liberating and prophetic presence."[22] Douglas's emphasis is on finding Christ in the struggle for wholeness.

Douglas's interpretation of Jesus' significance for black women, while similar to Grant's, differs in its understanding of the problem and its solution. Douglas expands Grant's tri-dimensional analysis of black women's oppression to a multidimensional analysis that is both sociopolitical and religiocultural. Douglas also understands the blackness of Christ differently than Grant. Although Christ can be seen in the faces of the poorest black women,

Douglas's Christology does not center on the experience of oppression, but rather on the struggle against oppression. When Douglas identifies the Black Christ, she states that Christ is "found where Black people, men as well as women, are struggling to bring the entire Black community to wholeness."[23] Working for wholeness is the standard by which Douglas evaluates Christ. "Christ is a Black woman whenever Black women act to establish life and wholeness for the Black community."[24] Unfortunately, Douglas does not provide an image of her vision of wholeness. The reader is left to assume that wholeness is the opposite of the racist, sexist, classist, and heterosexist activities she decries.

Douglas's interpretation of the Black Christ also suggests a womanist construction of salvation. Douglas is forthright in acknowledging that womanist theology must aim for the wholeness of the black community. Black people need to be saved to social, political, cultural, and religious well-being. Salvation is not just the goal of that wholeness, but is found in *the struggle to attain* that wholeness. Douglas connects her perspectives on Christ with salvation by asserting that salvation comes from imitating Christ: "For Blacks, it is precisely by imitating Christ that we bring salvation to our community."[25] Blacks must not only identify with Jesus, but they must imitate Jesus' prophetic role of challenging even an oppressed community to rid itself of its own forms of oppression. Thus, Douglas's focus on the life and ministry of Jesus indicates that the way of salvation comes from doing as Jesus did. To be saved, one must imitate the Savior; one must be willing to challenge oppression wherever it is found. Salvation is about achieving wholeness, and it is found in the continual actions of those who are working for that wholeness.

Delores S. Williams

Delores S. Williams believes that salvation must address black women's experiences of suffering and evil. There are two key elements in Williams's doctrine of sin and salvation. First, both sin and salvation are social. Second, sins are committed against the very personhood of black women, particularly against black women's bodies. Salvation, then, must deny any sacrifice or suffering in the body and be located in a vision of right relationship between black women and their bodies, black men, white women, and the world at large.

In the essay "A Womanist Perspective on Sin," Williams constructs a womanist doctrine of social sin from the ideas about sin found in spiritual songs, the autobiographies of ex-slaves, and the autobiographies of nineteenth-century African American women. From these sources, she concludes that the black community describes its experience of sin as being troubled or burdened. While the black community demonstrates a notion of individual sin in particular wrongdoings, there is a much larger idea of sin as social. Social sin occurs when one group commits wrongdoing against another group. According to spiritual songs and the testimonies of ex-slaves, "white" is not devalued, nor is it synonymous with evil. Sin is found in the negative behavior and unhealthy structure of relationships between blacks and whites: "Rather, certain patterns of human relations that yield cruelty and enslavements are thought to be evil and sinful."[26] Sin is social because it involves the evil and suffering inflicted upon groups of people by other groups of people. Sin is found in the behaviors of groups of people and in the systems that perpetuate this behavior.[27]

Williams's doctrine of sin also involves individual participation. The writings of nineteenth-century black women reveal an identification of sin and their own "unworthiness." Williams links this sense of unworthiness to the elevation of white womanhood, the consequent devaluation of black womanhood, and to the fact that the exploitation of black women's bodies (through lynching, overwork, and rape) was ignored by the American legal system. Therefore, Williams concludes that the devaluation of black women's sense of self is also sinful. For this type of sin, Williams charges society at large, the African American community, and even black heterosexual women who devalue the full humanity of black lesbians. So, sin is also participatory: "Individual sin has to do with participating in society's systems that devalue Black women's womanhood (humanity) through a process of invisibilization—that is, invisibilizing the womanist character of Black women's experience and emphasizing the stereotypical images of Black women that prevail and are perpetuated in the larger society."[28] The devaluation of the body, sexuality, humanity, and self-esteem are the womanist sins that can be seen as social and individual through participation.

Williams addresses sin with a concept of salvation that is both social and participatory. She hints at the need for salvation to address the needs of black women at micro and macro levels. Salvation needs to address the individual needs of black women, "thus elevating and healing Black women's self-esteem figures into womanist notions of what constitutes salvation for the oppressed African-American community."[29] Yet Williams also asserts that salvation is concerned with more than the individual acts of sin. Salvation occurs in the process of addressing sin. Referring to African American spiritual songs, Williams writes, "[S]laves seem more concerned about a process of moving toward positive transformation and destination than with identifying individual acts as sinful."[30] This is the first place where Williams suggests that salvation, like sin, is not found in one act, but in the process of alleviating collective behaviors that are sinful.

Williams's assertion that salvation addresses the social nature of sin means that salvation also alleviates sins and evils in the temporal world. In her essay

"Straight Talk, Plain Talk," Williams insists that salvation is this-worldly, and that churches should work for the social salvation of the black community. Williams has no need for salvation that focuses on heaven or any place outside of this world: "I contend that the need for social salvation then and now presents a necessary and serious challenge to all black Christians. It prods them to leave heaven and 'otherworldly' pursuits to the business and judgment of God. There is only the material world in which to work out a place of salvation for Black people and the Black community."[31] She believes that many young black people have given up on the promise of heaven and life after death. Salvation, therefore, is not about making it to heaven or defeating death. Salvation is about surviving, finding meaning and quality of life.[32]

Williams suggests three "in-house strategies" that black churches can use to effect this social salvation. Black churches should renew the memory of black heroes and heroines whose actions show how racism has historically oppressed black people. Williams cites Malcolm X and Angela Davis as two such examples. Second, churches should develop community consciousness and actions that assist black people in getting beyond oppressive systems. This strategy might entail starting educational institutions and making social, political, religious, and economic alliances with non-black groups and organizations that support black advancement. Lastly, black churches should encourage constructive critical thinking and planning. She concludes that if the church does not participate in the work of bringing social salvation to the suffering and violated ones, it has no mission. When black churches support the "quest for salvation on earth," they also support the historical beliefs of the black community and the theologies of black male and womanist theologians. Salvation is social, this-worldly, and, with the active participation of black churches, institutional.

Williams's second discussion of sin focuses on the devaluation of black women's bodies. Unlike Grant and Douglas, Williams does not define black women's experiences of sin as the multidimensional oppression of racism, sexism, and classism. In "Black Women's Surrogacy Experience and the Christian Notion of Redemption," Williams argues that an interlocking system of classism, racism, and sexism is not the exclusive experience of black women. "Jewish, Hispanic, Asian and other women of color in America can also experience this reality."[33] Williams seeks to particularize the experience of African American women in their historical and contemporary roles as surrogates.

Williams identifies two kinds of surrogacy—coerced and voluntary surrogacy. During slavery, black women's surrogacy was coerced. White men and women forced black women to provide labor and children. Whites exploited the biological functions of black women in order to generate a steady supply of slaves for the developing capitalist economy, gratify sexual desires, and supply wet-nurse services for suckling white babies. Black women not only managed white people's homes, cooking, cleaning, and caring for their children, but they also labored in the fields. Their labor substituted for that of white women, white men, and black men. Black women's labor in the postbellum period constitutes voluntary surrogacy. Black women were relegated to subservient positions; moreover, many black women continue to be circumscribed to these social roles and constitute a class of servants to white people.[34] As more and more black men are criminalized and incarcerated, black women are taking on the roles of mother and father to their children. Black women have taken on the roles of white men, white women, and black men. Their roles as surrogates are still perpetuated.

Although black women are not the only group to suffer and experience violence toward their bodies, black women experience this in particular forms. Theologian A. Elaine Crawford affirms Williams's discussion of black women as historical and contemporary surrogates:

> To be sure, suffering is a part of the human condition and all peoples have experienced suffering. Abuse and violence pervade the lives of women of every ethnicity. Yet, African American women have had a legacy of abuse and violence perpetrated against their bodies that has been justified through sexualized stereotypes and mythologies that denied the presence of God in them. It denied that they were created in the image of God.[35]

Crawford explicitly connects the unique context of the physical abuse of black women in America with interpretations of their relationship to God. Whereas Crawford feels that this abuse stands in direct opposition to the concept of *imago Dei*, Williams likens the abuse of black women with traditional concepts about salvation through Jesus Christ.

Williams matches the theme of black women's surrogacy with views of the atonement that cite Jesus' death as a vicarious sacrifice for the sake of sinful humanity.[36] If Jesus died for humanity, he was the ultimate sacrifice and should not be emulated by black women:

> In this sense Jesus represents the ultimate surrogate figure standing in the place of someone else: sinful humankind. Surrogacy, attached to this divine personage, thus takes on an aura of the sacred. It is therefore altogether fitting and proper for black women to ask whether the image of a surrogate-God has salvific power for black women, or whether this image of redemption supports and reinforces the exploitation that has accompanied their experience with surrogacy. If black women

accept this image of redemption, can they not also passively accept the exploitation surrogacy brings?[37]

Williams's womanist doctrine of salvation will not affirm any idea of Jesus as a substitution of the sins of humanity: "There is nothing divine in the blood of the cross."[38] In spite of her rejection of the cross, Williams understands Jesus as crucial to a theory of salvation. She states: "The fish and loaves, the candles we are to light, that our light will so shine before people so that we can remember that this message that Jesus brought, I think, is about life, and it's about the only two commandments that Jesus gave; they were about love."[39] Williams believes that Jesus' life constitutes a vision that is salvific.

Williams focuses on the vision offered in the ministry of Jesus as represented in the Synoptic Gospels. She focuses on the way Jesus models "right relationships." She describes Jesus in this way:

> Jesus showed humanity a vision of righting relations between body, mind and spirit through an ethical ministry of words (such as the beatitudes, the parables, the moral directions and reprimands); through a healing ministry of touch and being touched (for example, healing the leper through touch; being touched by the woman with an issue of blood); through a militant ministry of expelling evil forces (such as exorcising the demoniacs, whipping the moneychangers out of the temple); through a ministry of prayer (he often withdrew from the crowd to pray); through a ministry of compassion and love.[40]

Jesus saves because of what he does. Jesus teaches, heals, condemns evil, prays, and loves. Williams believes that God is acting through Jesus to invite humans to participate in this ministerial vision. Salvation comes from this *vision* we see in the life of Jesus. Williams states this directly: "Redemption had to do with God, through Jesus, giving humankind new vision to see resources of positive, abundant, relational life—a vision humankind did not have before."[41] This is a vision for black women.

The ministerial vision of Jesus is a vision, not only for liberation, but for survival and quality of life. In *Sisters in the Wilderness*, Williams uses the Abraham-Sarah-Hagar stories from the book of Genesis to assert that the God of womanist theology is not just a God of liberation, but also a God who is interested in the survival and quality of life of black women. In this biblical narrative, God promises a child to Sarah and Abraham when Sarah is beyond child-bearing age. Sarah gives Abraham permission to impregnate her Egyptian maidservant, Hagar. Hagar soon becomes pregnant but experiences mistreatment from Sarah as her pregnancy continues. Hagar decides to leave the home of Abraham and Sarah, but after finding herself helpless in the desert wilderness, she quickly returns. She eventually gives birth to Ishmael and leaves (through the desert wilderness again), with her son carrying provisions from Abraham and Sarah.

Williams notes that when Hagar first leaves Abraham and Sarah, God sends Hagar back to their home. Hagar is not liberated from her place of oppression, but she is given an opportunity to survive and have quality of life—things that are possible in the home of her oppressors and not in the desert wilderness. Survival and quality of life are now guiding principles for womanist theology. Williams writes, "On the basis of the reconstruction and redemption in this book, an ethical principle emerges as a guide in identifying what is to be revalued. The ethical principle yielded is 'survival and a positive quality of life for black women and their families in the presence and care of God.'"[42] Williams connects her understanding of Jesus' ministry and the Hagar story into a theory of salvation in which God gives individuals the vision to see the resources that promote their survival, quality of life, and right relations with the self, the world, and God. Black women's history reveals that this salvation is often obtained through resistance and survival strategies.

Williams's womanist perspective on salvation focuses on the idea of vision. Jesus' life demonstrates a ministerial vision of teaching, condemning evil, praying, and loving. This vision allows both individuals and groups of people to see the resources that God makes available for salvation. For Williams, salvation is the combination of vision and action that rejects all suffering and leads toward survival and quality of life.

JoAnne Marie Terrell

JoAnne Terrell understands salvation by focusing on the saving power of the cross of Jesus Christ. In *Power in the Blood?* Terrell agrees with Williams that God does not condone the violence of the cross, black women's surrogacy, or the present state of affairs. She also agrees that Christians need to look at the life-affirming images in the ministry of Jesus. Terrell maintains the feminist and womanist critique of *sacrifice* defined as permitting injury or disadvantage to someone or something for the sake of someone or something else. Like Delores Williams, Terrell criticizes any salvation found through surrogacy. Nevertheless, Terrell critiques Williams for ignoring the biblical evidence that God did indeed send Jesus in part for the purpose of dying. Terrell strives to understand how the cross has remained such a strong and important metaphor in African Americans' theories of salvation, and how, through the experiences of black women, an understanding of the cross can be life-giving and redemptive.

Terrell focuses on the oppression that black people experience at the hands of the government. Like other black male and female theologians, Terrell agrees that there are strong similarities between Jesus and African Americans in their experiences of betrayal, imprisonment, suffering, and torture. Yet she also points out commonalities between African Americans and the martyrs of the early church, since they both struggled to comprehend their oppression within the theological framework of the Christian story: "[T]he Christian and the slave community emerged in an ethos of repression, subjugation, idolatry and death imposed by their state apparatus."[43]

As a result of their oppression and adoption of the Christian story, early Christians and African American slave communities operate with two understandings of the cross—a hermeneutic of sacrifice and a sacramental witness. The hermeneutic of sacrifice interprets Jesus' death on the cross to mean that personal sacrifice imitates Christ and demonstrates Christian character. The way of sacrifice understands the sufferer as one who mediates the presence of God to those who witness their pains.

Terrell acknowledges the negative consequences of adopting the hermeneutic of sacrifice as an interpretation of the cross. The Christian understanding of sacrifice as necessary for salvation has inflicted and continues to inflict violence against groups and individuals around the world. It has led many blacks to "leave white authority unchallenged, or constrained them to veil whatever challenge they did or could pose."[44] More specifically, this interpretation of sacrifice contributes to the justified abuse and suffering of women in situations of domestic and sexual violence. Terrell is quick to denounce this interpretation: "I simply want to indicate the endemicity of violence in the world we know and to point out that this sense of sacrifice—*permitting injury or disadvantage to someone or something for the sake of someone or something else*— does *not* have divine sanction and is precisely a betrayal of Yahweh's insistence on righting relations."[45] For Terrell, this sacrifice can only begin to have validity if the sufferer has agency in the decision to suffer.

Terrell argues that the cross is redeemed through an understanding of the cross as sacramental witness. Sufferers can understand their suffering at the hands of the state as an act, in part chosen by the sufferer, which will highlight the strength of the sufferer's convictions and inspire future generations to fight against injustice. Terrell gives several examples, including the lives of early Christian martyrs, Sojourner Truth, and Martin Luther King Jr. Terrell asserts that the cross can be understood as a symbol of God's presence with the sufferer. The cross is seen as divine assistance to the sufferer to gain victory over suffering: "The empty cross is a symbol of God's continuous empowerment."[46]

Terrell's emphasis on the cross pays particular attention to the language of Jesus' blood as one of the vehicles through which humanity is restored to right relationship with God. She begins by evaluating the Hebrew tradition of offering the blood of animals as a vehicle for reconciliation between God and God's people. Referencing the tradition of animal sacrifice among the Israelites, Terrell concludes that the shedding of blood indicates "the seriousness of [the Israelites'] intent to live in right relations with God and neighbor."[47] God's acceptance of the sacrifice implies that God does not simply require blood; rather, God reveres blood. Thus, the Christian idea that Jesus' death and blood sacrifice is offered "once and for all for the sins of the world" asserts that Jesus' blood-loss has eternal efficacy. That God, in Christ, sheds God's own blood signifies that there is something of God in the blood of the cross. It does not affirm the hermeneutics of sacrifice. On the contrary, it means that God loves humanity and can be seen in the blood of those who are suffering. Ultimately, Terrell develops a subjective theory of the atonement when she asserts that Christ's example can teach and save humanity.[48] "I believe that anyone's death has salvific significance if we learn continuously from the life that preceded it."[49] A sacramental witness is defined by the individual's convictions, not victimization.

Terrell believes that the African American community has particular cause to find significance in Christ's blood and blood loss on the cross. Terrell explores the stories of black women and men from slavery and the times of lynching, along with the contemporary blood-related issues of AIDS and black-on-black violence. Terrell also discusses the blood shed by black women murdered by their intimate partners. She believes that their lives, like the example of Jesus on the cross, can be a sacramental witness to the African American community:

> My mother's ultimate sacrifice [of death by the hands of a loved one] and those of countless other black women, who suffer abuse and die at the hands of patriarchal, violence-driven persons, whose deaths go unreported and under-reported, unprosecuted and under-prosecuted—are potentially liberating for women if they learn from their experiences, if we see how they exercised or did not exercise their moral and creative agency. This seems a much more relevant view of the atoning worth of women's blood.[50]

If a sacramental witness is applied to the cross and some of the violence contributed against black women, then black women's blood is not only sacred, but also contains the power of salvation.

Terrell finds salvation in the sacramental witness of Jesus on the cross. Despite the violence of Jesus' suffering on the cross, Terrell affirms that there is something divine in the blood shed in suffering. When we see God's presence in the sufferer and learn from the violence, we can be saved. Salvation comes from the lessons learned after instances of suffering. The very life force, the blood, of sufferers is part of the sacred means of pointing us toward salvation.

Karen Baker-Fletcher

Karen Baker-Fletcher's concept of salvation affirms the proposals of Grant, Douglas, and Terrell, while expounding upon their ideas and extending their views to include the natural world in her understanding of sin and salvation. Baker-Fletcher argues that environmental racism should be added to the list of unique oppressions. She also believes that the ministry and the person of Jesus Christ reveal salvation. She describes Jesus as an ancestor and emphasizes the importance of incorporating one's cultural and religious ancestors into the concept of salvation. Baker-Fletcher's emphasis on honoring Jesus, the cultural and religious past, and the earth leads to a holistic womanist understanding of salvation as a transformation of the human and natural world.

Although Baker-Fletcher does not elevate environmental racism as a sin that is more grievous than the sins that occur among humans, she understands the sins against the earth as critical offenses. In *My Sister, My Brother*, Baker-Fletcher names the oppression of the earth as the result of interlocking systems: "Our present context is not only one of xenophobia that creates isms against one group or another daily, but also one in which we risk losing the planet we depend on for daily physical bread because of abusive habits, negligence, the greed of an economic industrial elite, and the militaristic angst of nuclear-weapon-holding nations and terrorists."[51] Because humans depend on the earth for life, threats against the earth are connected to all other forms of intra-human oppression.

Baker-Fletcher acknowledges that all people must contend with the failing health of the created world, but argues black women experience the abuse of the land in particularized manners: "What makes Black women's oppression distinctive is that such evils are—*always*—combined with the evils of sexism *and* racism. Classism, environmental racism and heterosexism for Black women, then, take on a particularly *thick* character."[52] She notes that this "thick character" is evident in black women's lives—disproportionately living in poor urban and rural areas where hazardous waste, incinerators, and industry are placed. "[Black women] are more likely to work in polluted, unhealthy work environments."[53] Baker-Fletcher connects the abuse of the land, "mother earth," to the abuse of black women's bodies.[54] Both black women's bodies and the land have been exploited and raped for the economic gain of their oppressors.

Baker-Fletcher insists that we see the activity of God in the natural world. She describes the positive ways that God acts in nature: "God acts in nature in numerous ways—in the hurricane and in the morning dew, in ways that are awe-inspiring and in ways that are simple, refreshing, comforting."[55] Baker-Fletcher does not just focus on the aesthetic moments of nature. She also considers the times when humanity experiences nature as destructive: "Is God in the hurricane, the tornado, the earthquake? Or is that just nature living its own life, doing what it must to exist, to live, to express the fullness of its life-force? Is God in nature or not? Perhaps God is in nature, but nature is not God. Nature reveals God, because God is present in all that lives, in all that is."[56] Baker-Fletcher knows that God incarnates nature and that the forces of nature cannot be divorced from our understanding of the divine. The destructive effects of nature on humanity occur because humanity lives on shared land and sometimes interferes with nature's system of survival. Other times, humanity experiences (God in) nature as destructive because nature "has its own movement independent of [human] desires."[57] As Baker-Fletcher focuses on the need to save the earth, she also acknowledges that humanity experiences nature as both creative and destructive.

Baker-Fletcher interprets salvation as the transformation of the world. Baker-Fletcher combines Grant's and Douglas's emphasis on salvation as liberation and Williams's emphasis on the telos of survival and quality of life, and includes the natural world. "The task for a womanist theology of survival, liberation and wholeness is to address the brokenness of all of creation in a wholistic manner, ministering to body, mind, spirit, and the material world."[58] Lifting up the African American spiritual based on Psalm 27, Baker-Fletcher describes God as "strength of life." God as strength of life sustains self and the universe. God "provides light for envisioning survival and liberating resources, strength to carry out visions, and salvation through the transformation of life as it is to life as it should be."[59] God grants individuals the vision to see their available resources and use them to work for healing, wholeness, and sustenance. While God provides the vision, salvation also depends upon the freedom of humanity to work for the transformation of society. Baker-Fletcher writes that God can empower humanity: "[R]egardless of the presence of evil in human existence, believers are transformed by the empowering strength of God so that they no longer live in fear."[60] Salvation includes the personal hope given to people, and people are then equipped to effect salvation in the world.

As a Christian womanist theologian, Baker-Fletcher ties Jesus to her ideas about salvation. She believes that it is Jesus who empowers black women with the vision for resistance and survival resources. Like other womanists, Baker-Fletcher names the acts of Jesus' life and ministry as salvific: "[L]aying on hands to heal, sharing food and wine, empathizing with the woman with the issue of blood, loving widows and orphans, forgiving women condemned by society, passing on wisdom as a teacher, listening to Mary and Martha, weeping over and healing Lazarus, conquering death and evil in his historical life and beyond."[61] Baker-Fletcher summarizes the acts of Jesus' life, and the symbolism of his death and resurrection, as the power to heal, sustain, and liberate.

Yet Baker-Fletcher does not exclude the significance of Jesus' suffering, death, and resurrection in her Christology. The cross, or tree, is a symbol of life and death for Jesus and contemporary society. Jesus was crucified on a tree; blacks have been lynched on trees. Yet the life of Jesus, like the lives of so many African American freedom fighters, is sacred and gives hope for future generations to struggle for justice. As Jesus is abused and redeemed on a tree, so the natural world (trees, etc.) is abused and can be redeemed. The cross is also a symbol of the risk involved in working for salvation. "Jesus' ministry of resistance against evil and his empowerment of others involved the real risks of political persecution, character assassination, and even death. The cross must not be forgotten because such persecution is a possible consequence of standing up for what is morally right."[62] The resurrection, on the other hand, represents God's ability to constantly create anew.

Baker-Fletcher insists that a womanist Christology includes consideration of the natural world. She initially insists that Jesus and creation are struggling toward a liberating relationship. She takes this point further by comparing the sustaining qualities of the earth with the sustaining quality of Jesus' ministry: "Without the life-sustaining warmth of the sun, the quenching power of rain, the oxygen the air provides, there would be no hope for the physical sustenance of the bodies that enflesh our spirits. The entire cosmos, then, is engaged in God's activity of providing resources for survival and wholeness."[63] She concludes that we see Jesus not only in the faces of black women, but in the face of the earth, waters, wind, and sun. As humans, then, we must consider the earth as neighbor and extend the golden rule to the created world.

Baker-Fletcher considers the constitution of Jesus in her ecological emphasis. Baker-Fletcher's understanding of Jesus as fully human and fully divine translates into a naming of Jesus as fully dust and fully spirit.[64] That is, Jesus is a full incarnation of God in human form, while also identifying with the earth. Baker-Fletcher describes Jesus as *feeling* with the earth. She cites Jesus' interaction with water, wind, and trees as an example of this. "Jesus [is] one who is in harmony with all aspects of nature."[65] Because the earth is so often disregarded by humanity, Jesus' regard for creation is an extension of his care for "the least of these."

Baker-Fletcher also depicts Jesus as an ancestor. Drawing upon Pan-African theologians and African traditional religious understandings of ancestors, Baker-Fletcher describes Jesus as part of a community of ancestors who have lived, died, and continue to be remembered in the lives of the present. Jesus is, however, the greatest ancestor: "Spiritually and historically, Jesus is a member of an entire community of wise ancestors—similar to saints in the Christian tradition. What makes Jesus distinctive is his perfect wisdom and embodiment of God, who is Spirit."[66] Jesus lives on in the memory of the community, and there is an everyday consciousness of Jesus in the human and earthly community. As Baker-Fletcher describes Jesus as an ancestor, she directly relates this idea to ancestors in traditional African religions: "Moreover Jesus is like African ancestors in his power over death. Death fails to erase the power of his life."[67]

Baker-Fletcher wants to highlight the ways in which death cannot erase the power of anyone's life. She discusses the ways that African traditional religions focus on the role of the ancestors. "According to certain African cosmologies, the ancestors, which contemporary African Americans too often disremember, live on through 'children, relatives, *rituals of remembrance*, and significant deeds.'"[68] She believes that we must remember all of our ancestors— Jesus and "those ancestors whose names no one remembers."[69] According to Baker-Fletcher, ancestors have a memory of the past that is greater than that of the living. Referring to Toni Morrison's fictional character Beloved, Baker-Fletcher writes, "Beloved's memory holds knowledge of the experiences of the ancestors, extending to the slave ships of the Middle Passage. She has a memory of African mothers who died during the trans-Atlantic slave trade. Beloved represents not only the ghost of Sethe's [the main character's] dead daughter but also ancestors from Sethe's slave and African history."[70] Beloved has more extensive knowledge than the present generation, and she tells her memories to other characters in the novel. The implication is that this information is important for the survival of these characters. With this interpretation, Baker-Fletcher suggests that the remembering of the ancestors helps the present to incorporate its past into its current becoming.

This remembrance of the past is an important part of Baker-Fletcher's concept of salvation. The memory of Jesus, cultural heritage (especially the Native American and African cultural past of African Americans), and history are critical to effecting salvation. Baker-Fletcher writes about it in this way: "The wisdom and knowledge required to make decisions that promote survival, healing and liberation are dependent on the power of *memory*. The creative power to make meaning out of the past is necessary to give a sense of direction for present and future generations."[71] As Baker-Fletcher encourages black women to remember the past, she emphasizes the remembrance of the African and Native cultural pasts. *Rememory*, she states, involves "insurrection of subjugated knowledges about the history and ancestry of Africans in the Diaspora."[72]

Baker-Fletcher believes that black women, in particular, need to reconnect with their suppressed memories of their African history, the totality of their cultural heritage, and the techniques they have used to survive thus far in order to move fully into the future. While memory must be complete, only the aspects of the past that assist in the task of salvation should be recreated. Remembering the destructive aspects of the past allows people to avoid repeating them: "The purpose of memory is to build strengths and correct weaknesses in community relations in order to more effectively challenge sociopolitical and economic injustice."[73] Through memory, the past contributes to the present work of salvation.

There are distinct ethical implications in Baker-Fletcher's doctrine of salvation. Understanding the problem, empowered by God, and using the appropriate resources, she urges all people to challenge the status quo and assist in the work of salvation: "We are required to discern the truth of our participation in systemic societal injustice, to name systemic societal injustice, and to challenge the powers that be to transform dehumanizing, necrophilic (death-loving) socioeconomic practices into systems that value the worth of all humanity and creation."[74] The work of salvation includes being a good steward of the earth and helping to transform the earth with the rest of society. These goals are not attained in one instance, but in everyday ordinary acts: salvation has to do with the "daily moment by moment business of living."[75]

For Baker-Fletcher, salvation is a holistic way of living. Using Jesus as an example, Baker-Fletcher identifies saving activity as the work of healing, sustaining, and liberating. Human salvation, however, cannot be exclusive of salvation for the created world. Salvation comes from transforming this world and allowing the best of the past—the nameless ancestors, the ancestors who are known, and Jesus, the greatest ancestor—to inform the present and future ways of living.

Summary of Womanist Views of Salvation

From the work of the aforementioned womanist theologians, one can make some conclusions about womanist concepts of salvation. Womanist theologians who discuss salvation address the suffering and desperate situations of black women. The offenses against black women are variously identified as the tridimensional oppression of racism, classism, and sexism, as well as multidimensional oppression that includes heterosexism, environmental racism, domestic violence, and surrogacy. These offenses are part of the particular experiences of black women in U.S. history. God cares about the lives of black women and helps them to deal with and overcome these circumstances.

For womanist theologians, salvation flows from their understandings of Jesus Christ. Black women identify with the experiences of Jesus. Black women see similarities between their suffering and Jesus' suffering. Black women believe Jesus cares for them as marginalized individuals, because Jesus had a ministry to the outcasts of his society. Black women believe that Jesus' resurrection gives hope for their own liberation from oppression. Salvation comes by embracing the vision that Jesus provides throughout his life. With differing emphases on the life or death of Jesus, these womanist theologians assert that Jesus changed the world and that salvation occurs when people work for the transformation of the world by imitating Christ. For womanist theologians, salvation is always social.

These womanist theologies understand that salvation is not always liberation or freedom from all pain and suffering. Salvation is not a divine imposition or gift to creation. Salvation is also survival and quality of life, and it requires the cooperation of the world in which we live. While God offers salvific resources, humanity must take advantage of these resources to effect salvation. Womanist perspectives on salvation draw from black women's past cultural experiences and the creative ways by which they have survived and incorporated their experiences to make it this far. In vastly different ways, Terrell and Baker-Fletcher suggest that salvation involves learning from the lives of those who have died. This allows individuals to move past determinism and learn from the experiences of the past to create something good.

Most important, womanist discussions of salvation bring strong metaphorical language to a constructive womanist theology. Womanist theologians discuss salvation in concrete images: survival, quality of life, and discipleship. Womanist theologians use the ministry of Jesus to provide action verbs to the process of salvation: teaching, healing, praying, welcoming, suffering-with. In this way, they give pictures of what salvation looks like and how it is achieved. They expand understandings of salvation such that we can see salvation in black women, poor people, those marginalized because of their sexual orientations, and even blood and other natural elements. Womanist theologians use familiar and indigenous expressions of black women and black religion to add particularity and power to their analysis of what it is that makes us whole.

Making a Way Out of No Way

The concept of "making a way out of no way" best describes the ways that womanist theologians articulate salvation. Delores Williams best describes this concept as a theme to which many womanists feel connected. In *Sisters in the Wilderness*, Williams states that black people in general, and black women in particular, express their relationship with God as the one who "makes a way out of no way." She writes: "Many times, as a little girl, I sat in the church pew with my mother or grandmother and heard the black believers, mostly women, testify about 'how far they had come by faith.' They expressed their belief that God was involved in their history, that God helped them make a way out of no way."[76] It is a central theme in black women's experiences of struggle and of God's assistance in helping them to overcome struggle.

"Making a way out of no way" is more than Williams's naming of the relationship between black women and God.[77] Karen Baker-Fletcher acknowledges this:

> [Survival as a creative quality] has been metaphorically referred to as the power of "making a way out of nothing" in the work of [womanist ethicist] Katie Cannon and "making a way out of no way" in the work of Delores Williams. In [my first book] *A Singing Something,* I refer to this particular quality of God and Black women in my grandmother's words as "making do." All three metaphors refer to what Williams calls an ethic of survival and quality of life among Black women. The activity of the God who enables them with vision for such survival traditionally has been described as God's *sustaining activity*.[78]

"Making a way out of no way" is an expression that acknowledges God's presence in providing options that do not appear to exist in the experiences of the past. It is a weaving of the past, future, and possibilities offered by God; a weaving that leads to survival, quality of life, and liberating activity on the part of black women.

"Making a way out of no way" acknowledges both the role of God and of human agency as new ways break forth into the future. There are four characteristics of "making a way out of no way": (1) God's presentation of unforeseen possibilities; (2) human agency; (3) the goal of justice, survival, and quality of life; and (4) a challenge to the existing order.[79]

Taken literally, "making a way out of no way" suggests that a path forward appears out of nowhere, out of nothing. We should not understand it this way. Instead, "making a way out of no way" means that the way forward was not contained in the past alone, the only way that was known. A way forward, a way toward life, comes from another source. It comes from unforeseen possibilities. These possibilities come from God. Using the example of Hagar, Williams writes, "God opened Hagar's eyes and she saw a well of water that she had not seen before. In the context of the survival struggle of poor African-American women this translates into God providing Hagar (read also African-American women) with *new vision* to see survival resources where she saw none before."[80] God is the one who presents the way. A way is made more properly out of God than out of nowhere. Womanist ethicist Emilie M. Townes also acknowledges the grasping of possibilities as a part of womanist spirituality in general: "Living out womanist spirituality means integrating faith and life. . . .We are called to a new and renewed awareness of our humanness and our infinite possibilities. . . . God makes demands on us to live into our faith in a radical way. . . . out of the possibilities we have before us and not out of our well-acknowledged and believed shortcomings."[81] God's offering of possibilities is felt as a call into the future.

Williams is careful to note that the possibilities offered by God are not always *felt* as good. As mentioned earlier, Williams concludes that God is not liberating Hagar, but God is ensuring Hagar's survival. God has knowledge of a wider context than Hagar could have and offers this to Hagar. Although returning to the place of her oppression is not what Hagar wants, it is the best option for her in her given context. For Hagar, salvation can look like a safe place with food and shelter for the delivery of a baby. Baker-Fletcher describes salvation as a group of teenagers in Los Angeles who grow their own food in a community garden and sell it at a local farmers' market.[82] Survival is often inadequate in terms of full liberation, but it is one of the ways in which God saves.

God does not force possibilities onto Hagar, or any human, when "making a way out of no way." There is always human agency involved. "God gave [Hagar] new vision to see survival resources where she had seen none before. Liberation in the Hagar stories is not given by God; it finds its source in human initiative."[83] Williams is so careful to emphasize the role of human freedom that she speaks about "making a way" as something that the human being does *with God's help*. This is why she uses the stories of Hagar: "The Hagar stories are those which suggest that an *ex-slave* mother could, with God's help, be in complete charge of furnishing her son with survival strategies. There are no other stories like this in the Bible."[84] "Making a way out of no way" is, therefore, a combination of God's presentation of possibilities and human decision.

"Making a way out of no way" includes an ethical goal of justice. Womanist theologians have long understood justice as part of God's vision for the world and the goal of salvation. By looking specifically at the experiences of black women in America, they discuss the ways in which the vision of God is manifest in a particular situation. The goal of justice is a logical component of a constructive womanist theology because of the ways in which the problematic is described. The sufferings of black women are a result of the unjust social, legal, political, and economic systems that give greater value and preference to the ideals of wealth, whiteness, maleness, heterosexuality, and anthropocentrism. Grant writes about this in terms of humanity: "In general, womanist principles accent the move toward full humanity for all. To this end, the eradication of all forms of oppression is primary."[85] Townes specifically references the need for justice: "God's love moves out to grow in compassion, understanding, and acceptance of one another. It helps begin the formation of a divine-human community based on love that is pointed toward justice."[86] Seeking justice challenges the societal structures we currently experience. Justice for the African American community will necessitate an eradication of the existing structures that oppress people on the basis of racism, sexism, classism, heterosexism, and ecological injustice.

"Making a way out of no way" challenges the wider society and our own personal comfort. As in the case of Hagar, it moves us into the wilderness. While the wilderness is a difficult place to be, Williams asserts that it is a meeting place for God and humanity. There, God teaches and guides humans into a sense of identity and strength in order to continue the struggle.[87] Womanist theologian Renee Hill pushes all black theologians (womanists included) to question where we currently are and what we currently believe. A norm of love and justice will necessarily lead to this questioning: "It is this love and justice that ultimately disrupts all that we take for granted, whether theological reflection or our understanding of who and what we are. It is this love and justice that disrupts cycles of oppression and calls us to new and powerful ways to live in all of the intersections of our lives."[88] "Making a way out of no way" is sometimes experienced as release and joy; other times it is experienced as resources in the midst of oppression without release. Either way, it disrupts the past from continuing on as it would without the possibilities offered by God.

"Making a way out of no way" is the way of life that appears in situations that threaten death. Williams reminds readers that African American women have not been passive "in the face of the threat of destruction and death."[89] Again, the story of Hagar is illustrative: "One of the constituent ideas in the Hagar-in-the-wilderness symbolism is Hagar's, black women's and black people's encounter with the threat—and often actuality—of death-dealing circumstances. Alone in the wilderness, pregnant on one occasion and alone with her son in the wilderness on the other occasion, Hagar and child surely would have died had not God intervened."[90] When black women rebel against death-dealing situations and God offers possibilities that were previously unforeseen, a way is made out of no way.

Womanist views on salvation can be articulated in the expression, "making a way out of no way." It is an expression that acknowledges God's role in providing possibilities that are not apparent in the experiences of the past alone. It weaves the past, future, and possibilities offered by God into decisions that lead to survival, quality of life, and liberation for black women. This concept acknowledges both the influence of God and of human agency as black women live into their futures. "Making a way out of no way" expresses black women's experiences of struggle and of God's assistance in helping them to overcome tribulations. This womanist concept of salvation involves God's presentation of unforeseen possibilities, human agency, the goals of justice, survival, and quality of life, and a challenge to the existing social order.

Postmodern Challenges

"Making a way out of no way" must be able to speak to the realities of today's world. Religious pluralism is one of the biggest challenges that contemporary society poses to any theological construction. While a plurality of religious faiths and experiences is not new, postmodernism reflects openness to the validity of multiple religious perspectives. The reality of religious pluralism is particularly important for black religions in the United States because it represents the ways in which the slaves and their descendents interacted with African traditional religions and other religious traditions. In order to speak to today's realities, a womanist theology cannot require a belief in Jesus Christ for salvation, and it must uphold a religious framework that can discuss the relationship between God and the world for more than one single religious tradition. All the while, this womanist theology cannot contradict the ways we interact with science, technology, and economics in today's world.

African Traditional Religions

The aforementioned womanist concepts of salvation are intertwined with each theologian's understanding of Jesus Christ. Jacquelyn Grant and Kelly Brown Douglas affirm that for black women, the historical Jesus is primary.[91]

Jesus' lowly birth, ministry to the poor and outcast, wrongful death and resurrection, and struggle against injustice allow black women to identify with Jesus, and Jesus with black women. This co-suffering and identification are so strong that Jesus can be seen as a black woman. Delores Williams concludes that redemption depends on black women's participation in the ministerial vision of Jesus. Joanne Terrell focuses on the saving power of Jesus' blood on the cross, and Karen Baker-Fletcher identifies Jesus as the greatest ancestor. As they emphasize Jesus' life or death as salvific for black women, these womanist understandings of Jesus do not make any specific reference to the divine-human constitution of Jesus.[92] Without such references, it is impossible to ascertain how these womanist theologians understand the uniqueness of Jesus Christ within Christianity and among non-Christian religions.

Womanist reflections about Jesus focus on images of Jesus, but womanist theologians are broad and conflated in their language about God. Although Grant focuses on the humanity of Jesus, she still knows that black women understand Jesus as God.[93] Christology and theology are nearly identical. She writes, "In the experiences of black people, Jesus was 'all things.'"[94] Jesus is described as mother, father, sister, and brother. Williams says it in this way: "Black women's stories . . . attest to Black women's belief in Jesus/Christ/God involved in their daily affairs and supporting them. Jesus is their mother, their father, their sister and their brother. Jesus is whoever Jesus has to be to function in a supportive way in the struggle."[95] These womanist theologians use the term "Jesus" to refer to all acts they consider divine. Baker-Fletcher notes the same trend in the religious language of black women: "Among many Black Christian women, there is a tendency to conflate God (Creator), Jesus, and Holy Spirit during the ordinary, everyday eloquent prayers in homes, churches and gatherings."[96] A. Elaine Crawford describes this trend as a high Christology: "Womanists employ a very 'high' Christology. It is high, not in the typical western perspective meaning to emphasize his divinity, but high in the African American sense, indicating that Jesus has an integral place, a real consuming presence that empowers the life of the believer."[97] While echoing the centrality of Jesus for some black Christian women, womanist theologians discussing salvation have made no substantive distinctions between Jesus, Christ, and God, and affirm a close but unspecified relationship between Jesus and God.

The same critique must be addressed to the expression of "making a way out of no way." The model of "making a way out of no way" necessarily involves God. But what about Jesus? The aforementioned womanist theologians generally describe both "Jesus" and "God" as the divine agent in "making a way out of no way." They make no distinction between Jesus and God when it comes to the source of the divine activity in "making a way out of no way." Williams writes that it is Jesus who performs the role of "making a way out of no way": "African American Christians have, for generations, believed in salvation through Jesus Christ. Referring to God and Jesus interchangeably, they have understood the gospel (or good news) to be Jesus' power to deliver the oppressed, Jesus' power to provide healing sustenance and to guide humankind toward a positive quality of life."[98] Williams does not carefully identify whether or not it is Jesus or God who helps to "make a way out of no way."[99]

While Crawford's redefinition of a "high Christology" seems to reflect what other womanist theologians note about the language and experiences of ordinary black Christian women, it limits the scope of a womanist concept of salvation to Christian religious experiences in general, and high Christological perspectives in particular. For womanist theologians writing in a Christian context, the necessary connection between Jesus and salvation is comprehensible. In their failure to address the constitution, uniqueness, and divinity of Jesus, however, they do not answer critical questions about Christian belief and identity. Is Jesus a unique and one-time incarnation of God? Or is Jesus one of many of the historical and cultural ways that we experience God among humanity? Is Jesus part of a Trinity that existed before the foundation of the world? Or is Jesus reflective of a divine presence we cannot understand outside of his historically situated birth in ancient Palestine? Affirmative answers to all of these questions can be found in the spectrum of Christian beliefs. Current womanist theologies on Jesus Christ and salvation do not reflect these Christian theological (and often denominational) differences. Most importantly, in tying the pursuit of justice, wholeness, health, and quality of life to Jesus, these womanist theologies reflect what womanist ethicist Melanie L. Harris laments as "the elevated and exclusive status Christianity holds within womanist theology."[100]

Indeed, womanist theologies are still growing in their ability to engage non-Christian religious traditions.[101] Womanist Muslim religious scholar Debra Mubashir Majeed notes the Christian character of womanist religious scholarship: "Arguably, most African Americans self-identify as Christians. Their allegiance supports the 'natural tendency' in black America and the academy to *speak* of African American religion and *mean* Christianity."[102] A postmodern womanist theology must begin to embrace the religious diversity of black women's religious experiences. Reflecting on the twenty-year history of womanist religious scholarship, Harris calls for such diversity in womanist theologies: "Beyond its comfortable settings of Christian categories and perspectives, womanist theology is now at a point whereby its voice must speak for the liberation and religious expression of black women in a variety of religious traditions."[103] While black women practice widely identified world religions such as Christianity, Judaism, Islam, and Buddhism, discussions of black religiosity demand openness to religious plurality.

Black religion is a syncretic movement that includes the influence of European Christianity and its adaptation by slaves and nineteenth- and twentieth-century believers. Black religion includes significant influences from indigenous religions, particularly African traditional religions. In his religious history of African Americans, Gayraud Wilmore writes, "ATR [African traditional religions] were found in some form, however attenuated, in the slave community and were absorbed to some degree into black Christianity."[104] Although womanist theologians desire to represent the uniqueness of black religion in an American context, a concept of salvation based primarily on Christianity limits their ability to account for the non-Christian dimensions of black religions.

As womanist theologians study the religious experiences of black women, they acknowledge the multiple cultural and religious influences that constitute African American religion. In the crucible of slavery, African Americans blended their African religious sensibilities with the Christianity introduced to them by their captors. As a result, African American Christianity reflects both the tenets and practices of Western Christianity and African traditional religions. Yet, as Maulana Karenga adds, African Americans currently participate in a variety of African-based religious traditions:

> The religion of Black people in the United States is predominantly Judeo-Christian, but Islam, both Black and orthodox, and ancient African religious and ethical traditions, are growing among African Americans. Among these other varied traditions are the Black Hebrew tradition, the Rastafarian tradition, and the Yoruba tradition which is an international tradition including a Continental Yoruba practice, a Santeria Yoruba practice, and a Candomblé Yoruba practice. Also in recent years, the Maatian tradition from ancient Egypt has emerged.[105]

Thus, African American religion includes both the unique ways in which African American Christianity syncretized Western Christianity with the religious heritage of the enslaved Africans, *and* the contemporary diversity of religious practice by African Americans.[106]

In summary, womanist theologies have focused on the experiences of black women in African American Christianity. Womanist theologies acknowledge the influence of syncretized forms of African traditional religions in its interpretation of spirituals, conjure, ecstatic dance, and other African American religious practices. However, most womanist theologies have only dealt with forms of African traditional religions as they relate to African American Christianity. Black theologian Gayraud Wilmore argues that black theologies must go beyond discussing Christianity and give more attention to African traditional religions: "But it is still possible and desirable to recover some of the great enduring values of the traditional religions of Africa for the revitalization and enhancement of religion in the United States. This is unlikely to happen, however, if African and African American scholars do not take the initiative to uncover the African religious inheritance for the benefit of the whole human family."[107] Wilmore implies that African Americans, regardless of contemporary religious affiliation, encounter African traditional religions and that this cultural encounter influences, to one extent or another, black religiosity.[108] Womanist theology, therefore, has the responsibility and potential to address the diversity of black religion—including a specific focus on forms of African traditional religions.[109]

Some womanist religious scholars argue that African traditional religions offer resources that are either complementary to the goals of Christian womanist concepts of salvation or even better able to achieve these goals. In her essay "The Sweet Fire of Honey: Womanist Visions of Osun as a Methodology of Emancipation," Shani Settles argues that African traditional religions offer religious resources for the attainment of freedom and justice: "[African-derived religions] were and continue to be powerful oppositional and differential resources for liberation projects because they embody and engender a 'methodology of the oppressed,' methodologies for emancipation that create models of revolutionary modes of being."[110] A theology interested in freedom and justice can be based on African traditional religions as well as Christianity. Religious scholar Tracey E. Hucks investigates the spirituality of an African American woman who maintains dual affiliation as a religious leader in a black Christian denomination and a Yoruba-based religious tradition. Hucks argues that African traditional religious affiliation can serve as a complementary or additional resource for fulfilling necessary mental, emotional, physical, and spiritual needs of black women and communities in ways that are not available in Jewish, Christian, and Islamic traditions.[111]

Karen Baker-Fletcher is the only womanist theologian to explicitly reference the inclusion of African traditional religious elements in her construction of salvation. She states that ancestors and traditional African religions are critical to how the present generation understands the best way to survive and thrive in its current context. Even in her construction of salvation, there are roadblocks to a more in-depth consideration of African traditional religious elements. First, she maintains that Jesus is the greatest ancestor, and perpetuates the Christocentric focus of the womanist discussion on salvation. In African traditional religions, ancestors refer to those deceased members of one's family lineage. Without a direct familial lineage to Jesus, one could not rightly assert Jesus as an arch-ancestor. (There will be more discussion of this issue in chapter 4.) Second, she does not discuss *how* the present generation learns from the ancestors. Do we, as Terrell suggests, just look at their lives and glean some lessons from their mistakes and triumphs? Or are the ancestors active in the present—as Baker-Fletcher suggests with her continued reference to Beloved and the appearance of this "ghost" in the temporal world? And, like Beloved, do ancestors return to share their knowledge and help the living?

Given these reflections on the limited discussion of Jesus Christ in womanist conceptions of salvation, the Christian dominance in womanist theology, and the importance of African traditional religions to the development of black religiosity, we must distinguish between Jesus and God so as to offer a religious framework that can account for both Christian and non-Christian religions. This will be one of the goals of "a constructive womanist concept of salvation." Identifying the divine agent of "making a way out of no way" as God rather than Jesus opens the concept of salvation to diverse understandings of the relationship between Jesus and God. Dropping the necessary connection to Jesus and the language of Jesus as being identical to God allows this constructive womanist concept of salvation to be informed by womanist understandings of Jesus without being tied to a single religious understanding of Jesus as Christ. Salvation then becomes the concern of people with different understandings of Jesus. Life lived with a desire and quest for health, strength, wholeness, quality of life, justice, and freedom may have, but does not necessitate, a belief in Jesus as uniquely God. "Making a way out of no way" declares that there is a relationship between God and humanity that allows new ways to break forth into our current realities. This relationship is qualified by God's offer of new possibilities, human agency, and a challenge to the current social, political, economic, and cultural forces that derail black women from achieving the goals of justice, survival, quality of life, and wholeness.

Philosophical Metaphysics

A constructive womanist concept of salvation looks to philosophical metaphysics for a religious worldview that can account for multiple religious traditions. Metaphysics seeks to describe how the world operates and, more specifically, how God and the world relate to one another. Systematic theology, on the other hand, provides a method of classifying and defining various themes within a specific religious tradition. That is, systematic theology can be understood as an ordered expression to what is stated in doctrines. Drawing on the resources of philosophy and other disciplines, systematic theology, in its most traditional form, tries to place various doctrines within a framework of thought—each one relating to the others—that can sift through the inconsistencies of different cultural and historical contexts.[112] Theologian John Macquarrie uses comparable language in defining systematic theology as "the intellectual discipline that seeks to express the content of a religious faith as a coherent body of propositions."[113] Although there is no formal starting point for systematic theology, most contemporary Christian systematic theologies, like their predecessors, begin with the doctrine of creation, go on to the historical events associated with Jesus Christ, and end with eschatological expectations.[114] Macquarrie also identifies two ways of systematizing theology.[115] One approach takes a central theme from the Christian tradition that serves as a doctrinal center. One example might be liberation theology's focus on the theme that God is on the side of the oppressed. A second approach to systematic theology identifies a sympathetic philosophy that unifies the other concepts. Looking again at liberation theology, one may identify Marxism as one such philosophical foundation.

Metaphysics and theology have long partnered in the expression of theology. In the early centuries of the last millennia, Islam, Judaism, and Christianity borrowed conceptual tools from Greek philosophy to discuss the relation of God and the world and the world operating in reference to God. This is perhaps most clearly revealed in the creeds of Nicea and Chalcedon, which readily borrowed the Greek concepts of substance, nature, and person in their articulation of the humanity and divinity of Jesus Christ. But metaphysics was not the exclusive domain of Christian philosophers and theologians. Avicenna and Maimonides incorporated classical Greek philosophy into their understandings of Islam and Judaism, respectively.[116] A shift occurred in the theological use of metaphysics during the Enlightenment. David Burrell argues that the development of the natural sciences pressed theologians to "recover those portions of metaphysics compatible with a new natural science and indispensable to articulating a faith."[117] Burrell identifies the philosophical theologies that employ metaphysics as "a burgeoning enterprise" in the theological disciplines.

The modern use of metaphysics follows in the tradition of empirical and speculative philosophy to articulate a model that describes and accounts for every aspect of reality. Like empirical philosophy, metaphysical theology treats experience as the primary source of religious knowledge. Influenced by the eighteenth-century British empiricists, empirical theologians variously refer to a sixth sense of perception, be it moral, aesthetic, or religious.[118] Speculative philosophy, in the words of philosopher Alfred North Whitehead, is "the endeavor to frame a coherent, logical, necessary system of general ideas in terms of which every element of our experience can be interpreted."[119] Again, taking the occurrences of the actual world as its source, Whitehead describes metaphysics as nothing more that "the description of the generalities which apply to all the details of practice."[120] Metaphysics is, one might say, our best ideas given what we know; according to Whitehead, "Metaphysical categories are not dogmatic statements of the obvious; they are tentative formulations of the ultimate generalities."[121] Thus, metaphysics does not take priority over the facts given to us by the actual world. It is, rather, informed theory about the workings of the entire world—including the world's relation to the divine. Although metaphysics can and has been used in Christian traditions, the system itself does not require or presume such a starting point. As has been done historically, metaphysics *can* be used to discuss non-Christian religious traditions, as well as their relation to one another within the world and the divine.

As black and womanist theologians have applied the tools of systematic theology to the study of black religions, they have, for the most part, limited their study to Christianity. Working within the particular categorical confines of Christian systematic theology, black and womanist theology has focused on African American Christian evaluations of the doctrine of God, Jesus Christ, salvation, heaven, and so forth. Although it is possible to conduct a systematic theology of some non-Christian religions such as Judaism and Islam, this approach is still limited because it only serves to describe the doctrines *within* the bounds of the singular faith tradition. Because metaphysics describes the operation of the entire world, it allows for a variety of religious and cultural understandings about the relationship between God and the world. This is particularly important for the study of black religions, which have long asserted the impossibility of distinguishing a religious sphere from the social, economic, and cultural spheres of lived practices. If womanist theology uses a philosophical metaphysic, it will have greater capacity for the study of non-Christian religions.

I offer process metaphysics as a postmodern theological framework that addresses the challenges that today's context poses to a constructive womanist theology. As a philosophical metaphysics, process thought offers a religious perspective that describes how the world works with specific views of God and human agency. Process thought discusses the relationship between the world and God without particular reference to Christianity, and is able to account for lived experiences across the boundaries of religious traditions. As a postmodern philosophy, process metaphysics presents a view of the world that is compatible with today's knowledge about the world. A postmodern approach is important for a constructive womanist theology that affirms the expression, "making a way out of no way," which is grounded in the particular historical experiences of black women. In order to speak to contemporary black women, "making a way out of no way" must also resonate with postmodern understandings of the world. This integration with an intention-ally postmodern perspective will reveal "making a way out of no way" as a womanist theology that can reflect the lyrical, metaphorical, cultural, and his-torically attentive strengths of womanist theology while speaking to religious diversity and the realities of black women's lives in the late twentieth and early twenty-first century.

Two

A Postmodern Framework
Process Theology and Salvation

Why is God letting this happen to me?—"Lisa"

Postmodern theology describes the relationship between God and the world in ways that are consonant with life in the late twentieth and early twenty-first centuries. It honors that we live in a technological and global society where we are constantly interacting with those who are radically different from us. Postmodern theology is based on and assessed by what we know about the world in which we live. As a philosophical metaphysics, process thought offers a depiction of reality as a whole, including atoms, amoebas, dolphins, human- ity *and* God. More specifically, process theology explains the constant sense of change in the world and how we exist in the midst of stability and instability. As process theology discusses how we move into the future with influences from the past and the possibilities available to us, it also analyzes the factors that prevent the world from being the beautiful, harmonious, adventurous place that God desires.

As process theology accounts for our experiences in the world, it includes the beautiful and life-giving parts of our lives as well as the death-dealing and destructive parts of our lives. Process theology understands that evil and suf- fering are built into the structure of the world. Process theology does not attribute evil to God or a satanic figure; rather, our freedom to pursue our own ends is often the source of loss and pain throughout the world. Although the changes we experience always involve some loss, evil need not have the final word. There are always ways to preserve life. A postmodern response to Lisa's question, "Why is God letting this happen to me?" will investigate issues of loss, freedom, and immortality.

This chapter focuses on how Alfred North Whitehead, the philosopher on whose work contemporary process theology is based, describes evil and its resolution in a postmodern framework. As Whitehead synthesizes his understanding of physics, religion, and culture, he offers various understandings of evil, the suffering it often causes, and opportunities for redemption. Thus, this examination of Whitehead's thought will investigate three of Whitehead's central works on his philosophical metaphysic. From Whitehead's explanations of evil, freedom, and immortality, I will offer a postmodern theology that describes the creative and destructive aspects of life as choices made amidst the powerful influence of the past and the promise of the future heard within God's calling to each of us.

This postmodern theological framework emphasizes the ongoing processes of life, individual ability to exercise power, the inevitability of relationships on all levels of reality, the eternal vision of God, and opportunities for immortality in the midst of pervasive loss. While Whitehead does not refer to these characteristics of his system as a theory of salvation, they compose the efforts to salvage hope, life, and justice in the midst of forces that often prevent such goals. This postmodern theology becomes a way of understanding how we all function in the world and God's role in helping us to create a world of harmony, complexity, beauty, and adventure.

While process theology is philosophical speculation about the world at large, it can still speak to the religious experiences of black women. Critics of process theology assert that its goals of beauty, adventure, and zest fail to address the issues of systemic oppression and injustices faced by many of the world's inhabitants. Indeed, Whitehead's description of God's vision poses a couple of questions to process theology: Does God's vision for the world include any understanding of justice? Is the philosophical language of process theology compatible with the kind of metaphorical language and emotional experiences that have served black women during their most difficult times? In order to serve black women, a postmodern framework needs to account for the pursuit of justice and some components of black religious experiences.

Process Theology as Constructive Postmodern Thought

Postmodern thought represents the attempt to move beyond the limits of the modern period. Many Western philosophers divide intellectual and cultural history into three periods—premodern, modern, and postmodern—and center on "the modern period." Each period is characterized by shifts in politics, economics, religion, education, and science.[1] Postmodernists believe that many of the lessons of the modern period were inaccurate, inadequate, or destructive. They want to acknowledge new information about the world and overcome some of the shortcomings of the modern period. Constructive postmodern thought wants to transcend the limitations of modernity without negating the wisdom of the modern and premodern periods. A constructive postmodern theology attempts to construct a worldview by which we can be faithful to a concept of the divine without ignoring what we currently know about the world in which we live.

Between the medieval period and the Enlightenment, particular shifts occurred in the life and consciousness of Western societies. Before the fifteenth and sixteenth centuries, one's past and outside authorities generally determined one's knowledge and the quality of one's life. One's social position was subject to a kind of determinism. That is, a peasant's child would be a peasant; an aristocrat's child would be an aristocrat; a tailor's child would grow up to be a tailor. This was, in part, a reflection of European feudalism, where people were subjects of lords and aristocrats rather than citizens of a nation or state. This kind of hierarchy was also pervasive in religion. Most Western Europeans were Catholic under the guidance of papal leadership in Rome (with most of Eastern Europe affiliated with the Orthodox Church, centralized in Byzantium). The government supported Catholicism as a state religion, tolerated Jewish communities, and allowed for heretics to be put to death. The Catholic Church established the content of faith—proper doctrines and interpretation of the Bible. Most individuals were illiterate, and religious education was discouraged for laypeople. For the educated, authority was placed in traditional sources like the Bible, the writings of ancient church leaders, and philosophers like Aristotle. The educated were trained to interpret these authoritative sources for either deeper spirituality or greater knowledge about tradition. It was also an accepted fact that the earth stood still at the center of the universe. The sun and other planets were understood to revolve around the earth in exact circles. Together, these conditions compose what many philosophers refer to as the "premodern" period.

In the fifteenth and sixteenth centuries, politics, economics, religion, and science underwent substantial changes that led to the "modern" period. Society began to affirm that all people have certain rights granted to them regardless of the circumstances of their birth. The economy shifted from an agrarian society to one of specialized labor, in which each person perfected a particular craft or task and fulfilled that role in either assembling a particular product or in society at large. These different tasks were now governed by a centralized power, not as a source of authority, but as a central way of solving problems. In politics, this trend translated into social programs (including socialist politics and programs) governed by a national center. The Protestant Reformation declared that Scripture, rather than the Catholic Church, was the authority for Christian faith. Increasingly, the Bible was translated from Greek and Latin into the languages of the people, and they were able to read and interpret it for themselves. This time period also saw the birth of Unitarianism: a denomination that rejects the idea of the Trinity, studies Jesus as a historical figure, and includes deists—individuals who believe God set the world in motion and then ceased to become involved in its affairs. Education began to emphasize experimentation and critical scrutiny of previously held concepts.

Westerners also began to see themselves differently in terms of the wider universe. Nicholas Copernicus asserted that the sun was the center of the universe; Galileo noted that the sun and moon were not perfect globes (in comparison to the earth), but that they contained sunspots and valleys and craters, respectively. In his famous statement "I think therefore I am," René Descartes epitomized the modern view that humanity has the unique ability to reason, and that reason constitutes both identity and hope for the future of society. Democracy, capitalism, communism, and socialism are all modern ideas. Philosopher Heath White summarizes the attitude of the modern period with this statement: "With the encouragement and cultivation of reason . . . we can expect progress in science and society. The only obstacles are ignorance and fear, and those can be overcome with education and courage."[2] The modern period is typified by a belief in reason, or our own thinking, to serve as a foundation for society and overcome any problem encountered.

Modernism failed to live up to many of its hopes.[3] Many people believed that humanity would use its increased knowledge of the world for good rather than for evil. The two world wars, however, revealed the modern capacity for violence and the shortcomings of centralized political power. Likewise, the same science that created a smallpox vaccine also developed weapons of mass destruction. In their own ways, communism, socialism, and democracy were seen to represent the progress of humanity and the ability to eradicate social problems. Although these systems of government were able to achieve great good, they also contributed to economic decline, human rights violations, and increased poverty, crime, and racial tension. Modernism expected religion either to dissolve into a faith in reason, or to transform into a rational faith with no claims to supernatural revelation. But the religious violence of the twentieth century and the fundamentalism of many of the world's religions indicate that modernism's projections were incorrect. Modernism's elevation of reason as the distinguishing characteristic of humanity led to the belief that human beings can dominate and use the resources of the natural world for its own progress. We are learning that there is not an endless supply of clean air, water, and land to sustain the growth and prosperity of humanity for an indefinite period of time.

New scientific discoveries also challenged the assertions of the modern period. Today, most people believe that there is more than meets the eye when it comes to the way things are constituted. For example, when we look at a mountain and call it a solid, we confess that it is not really a solid. That mountain is composed of many molecules, and those molecules are made up of atoms with moving particles within them. The same is true of the air we breathe. We can no longer assert that something is either there or not there. We can no longer assert that something is either standing still or moving. Rather, we agree that there are always some kinds of moving particles within the mountain, the air, and even ourselves. We also acknowledge that something as big as a mountain is affected by the erosion caused by wind and rain. This kind of knowledge challenges the dualism of the modern period—that it's there or it's not; it's still or it's moving; it's permanent or it's subject to change.

The dualism of the modern period reflects the privileging of Western categories of reason and a search for a universal truth. Modernism held that the development of reason was best revealed in Western European countries, and one of modernism's goals was to bring the rest of the world to the enlightenment and civilization of Western Europe. In the process, Western Europe colonized most of Asia, Africa, Central and South America, and the indigenous peoples of the United States. Referring to colonialism, Heath White notes that the rhetoric used to "civilize" non-Western societies often had barbaric results: "The agenda of the colonial powers, or at least its effect, had been in one way or another to erase the native cultures they colonized, on the assumption that enlightened, rational European culture was the pinnacle toward which all others should aspire."[4] These points demonstrate that the dualism of modernism was usually hierarchal; that is, one of the items compared was valued more than the other—men over women, European over African, white over black, permanence over change, reason over emotion.

The search for universal truth also leads to conflict in a society where diverse peoples are interacting more and more. Truth grants power. A good example can be seen in the realm of science. Most people today agree that the earth is round. Few of us have tested this for ourselves—we have not walked or sailed around it for ourselves, and we have not traveled to space and seen the round earth ourselves. We trust in this scientific discovery, and most of us would ridicule anyone who asserted that the earth is flat. We've granted science the power to tell us what is true. This proves White's point that truth is power: "The authority to determine what counts as true is also the power to determine who counts as important."[5] When authority is given to a universal truth in moral and ethical spheres, the authority is allowed to determine who is right and who is wrong; who gets punished and who does not; who gets to live a good life and who does not. The problem is that Truth with a capital *T* changes. Science once told us that the earth was flat and that certain races were biologically superior to other races. This is equally true for religious claims to one Truth. The belief in one single religious tradition or intellectual position as Truth invalidates the moral and ethical lives of many of the world's inhabitants. This is one of the reasons why process thinker David Ray Griffin asserts that "we can and should leave modernity behind—in fact, that we *must* if we are to avoid destroying ourselves and most of the life on our planet."[6]

Constructive postmodern theology is one response to the limits of modernity.[7] According to Griffin, constructive postmodernism seeks to go beyond the faults of modernism without negating its strengths or denying the wisdom of the premodern period. He writes about it in this way: "[Constructive postmodernism] seeks to overcome the modern worldview not by eliminating the possibility of worldviews as such, but by constructing a postmodern worldview through a revision of modern premises and traditional concepts."[8] A constructive postmodern theology that affirms premodern sensibilities will cling to what Griffin calls "premodern notions of a divine reality, cosmic meaning and an enchanted nature."[9] That is, a constructive postmodern theology insists upon a belief in God, a cosmic purpose to our lives, and that it is possible, even advisable, to have a sacred relationship (as opposed to one of domination) with the earth. It will also honor the insights and practices of indigenous and traditional religions. Goddess theologian Carol P. Christ believes that this is one of the strengths of this kind of postmodern thought: "[This] philosophy can help us to recognize and to persuade others that certain elements of premodern, nonwestern, and indigenous worldviews express truths that the modern scientific worldview has denied. These premodern insights which are also found in eco-spiritualities can thus be seen to be compatible with postmodern scientific understandings."[10] The ability to find value in premodern concepts poises a constructive postmodern theology to engage the African traditional religious aspect of black religiosity in America.

To overcome the shortcomings of modernity, a constructive postmodern theology will have to transcend the individualism, anthropocentrism, patriarchy, mechanization, economism, consumerism, nationalism, and militarism of the modern period. For this reason, Griffin adds, constructive postmodernism supports ecology, peace, feminist, and other liberatory movements.[11] Thus, many liberation theologies—ecological, feminist, and so forth—are postmodern theologies. Constructive postmodern theology cannot value men over women, reason over emotion, stability over change, one race over another. Thus, a constructive postmodern theology will affirm that God desires wholeness and life for the world's inhabitants.

I continue in the same vein as Griffin and many other process thinkers[12] who identify the philosophies of Alfred North Whitehead (1861–1947) and Charles Hartshorne (1897–2001), Whitehead's student, as examples of constructive postmodern theology. Having spent much of his life as a mathematician and physicist, the British-born Whitehead taught at Harvard University after 1924.

Thus, his ideas are often considered part of the American philosophical tradition. Aware of the new insights in science during his time, Whitehead wanted to construct a way to think about the world that accounted for what science was saying about energy and subatomic particles. What Whitehead calls the "philosophy of organism" has been categorized as process theology or neo-classical theology by his followers.[13] He articulates these ideas primarily in his books *Science and the Modern World* (1925), *Religion in the Making* (1926), *Process and Reality* (1929), and *Adventures of Ideas* (1933).

It is important to note that the principles of process thought, while constituting a constructive postmodern worldview, are not unique to Whitehead and his followers. Philosopher Nicholas Rescher notes that the central themes of process thought can be found throughout Western intellectual thought, including Plato and his Greek predecessor Heraclitus (sixth century B.C.E.).[14] I am not surprised to find resonances between process thought and African traditional religions. The earlier description of Western philosophical history and the identification of process theology as a constructive postmodern theology do not assume that the principles of process theology are "new," that they are particular to Western philosophy, or that they originate in European culture. I use Whitehead's description of the philosophy of organism because he attempted to devise a philosophical system based on the ongoing changes occurring in every element of the world. Whitehead's philosophy also serves as the theoretical base for many contemporary theologians who identify with the process theological movement. Thus, Whitehead functions as a leading figure in twentieth- and twenty-first-century process thought. The proposed postmodern framework understands itself as a constructive postmodern theology, as Griffin describes. It is a process theology based on Whitehead's philosophy. For the sake of clarity, this construction will be called "a postmodern theological framework."

In process theology, everything that happens is a product of the past, what's possible, and what we do with those things. Whether you are a quark, an amoeba, or a person, you undergo this continual process of sorting through these three inputs: what you inherit from the world, what's possible in your context, and what you do about it. This is the cause of our freedom. We are not bound by the past. It is not a deterministic system. We can do something new. God is the one who offers the possibilities to the world, urging us to choose the paths that lead to a vision of the common good. While the principles of God's vision do not change, the way it gets played out on earth depends on what is happening in the world. God takes in, or incorporates, the events of the world into who God is. God then relates those events with God's vision for the common good, searching for the best of what has happened in order to offer those aspects back to us in our next instance of becoming. In sum, our experiences in the world influence who we are and what we do. We then go on to influence those around us. What we do also affects God and how God relates to the world.

Whitehead on Evil, Freedom, and Immortality

Alfred North Whitehead's philosophy contains the elements necessary for discussing the attainment of wholeness and quality of life. As Whitehead articulates a metaphysics that describes the workings of the world, he also gives an account for evil. He variously describes evil as suffering, loss, and the feeling that accompanies overwhelming loss. Evil can be overcome through the freedom granted to the world's inhabitants, the activity of God, and the relationality of the system. This postmodern theological framework focuses on Whitehead's concepts of immortality, the acceptance of some levels of evil, and responses that aim for higher forms of beauty. In these ways, Whitehead describes God's attempts to save what is lost and find value in every aspect of the world. In the following section, I examine Whitehead's concept of evil and its resolution to reveal key elements for a constructive postmodern framework.

Whitehead understands that the issue that makes a functional theology so difficult is the attempt to reconcile a good God with the reality of evil in the world and our experiences of suffering. In *Religion in the Making*, Whitehead writes, "All simplifications of religious dogma are shipwrecked upon the rock of the problem of evil."[15] Whitehead gives great attention to the source and description of evil and the ways that his metaphysical system addresses it. Evil does not come from an "other" that opposes God, nor is it part of God's nature. For Whitehead, evil is part of the system, the way in which the world operates. Whitehead discusses evil differently as he develops his metaphysical system. In *Religion in the Making*, *Process and Reality*, and *Adventures of Ideas*, Whitehead discusses evil and the ways that God and the world respond to it.

In *Religion in the Making*, Whitehead describes the evolution of religions in history as a process of becoming. That is, the great "rational religions," which he identifies as Christianity and Buddhism, are a result of the emergence of a religious consciousness. The rational religions progressed through four stages: ritual, emotion, belief, and rationalization. Ritual is the habitual repetition of particular actions. It is characteristic of collective tribal and highly social societies. Ritual produces and sustains emotion. Eventually, myth emerges as a way to explain rituals and emotions, and later to form a basis for belief.

Myth is powerful because it is pragmatic—it works for its adherents. A rational religion is a religion in which beliefs and rituals are organized into a coherent order for life. Rational religions are the result of a gradual transformation of their former forms in ritual, emotion, and myth. In this transformation, rational religion emphasizes the individual (as compared to the social nature of "ritual religions"). *Religion in the Making* describes some of the specificities of evil—how we commit evils, how we feel them, and how our actions affect those around us.

In *Process and Reality*, Whitehead offers a more detailed explanation of the process of becoming and, thus, a deeper discussion of evil and the ways that the system addresses it. From this work, one can conclude that evil is loss, and that it is overcome by the way we remember the past, the way that God remembers us and searches for the best in us, and through the vision for the common good that we can experience in God's calling.

In *Adventures of Ideas*, Whitehead describes the progress of civilization as a continual advance toward newer heights and greater complexity within society. Here the process of becoming is also the progress of civilization. For Whitehead, civilization, or the world, is guided by God's ideal vision. God's vision is that the world would be characterized by the ideals of truth, beauty, art, adventure, and peace. Within the world, the ideals work in the following way: Truth occurs when what we experience corresponds to what is real. Beauty appears when there is harmony among the things that influence us as we become. Adventure is the search for new experiences. Art is produced when the occurrences of the world reflect new experiences. Peace is faith in the ideals to which God is calling us. As Whitehead describes the ideals of God's vision, he notes that the real occurrences in the world are less than ideal. In fact, suffering is often the result of conflict in the world. Whitehead identifies various responses to suffering and privileges the responses that heed the calling of God to new opportunities.

The differences between evil in the world and the resolution of evil in the world are often artificial distinctions made for the sake of clarity; similarly artificial is the distinction between our role and God's role in these activities. In reality, some of the same forces that create or perpetuate evil can also resolve it. Likewise, the roles that we play in producing evil, or resolving it, are not neatly separated from God's calling to and vision for the world. We act in response to God, and God acts in response to us; there can also be cooperation between God and the world. Sometimes we experience conflicting goals, and that produces discord; the same is true of God as well.

Evil in the World

The Freedom of the World

In *Religion and the Making*, Whitehead describes the process of the world's becoming as occurring through the interrelation of God, what's possible, and the inhabitants of the world. He describes God as the principle that provides relevant possibilities to the world. God contains all the possibilities of the world and offers them to us based on the particularities of our context. The possibilities we consider when we make decisions come from God. God orders these possibilities, urging us, or to use more process language, luring or persuading us, to choose those options that lead to a vision of the common good. Some theologians have called this urging the voice of God, the whisper of God, intuition, God's love for the world, or "that voice inside." God calls us—indeed, the entire world—toward God's vision for the common good. In this calling, God begs to be recognized, and yet God can also be ignored.

I intentionally use the language of "God's calling" to describe God's activity in the world. The language of "call" resonates with the language of religious communities that understand the ideal spiritual life as one lived in response to a "call" from God. The word *calling* goes beyond the singularity implied in the word *call*. The "call" may not be experienced as a clear sentence or directional order. "God will indeed offer guidance, but the guidance will not be in the form of a clear voice in the night, but in the form of options to weigh, factors to consider, friends to consult."[16] In addition, God may "call" us more than once, and to more than one thing. Indeed, there is repetition in the kind of "calling" that Whitehead designates.

God's calling is individual and general. It comes to us as individuals, but also as communities. Sometimes, as we become, we operate and make decisions and act in ways that conform to God's calling. Sometimes we do not. We are genuinely free to become in the ways that God is calling us. Or not. This is not a singular or one-time calling. In every moment, in every context, God is calling us. Over and over again, we have the opportunity to align ourselves with God's calling. Or not. The world is harmonious when it responds affirmatively or conforms to God's calling. Whitehead puts it this way: "There will be some measure of conformity and some measure of diversity. The whole intuition of conformity and diversity forms the contrast which that item yields for religious experience. So far as the conformity is incomplete, there is evil in the world."[17] To the extent that we use our freedom to diverge from God's calling, there is evil in the world.

To make matters worse, evil is not an isolated event. This is because of the interdependence of the world. The process of becoming makes the world radically relational. When we decide what to do in the world, we consider ourselves and our own values, but we also consider others and the wider world at large.[18] Because we consider our past and our future possibilities when we decide what to do in the world, relations are internal. What that means is that we do not *have* relationships. We are not discrete selves that can choose whether or not we want to relate to one another. Rather, we *are* relationships. Whitehead puts it this way: "The individual is formative of the society and the society is formative of the individual."[19] There is nothing outside of relationship.

We often think of these kinds of actions as "sin," as they depart from what God would have for us. Sin is easily perpetuated and systematized because we are so influential. We shape our futures and those around us. They have to live with what we have done. We have to live with what others have done.

In the interdependence of the system, evil cannot affect only one entity or person. When one of us chooses to operate in a way that is divergent from God's calling, it influences all of us. We all live with the consequences of those actions and have to work with them in our own lives and processes. In fact, when any of us act and live as if our actions and decisions only affect us, when we deny the interdependence of the world, when we act as if we are not all connected and in need of each other, we produce evil. Thus, Whitehead concludes, "Particular evils infect the whole world."[20]

Evil is destructive. This seems somewhat obvious. Evil often manifests itself in physical and mental suffering. But there is an even greater loss. Choosing to live, operate, or act apart from the principles of God's vision means that we have not chosen the most creative and positive option. There is evil in that we have not become what we could have been. We are not living up to our potential. We are prohibited from being all that we could be, all that God would have us be—and oftentimes this happens because of the evil we have to work and live with that we may not have created. And this becomes a greater evil because the social environment experiences a loss.

So often, we use our freedom to ignore the voice and the vision of God. We make decisions as if our actions do not affect the world around us. We make decisions without caring regard for others. We treat the earth as if it exists to be used for our own personal pleasure, and yet we become angry when the natural elements do not move in accordance with our desires. We isolate ourselves from other people, establishing hierarchies and superiorities in order to perpetuate our own selfish desires. We do this repeatedly within systems of power and influence, and create greater problems—systemic evils.

Evil Is Loss

There is another way to think of evil, as well. This way is much less individual. This understanding sees evil as part of the world we are born into. In part five of his tome *Process and Reality*, Whitehead writes that evil is the fact that the past fades. That is, who we are today is not who we were yesterday; and who we will be tomorrow is different from who we are today. We are changed by the new experiences we have, and who we were, that person, is gone. We can't get that person back. We are constantly becoming in every moment as we have new experiences to incorporate and new possibilities before us. And as we are constantly becoming new creations, we stop being who and what we were. As we engage and accept opportunities to be "born again," we are also constantly dying to our pasts. There is a constant or perpetual perishing. Whitehead puts it this way: "The ultimate evil in the temporal world is deeper than any specific evil. It lies in the fact that the past fades, that time is a perpetual perishing. Objectification involves elimination. The present fact has not the past fact with it in any full immediacy. In the temporal world, it is the empirical fact that process entails loss."[21] It is evil that so much is lost in the process of becoming. We decide what to do with what we have inherited and what could lie in front of us. We are selective in this process. We want to incorporate and perpetuate some things from our past. Other things we want to eliminate. Sometimes we want to keep conflicting aspects of our past with us as we move into the future, but we are unable to. People often call this "wanting to have your cake and eat it too." We have to choose. Something has to go, and that is a loss. It is a kind of evil.

At first glance, this definition of evil can seem like a rather weak way of understanding the radical manifestations of evil in the world. "The past fades," Whitehead says. That doesn't seem to account for the injustices of a country that can afford but will not ensure food for hungry children or health care for sick people. "The past fades." It doesn't seem to account for the broken bodies hanging from southern magnolia trees, which characterized decades of unprosecuted lynching. "The past fades." It doesn't seem to account for the people who beat and murder people who don't want to be in their gang, or who have somehow disturbed illegal drug trafficking. "The past fades." That doesn't even begin to account for the evil of this world.

It's more than that, though. "The past fades" says, "we continually lose." We lose the things we want to hold on to. We lose the things that are important to us. We sometimes lose our values; we lose our good sense; we lose our way. We lose our sense of self; we lose our slippery hold on what is right, just, and divine in many situations. We're constantly losing. So many times, this loss causes and is experienced as suffering and evil. And this kind of loss—it's just part of how things are. It is part of the world we inherit. We are born into it. We participate in it just by the accident of our birth.

Evil is part of the process of life in this world, and yet the process of becoming provides the means of avoiding evil as well. In other words, not all loss is evil. Some of the things that we lose and eliminate and leave behind are best left behind. We want to leave them behind. But we always have to choose. We can't have it all. "Selection is at once the measure of evil and the process of its evasion."[22] The selection process we engage in when we become something new can allow us to eliminate some evils of the past. For example, a woman may be the child of a mother who abused her, and perhaps her grandmother had abused her mother. This woman may choose not to abuse her daughter, though. In this choice, she has used her freedom, despite the powerful influence of the past, to eliminate something that she has experienced as evil. There is a kind of intrinsic evil because something has been lost, but for the world and for us in the world, evil has been, in whatever small way, evaded. Whitehead likens this system to a barrier reef: "A chain of facts is like a barrier reef. On the one side, there is wreckage, and beyond it harborage and safety. The categories governing the determination of things are the reasons why there should be evil; and are also the reasons why, in the advance of the world, particular evil facts are finally transcended."[23] The system itself contains both evil and the method for avoiding evil.

There is an additional way in which evil as loss is built into the operation of the world. God's calling as contextual and encompassing can sometimes generate loss in the world. Because God's calling responds to the conditions of the world and is tailored to each particular circumstance, God works with what the world provides. Some situations give very few options. Sometimes the way forward is still a march into danger or death. Sometimes we are "backed into a corner." Some circumstances are so desperate that God's calling is toward "the lesser of two evils." Sometimes none of the available possibilities for a particular circumstance fall under things we would normally identify as good. God's calling toward the more preferable of the available options may still result in loss, pain, and suffering.

Likewise, God's call to all of creation often leads to a level of loss and discord. What may be optimal for the well-being of one aspect of creation may not promote the health and well-being of another aspect of creation. For example, the food required to sustain the life of animals and human beings will necessarily cause a loss for, at the very least, some bacterial and plant life, and possibly other animals as well. Yet God still desires the well-being of all of creation, aiming for that which promotes the common good. These losses or evils are realities of the system. The ongoing process of becoming entails loss. Some circumstances within the world offer so little that even an adaptation of God's calling cannot eliminate loss and suffering. Finally, the conflicting interests in the world's diverse constituencies may also cause loss for some elements of the world. These are unavoidable evils. In *Process and Reality*, Whitehead defines evil as something that is built into the system of the world.

Discord and Suffering

Whitehead reminds us that evil is not just a fact, but also a feeling. We can experience certain things as evil. As mentioned earlier, our selections, actions, decision making, and experiences come with feelings. In this process, there is always loss, and this loss often hurts. It literally and figuratively hurts to lose so much so often in so many ways. Even if we know that we are moving on to something better, it often hurts to lose. But when we are not moving on to something good—when loss compounds upon loss and that compounds upon more loss, when we experience destruction and pain and violence and loss *more* than hope and life and beauty and grace—destruction is the dominant fact in the experience. We "feel" evil. We feel the discord and the conflict. We suffer.

And as it turns out, suffering does not bring out the best in us. In *Adventures of Ideas*, Whitehead describes three main ways that we often respond to suffering. First, when suffering becomes terribly intense, we don't want to experience the world with any feelings. We block those out, or inhibit feelings, from our experiences. We go numb. Second, other times we feel evil in great and overwhelming ways. This destroys our ability to feel beauty around us. Whitehead writes, "This is the feeling of evil in the most general sense, namely physical pain or mental evil, such as sorrow, horror, dislike."[24] When loss is dominant in our experience, we suffer, and we begin to lose hope that things will get better.[25] We can have a variety of experiences where there is only conflict; sometimes there is no harmony present at all. These experiences cause us to suffer, and we see the future through our lens of pain. These feelings of evil make it harder to see beauty and hope ahead. We live in this space, in this place. Third, we try to readjust the ways that we feel the vast evil in the world. We keep feelings of evil and suffering at a lower intensity as a background so we can have some clarity in the more active parts or foregrounds of our lives. In other words, we try to keep the bad things at the back of our minds and consciousnesses so that we can focus on other things—presumably things that demand our immediate attention. It makes sense. The knowledge, let alone the feeling, of the evil in our midst can be overwhelming, paralyzing, and numbing. And yet many of us do not have the option of paralysis. We must get up in the morning; we must raise our children, go to work, and find ways to eke out a life in the midst of suffering and pain. This does not eliminate the suffering or pain. It pushes it to the background, often for the sake and necessity of functionality.

The Resolution of Evil

Like the process of becoming itself, both God and the world are needed to address evil. God addresses evil through God's desires and calling to the world, God's memory of the world, and God's vision for the world. Those of us in the world can also respond to evil. As we embrace beauty and novelty, remember our pasts and maintain faith, we are able to help reduce experiences of evil. The interaction of these multiple factors can offer life and beauty to the world.

What God Can Do

God Aims for the Elimination of Evil

In *Religion in the Making*, Whitehead states that evil is to be combated and that God is involved in this combat. This happens in two ways: (1) through God's activity in the world and (2) within God's nature. Although we can reject God's calling, God is still calling us to be the best that we can be in every context. This constant calling is what saves us. Even Whitehead uses the language of salvation. Whitehead says that through us, "[God's] ideal vision is given a base in actual fact to which [God] provides [God's calling] as a factor saving the world from the self-destruction of evil. The power by which God sustains the world is the power of [God]self as the ideal."[26] The power to save the world is in God's calling. God provides a vision for the common good to each one of us, to the world. God does this over and over again and, thus, attempts to avoid evil.

Here, process theology differs from classical ideas of God's power. Process theology affirms the omnipresence of God. Indeed, God is everywhere at all times, embracing the world, feeling the world, and responding to all aspects of the world. But God's power and knowledge are conceived of differently than in orthodox conceptions of God. Process theologians believe that God embraces the highest form of power. Unlike classical models of God in which the highest form of power is an authoritative or coercive power, in process thought, God's power is a persuasive power. God cannot make us do one thing or another. Rather, God influences, persuades, lures, or "calls" us to embrace the principles of God's vision in every context.

Process theology describes two aspects of God—a primordial nature and a consequent nature or as having creative love and responsive love. In the primordial nature or creative dimension of God, God offers the world possibilities that are relevant for our current context. These possibilities are ordered according to a vision that calls us toward principles of beauty, truth, adventure, and art. As God influences the world, God literally becomes a part of every aspect of creation. In other words, incarnation is universal. On the other hand, God also responds to us or takes the world into God's self. God feels, or gathers into God's self, the events of the world, and they live on in God. God knows us and knows what happens to us. This is how God rejoices with us and suffers with us. We are a part of who God is. God is not identical to the world, but God is not set apart from the world in opposition to what the world is. God is in us, and we are in God.

Whitehead affirms both God's goodness and God's ability to search for value in even the greatest tragedy. For Whitehead, God is always good, and there is a part of God that never changes. He writes about it this way: "[God's] nature remains self-consistent in relation to all change. There is some consistency in creative action because of God's immanence. We cannot attribute evil to God's determinism."[27] Although the world is constantly changing and becoming, God's vision for the common good and continual calling to the world do not change. This is the primordial nature of God, or God's creative love. In *Religion in the Making*, Whitehead describes the consequent nature or responsive love of God as the kingdom of heaven. God receives the entire world into God's own nature. God then evaluates the experiences of the world and relates them to the vision for the common good. In so doing, God is able to find value in even the greatest evils.

In the kingdom of God, evil is overcome by good. Whitehead writes about this in greater detail:

> The kingdom of heaven is not the isolation of good from evil.
> It is the overcoming of evil by good. This transmutation of evil
> into good enters into the . . . world by reason of the inclusion
> of the nature of God, which includes the ideal vision of each
> actual evil so met with a novel consequent as to issue in the res-
> toration of goodness. God has in [God's] nature the knowledge
> of evil, of pain and of degradation, but it is there as overcome
> with what is good.[28]

In other words, inside God, God knows of all evil, loss, and destruction, but within God's nature, it is overcome with what is good. Here, and only here, is the world really saved from the self-destruction of evil. This does not prevent evil from affecting our lives in this world, but it offers a concept of salvation outside of this world. Thus, salvation also comes inside God in the form of the kingdom of heaven.

In *Religion in the Making*, evil is the result of the freedom of the world. Sometimes we choose to ignore God's calling, and this decision has consequences for us and the surrounding world to which we are related. God's goal is to eliminate evil. That is, God tries to save the world from evil. God saves the world through the vision that comes to each of us in God's calling. God saves the world by offering Godself to the world. And yet God also saves the world within God's self—by perfecting the evils of the world inside God's nature.

God's Memory of the World

The events, people, and creatures of the world are also immortal in God. As mentioned earlier, God feels, or gathers into God's self, the events of the world, and they live on in God. This is how God knows us and knows what has happened to us. But God does not just know us; God actually incorporates the events of the world into God's own nature. The world has an effect on and changes who God is: "There is a reaction of the world on God. The completion of God's nature into a fullness of physical feeling is derived from the objectification of the world in God."[29] Because the events of the world are always changing, there is a part of God that is ever changing, ever growing, with the inclusion of the occurrences of this world. In this sense, God is a true companion as God absorbs the experiences of the world into God's self.

As Whitehead intimates in *Religion in the Making*, what is lost in the world is not lost to God. As God incorporates all the events of the world into who God is, God also evaluates the experiences of the world—saving that which can be saved, relegating the evil to the edges. Sometimes there is very little good to work with, but God can find it and preserve it. Whitehead describes it in this way:

> The revolts of destructive evil, purely self-regarding, are dismissed into their triviality of merely individual facts; and yet the good they did achieve in individual joy, in individual sorrow, in the introduction of needed contrast, is yet *saved* by its relation to the completed whole. The image under which this operative growth of God's nature is best conceived as that of a tender care that nothing be lost [emphasis mine].[30]

God's preservation of what is good, even if it is minimal, from the past allows God to find something of value in even the worst occurrences in the world. God can find value in the most evil situations. Sometimes there is only a small amount of good to work with. Inside God, evil and the immediacy of sorrow and pain are transformed into something of value. Inside God, good is saved in relation to the whole. This is something that only God can do, because God has more knowledge than we do. We only have access to our actual world, our immediate surroundings. God has access to the entire world and the activities and feelings of the entire world. In that sense, God is always working with more information than we are. Since God is eternal, we have a kind of eternal life after death within God. Even after we die to the world, we live on in God. *This* is the kingdom of heaven.

Salvation is found not in God's ability to experience and incorporate the world into God's nature, but in God's evaluation of the world in this kingdom of heaven. God sifts the destructive evil from the good it nonetheless achieved. Whitehead identifies salvation as occurring here: "The consequent of God is [God's] judgment on the world. [God] saves the world as it passes into the immediacy of [God's] own life. It is the judgment of a tenderness that loses nothing that can be saved. It is also the judgment of a wisdom that uses what in the temporal world is mere wreckage."[31] God can transform everything into something valuable.

This, says Whitehead, is where we can locate the notion of redemptive suffering: "The sense of worth beyond itself is immediately enjoyed as an overpowering element in the individual self-attainment. It is in this way that the immediacy of sorrow and pain is transformed into an element of triumph. This is the notion of redemption through suffering which haunts the world."[32] This saving, this redeeming, all occurs within the nature of God. It is important to note here that Whitehead does not say that our experiences of suffering save us. Rather, within God's nature, in what Whitehead calls "the kingdom of heaven," God can find something of value. In this realm outside of the world in which we live, God can save everything.

The world is also immortal because of its redemption in God. God offers the results of this redeemed world back to us by ordering possibilities that the world can embrace. God orders these possibilities by a larger vision of ideals. Salvation occurs by assuring everlasting life for what is lost and by God's calling toward specific goals.

God's Calling

God relates God's incorporation of the world with the vision for the common good and with what is possible in the world. God takes in the events of the world, relates them to what is possible and to God's vision for the common good, and calls us once again. This is God's process of becoming. When God offers God's calling to the world, God considers the occurrences of the world, what is possible in a given context, and God's evaluation of these things. This is a reflection of the way in which we in the world become.[33] This is a significant aspect of process theology. In many theological systems, the world has the opposite characteristics of God. In those systems, we in the world are subject to change, we're mortal, and we cannot see into the future; God, on the other hand, does not change, is eternal, and knows what will happen before we do it. This understanding of God and the world sets up a hierarchical dualism in which things are understood in pairs and the attributes of value are attributed to God, while the world is devalued. Process theology asserts a different relationship between the world and God. God functions in a reciprocal relationship to the things of the world. Thus, process theologians say that rather than being the exception to the metaphysical principles of the world, God is the chief exemplification of the metaphysical principles of the world.

Since the "kingdom of heaven" is within God and is correlated with God's vision for the common good, in God's calling we are offered a vision of heaven. God weaves together the events of the world (located in Whitehead's "kingdom of heaven"), the vision of the common good, and the possibilities available to us. We can see now that the primordial or unchanging part of God is not just a collection of possibilities, but these possibilities as they are related to God's evaluation of the events of the world, which highlights the best part of what is available. The possibilities available to us are considered in light of heaven. Thus, heaven comes to us in God's calling. Heaven passes into the world through God's calling and qualifies this world so that all of us can include it as a factor in our experiences. "Thus the kingdom of God is with us today."[34] All of us have available to us aspects of heaven that can influence what we do and how we shape our world. But this is not the end of the story. Because what we do influences God, we can contribute to the content and vision of heaven. This then comes back to the world. It is a cyclical and reciprocal process in which the world receives God and contributes to God just as God receives the world and contributes to who we are and how we become.

Whitehead also describes God's aims as informed by a larger vision. This vision, the primordial vision, leads the world: "God . . . saves [the world]: or more accurately, [God] is the poet of the world, with tender patience leading it by [God's] vision of truth, beauty and goodness."[35] This vision, that I have been calling a "vision for the common good," is described as a vision of truth, beauty, and goodness. This vision shapes God's call to the world. That is, possibilities are ordered by the principles of this vision, and they come to the world in God's call. In this early description of the primordial vision, Whitehead is asserting that God operates by principles. God's "goodness" is accounted for in the primordial vision.

God Aims for Intensity

The calling from God not only contains a vision of heaven, but also brings novelty and order. Without God, we are completely determined by our past. Because God contains the possibilities that are available to the world, God is the source of novelty. It is because of God that we can become something new, something not available within our pasts alone. Yet God also brings order. The possibilities offered to us are not haphazard; they are ordered, and to the extent that we grasp them, there is order in the world. When God's calling is not completely embraced, there is disorder.[36] This departure from God's calling, what was described as evil in *Religion in the Making*, is in *Process and Reality* described as disorder. Yet order and novelty are not precisely God's goals. Rather, order and novelty *characterize* God's activity in the world: "Order and novelty are but the instruments of [God's calling]"; God's aim is actually "the intensification of [experience]."[37] Here, Whitehead begins to do something different. In *Religion in the Making*, God aims for the elimination of evil, but in *Process and Reality*, God begins to have different aims—order and intensity.

Intensity is a relatively large number of influences and feelings, without any reference to the qualities of the various feelings and influences. Intensity makes no reference to whether an influence is positive or negative, creative or destructive. It is like valuing diversity for diversity's sake. It simply refers to the number and variety of the factors that influence us. Because harmony reflects the absence of conflicting feelings and influences and intensity refers simply to numbers and varieties, the goals of intensity and harmony can themselves conflict and cause feelings of discord or suffering. One might say it in this way: the more influences there are upon us, the higher the likelihood for conflict. Whitehead refers to these conflicting feelings or feelings of discord as "feelings of evil." Thus, evil is not just loss or destruction, but, as Whitehead says in *Adventures of Ideas*, evil is more rightly "destruction as a dominant fact in the experience."[38]

God orders possibilities for the world toward the goal of intensity. Whitehead describes God's goal of intensity in this way:

> God, in [God's] primordial nature, is unmoved by love for this particular or that particular; for in this foundation process of creativity, there are no preconstituted particulars. In the foundations of [God's] being, God is indifferent alike to preservation and to novelty. [God] cares not whether an immediate occasion be old or new, so far as concerns derivation from its ancestry. [God's] aim for its depth of satisfaction as an intermediate step towards the fulfillment of [God's] own being. Thus God's purpose in the creative advance is the evocation of intensities.[39]

Whitehead's God does not desire repetition and changelessness in the temporal world. Nor does God promote constant change for its own sake. In other words, God does not want us to depart from the past just for the sake of doing so; nor does God want us to continue on in the past just for the sake of preserving it. According to this passage, God wants us to have intense experiences.

God's Vision for the World

In *Adventures of Ideas*, Whitehead identifies the components of God's vision with more detail than "harmony and intensity." Here Whitehead states that the vision that guides and shapes God's calling is constituted by truth, beauty, art, adventure, and peace. Whitehead's articulation of art, adventure, and peace are responses from the world. Truth and beauty comprise God's calling to the world.

Truth refers to the ways that our experiences correspond to reality. Reality is what is actually happening in the world. Truth occurs when what we experience corresponds to what is actually occurring. Whitehead admits that we need some basic levels of truth: "Apart from blunt truth, our lives sink decadently amid the perfume of hints and suggestions. The blunt truth that we require is the conformal correspondence of clear and distinct appearance to reality."[40] For human beings, sense perception is usually the most reliable of these truth-relations, but even the senses depend on a healthy functioning body. There will always be failure, interference, and partiality as we seek to find out what is true. Nevertheless, Whitehead feels that nature seems to contain within itself "a tendency to be in tune."[41] Although it is difficult to match up our experiences with what actually occurs in the world, we somehow manage (most of the time) to make it work.

Something has beauty if it is harmonious and intense. *Beauty* is defined by the way that we become what we become, and by the relationships within the world. Beauty is not just about the influences we experience; rather, beauty is known by *the way we incorporate* the past and the possibilities available to us. As we incorporate aspects of the past and available possibilities into our becoming, certain feelings accompany them. This process of becoming, the way we live in the world, does not just happen by rote. We *feel* these things. Our selections, actions, decision making, and experiences come with feelings. For example, a compliment may bring with it feelings of happiness or pride; the possibility of getting into college may bring with it feelings of excitement and nervousness. When the things that influence what we are going to do in a particular instance do not conflict and the feelings that accompany them do not hinder one another (as, for example, when the feeling of nervousness about the unknown tempers the excitement of going to college), then minor forms of beauty are attained. A minor form of beauty is present in the absence of conflicting feelings. A "major form of beauty" occurs when there are no conflicting feelings (minor forms of beauty) *and* when there are new contrasts in what we finally become. That is, we feel or become something different from what the influences alone provided for us. In the example of the compliment, the compliment brought with it the accompanying feelings of happiness and pride. If you respond with a word of thanks, then a feeling of gratitude (as well as the thankful response) is a new contrast. So beauty is also harmony. In other words, beauty occurs when there is harmony between the feelings that we have as we take in the influences of the past and the possibilities for the future. This harmony must occur both in terms of the details of how we experience these influences and in terms of what we actually do next.

What We Can Do

Art

Art is truthful beauty. On their own, beauty and truth are not necessarily connected. The universe aims for the production of beauty—of intensity and harmony—but beauty need not involve the attainment of truth. For example, a book of fiction may be beautiful, but its stories do not correspond to anything that actually happened in the world. Apart from beauty, truth is neutral; it is neither good nor evil. Good and evil are not found in the facts of what we become. Good or evil are the results of how we relate to one another in the world.[42] When what happens in the world is true and beautiful, there is greater harmony. Art is produced when what we actually become "summons up new resources of feeling from the depths of reality."[43] Thus, art promotes change. In so doing, it does not constantly perpetuate the past: "Art neglects the safety of the future for the gain of the present."[44] After all, adventure is best attained through a constant embracing of new possibilities when faced with the disharmony of the world, and art will promote adventure.

In his description of art, Whitehead affirms that there must be salvation outside of heaven. Although Whitehead has established that the true eradication of disharmony (or evil) is only found within God as the kingdom of heaven, he provides some way for the promotion of harmony in the world: "The good of the universe cannot lie in indefinite postponement. The Day of Judgment is an important notion: but that day is always with us. Thus art takes care of the immediate fruition, here and now; and in so doing is apt to lose some depth by reason of the immediate fruition at which it is aiming. Its business is to render the Day of Judgment a success, now."[45] We cannot just wait for heaven to experience relief from disharmony, discord, conflict, and feelings of evil and suffering. Our responses to these realities must also entail more than the feelings of numbness, living with feelings of evil, or trying to keep the bad things in the back of our minds. Some aspect of salvation must occur in this world. Whitehead believes it happens as the world moves toward new opportunities.

Adventure

There is a positive way of dealing with the disharmony and conflict in the world. We can focus on the new possibilities that are available to us rather than the influence of the past alone. According to Whitehead, this is the most radical approach to disharmony in the world: "This novel system is such as radically to alter the distribution of intensities throughout the two given systems, and to change the importance of both in the final intensive experience of the occasion."[46] We can radically alter our approach to dealing with discord and suffering by choosing a path that does not come from the past world alone. We can tune into the possibilities offered to us in God's calling. If, as Whitehead suggests, we change primarily according to the calling we experience from God, we can change the future of the world.

There is often conflict and discord in the world, but we can continue to search for something new. Conflict and discord result from the fact that modes of beauty are various and not necessarily compatible. It is very difficult to have a large number of influences without producing some conflict. But not all discord is bad, and discord is always preferable to becoming numb to the world. Discord and conflict are necessary factors in the process of change. Discord can produce hope just as easily as it can produce horror or pain. Discord can encourage us to go beyond merely repeating the past as we decide what to do with the world or circumstances that we inherit. Discord can encourage us to seek out new possibilities. Even if the past was something amazing and beautiful, it cannot last forever. We cannot repeat the same thing over and over and over again indefinitely. There will be some variation. There will be a drive toward diversity of experience. Whitehead refers to this search for newness as *adventure*.[47]

The path toward the ideals, toward newness, is better than remaining content with what we have already attained. This entire system is based on the principle that the inhabitants of the world have real freedom. Even though we are internally related to the world, we each still have a sense of individuality. We can still work with what we are given and become our own things. This quality is the essence of who we are. Whitehead believes that there is a "thrill keener than any prolonged halt in a state of attainment with the major variations completely tried out. Thus the wise advice is not to rest too completely in any continued realization of the same perfection of type."[48] To be adventurous is to embrace freshness and zest. We do this by exploring the alternatives that do not bring discord—the possibilities that come from God. This, Whitehead concludes, is the optimal approach to functioning in the world: "The best service that ideas can render is gradually to" lift various ideals into the parts of ourselves that hear the voice of God, so that these ideals can "become a program for reform."[49] The best thing that we can do is to tune into the calling from God and let God's vision guide us to create programs that will change the world.

The World's Memory of the Past

Another way that Whitehead's system discusses the response to evil is by addressing the issue of loss. The struggle with evil occurs in deciding how to include as much as possible while making a compromise because something must be lost. Because of the process of becoming, it is impossible to become something new without dying, in some way, to the past. Whitehead identifies this as the central issue in religion: "The most general formulation of the religious problem is the question [of how] . . . novelty does not mean loss."[50] A concept of salvation addresses evil in such a way that there is minimal loss. How, in the midst of this constant loss, this constant dying to the past, can we preserve life? In Whitehead's thought, a concept of salvation includes attempts to find some kind of immortality.

Whitehead addresses evil in his concept of immortality. As described earlier, we are changed by the new experiences we have, and who we were, that person, is gone. We can't get that person back. We have the memories of that person, of what has happened before. Those memories become part of the past that shapes who we are, but that actual person, those events, are gone. Thus, we may not be the same people that we were five or ten years ago, but we remember that person, that time, and the things that shaped us then. These memories may factor into what we decide to do today or tomorrow in a particular instance. This is also true of how others understand us. For example, two young sisters are fighting. One girl hits the other. The girl who was hit runs to the parent to report on what just happened, saying, "My sister is hitting me." The offending sister may respond, "I'm not hitting her now," because the action has ceased to happen. This is true. Nevertheless, the offended sister remembers what the other just did, and this affects what she does in the next moment. Thus, even though the past fades, the memory of it influences how we and others around us move into the future. We are always appropriating what is lost into what we do next.

The past is immortal to us as we remember it and incorporate it into who we become and what we do. This is Whitehead's concept of objective immortality: "All relatedness has its foundation in the relatedness of [the world]; and such relatedness is wholly concerned with the appropriation of the dead by the living—that is to say, with 'objective immortality' whereby what is divested of its own living immediacy becomes a real component in other living immediacies of becoming."[51] Although something is no more, we remember the fact of what has happened. Things live on after death, if only in the ways we remember the fact of what has happened. That is how something or someone is objectively immortal. It is easier to think of this in terms of people and larger periods of time. Whitehead argues that this kind of immortality is true on a moment-by-moment basis. It is as true for us as entire individuals as it is for the individual cells of our bodies. Even if we decide to eliminate a particular influence from the past, just the consideration of the past means that it leaves an imprint on us. In this sense, it too has a kind of immortality. The fact of it lives on after it is over. There is a still a kind of life after death. Thus, while parts of the world die in each moment as they become new things, they live on in the world they left behind. We are able to offer some kind of immortality to what has died. We are saved from this loss by the ability to preserve life. We are immortal in the influence and imprint we leave on those around us.

Faith

How do we do this? In the midst of conflict, suffering, discord, and the challenges that prevent us from getting to the truth, how do we continually seek out new possibilities? How do we manage to heed God's calling when there are so many forces that can keep us stuck in the past or the pain of our experiences? Whitehead believes that God promotes certain ideals for the world—ideals of intensity and harmony, of beauty and truth and art. But these are often conflicting goals. There will be disharmony and discord, and they will cause suffering within the world. Nevertheless, adventure and art should prevail. We must change and adapt. Whitehead acknowledges that this is no easy task. It will get discouraging. Whitehead argues that there is a mysterious principle that encourages the world toward art and adventure: peace.

Peace sustains us in the process of becoming. Peace is a positive feeling: "It is a broadening of feeling due to the emergence of some deep metaphysical insight, unverbalized and yet momentous in its coordination of values. . . . It is primarily a trust in the efficacy of beauty."[52] Peace is a gift that Whitehead also describes as faith. It kicks in "where reason fails to reveal the details."[53] Peace is not ignoring the reality of the world; rather, it prevents us from seeing the world as narrowly we otherwise might. Peace is a basic trust in the goodness of things. Peace is the feeling of salvation. Whitehead describes peace as that which reminds us that there is some value in everything, despite the loss.[54] Peace, in more traditional language, is faith. Peace helps us to believe and hope in the process of the organic world itself. It is not a passive belief, but a belief that sustains the actions and decisions of the world.

In *Adventures of Ideas,* evil is in the principle of incompatibility—that we cannot positively incorporate and synthesize all influences of the past and all relevant possibilities. They will bring conflicting feelings. God cannot surmount evil. In *Process and Reality,* Whitehead describes God as one who wants nothing to be lost, desiring to save the world. God is not aiming for mere preservation of the past or immortality. God is aiming for intensity and harmony. In *Adventures of Ideas*, Whitehead notes that these aims will often conflict. By necessity, discord and feelings of evil will arise.

The implication is that we will always have to deal with evil in the world. The elimination of evil can only happen in the consequent nature of God. God does, however, provide an ideal vision to the world through God's calling. Ideally, what we experience conforms to what occurs within the world. This is truth. God also desires a variety of detail with contrast, and a lot of it, within our individual experiences. This is beauty. Art aims at the coincidence of truth and beauty. That is, God desires harmony. Again, perfect harmony is only attained in God, but God urges us toward limited forms of perfect harmony on earth. In the process, God grants us peace. Peace is the gift from God that allows us to trust in the process. Peace allows us to believe that despite all that is lost, something valuable is gained as we continue to progress toward newer and higher forms of beauty.

Truth, beauty, adventure, art, and peace are the components of God's vision. God's vision is not just something that God has or sees or envisions. This vision is part of who God is. Many theologians refer to this as the unchanging character of God, or as God's unconditional love for the world. It is, more radically, part of who God is. When God offers this ideal vision to the world, when God calls us, God is offering Godself to us. According to Whitehead, the embrace of God's vision results in the advance of the world and the progress of civilization.

Summary of Whitehead's Ideas

From what Whitehead has written in the three works discussed above, one can make some conclusions about Whitehead's concept of evil and the ways in which it is to be addressed. Evil occurs when we do not follow or adhere to God's calling. When we freely choose another path, we cause evil—not just for ourselves, but for the world around us. Evil is also produced when we do not acknowledge the relationality of the world. That is, in this highly interdependent world, making decisions as if one is an "island unto oneself," ignoring all the ways that we influence the world around us, brings evil and greater discord into the world. These evils can be called "specific evils." In this sense, our freedom is the source of evil.

The ultimate evil is that so much is lost. Loss occurs through the fading of the past, and also when something is lost in comparison to what might have been. Loss is part of the process of becoming. It is part of the structure of the world. Still, evil is more complicated than that. Evil is produced by the conflict that often arises between harmony and intensity. Diversity, a vast number of influences on us, a complex past, conflicting goods, and a variety of opportunities before us do not guarantee harmony and pleasant feelings. The fact is that we can't have it all. We must choose. Sometimes there are few choices, and that need to choose often causes conflict and suffering. Suffering can be so painful that we have an even more difficult time moving forward, seeing new opportunities—in essence, hearing/recognizing God's calling.

Whitehead discusses various responses to evil in the world. Evil often causes suffering. Evil can produce physical pain and mental anguish. When these feelings of evil become dominant in our experiences, when we feel more pain than joy and hope, we often become numb or stuck in places of pain and anguish. Many of us strive to push our experiences of evil and suffering to the backgrounds, so that we function better in our daily lives. Yet we can also choose to go beyond the limitations of our past experiences, seek out new possibilities, and thus heed God's calling to us. As we conform to God's calling to the world, we can eliminate evil.

Efforts to preserve life in the face of loss also address the reality of evil in the world. We don't want our lives and experiences to completely fade, to lose all meaning and importance. Our pasts live on into the present and future as we remember them. These memories are factors for who we are and what we do in the present and future. Our pasts live on as impressions and influences on the present and future. In this sense, the facts of our past attain a kind of immortality. We also live on in God as the events of the world are absorbed into God. God relegates evil to the edges, saving that which is good within God's own self. This is the kingdom of heaven. Only here is evil truly eliminated. In God's calling, the world is offered a vision of heaven, and this allows us to participate with God in transforming evil into good. That is, as we enact a heavenly vision on earth and those events become part of God, we help to shape the kingdom of heaven.

Whitehead has various ways of describing God's role in responding to evil. In *Religion in the Making*, God seeks to eliminate evil. In *Process and Reality*, what is lost in the world has eternal life within God's nature. God is able to redeem evil within the kingdom of heaven. Here evil is described as part of the process of becoming. God no longer seeks to eliminate it in the world. Instead, God desires order and intensity for the world. God guides the world toward new experiences. In *Adventures of Ideas*, God's goals are intensity and harmony. These goals often conflict and result in feelings of evil or suffering. God is not precisely the source of suffering, but Whitehead suggests that God's hopes for the world will often produce conflict and discord. Sometimes conflict and discord lead to feelings of evil. Sometimes conflict motivates us to pursue new possibilities for our lives and the world. In the midst of all this,

God leads the world by a vision constituted by the ideals of truth, beauty, adventure, and art. To sustain our efforts to deal with evil, God gives us peace or faith. We can trust that, despite the conflicts and feelings of loss and suffering, the aims for harmony and intensity will create something that is preferable. There are sacrifices we must make for harmony, and peace allows us to bear with the evil that accompanies them.

Whitehead's philosophy depicts of reality as a whole. Whitehead's metaphysics reflect his understanding of religion, culture, civilization, science, and mathematics. It is a philosophy that seeks both to describe and theorize about the particularities of what actually happens in the world. Based on these understandings, Whiteheadian process theology strives to offer ideas about how the inhabitants of the world function and how we function in relationship to God. Yet this theology is not particular to human beings or to one religion or another. In this way, Whitehead's concepts of evil, freedom, immortality, and God are able to speak to the experiences of defeat and triumph, brokenness and wholeness, Christianity and non-Christian religions. Postmodern theology based on Whitehead's philosophical speculations can discuss salvation for all of creation as a way of living within the world and in relationship to God.

A Postmodern Theological Framework

A postmodern theological framework constructs a worldview that allows us to maintain belief in God within the context of the twentieth and twenty-first centuries. In today's society, technology facilitates interactions with people who are radically different from us. We are constantly dealing with different political systems, different religions, and people of different backgrounds and experiences. This has helped many of us to realize the problems of asserting the superiority of one category over another. We also know that there is more activity in the world than we can see at first glance: our skin cells die and regenerate when we are not paying attention; the most formidable mountain is composed of tiny, moving, sometimes unstable particles; the earth's resources can be depleted; and there may be life on other planets. As we become an increasingly complex society, we are also aware that there are vast inequities among the world's inhabitants. There are still great poverty, sickness, injustice, and death in the world.

A postmodern theological framework will seek to transcend the limits of modernity while also affirming the strengths of the premodern period. It will affirm constant change and movement in the world and reject hierarchical dualisms, such as those that value men, reason, and whiteness over women, emotion, and blackness. This postmodern theological framework will also affirm God's activity in the world, a divine purpose for our lives, and the sacrality and value of the nonhuman world. A postmodern theological framework will assert that God desires wholeness and life for the world's inhabitants. A postmodern framework will emphasize five qualities: (1) the ongoing processes of life, (2) individual ability to exercise power, (3) the inevitability of relationships on all levels of reality, (4) the eternal vision of God, and (5) opportunities for immortality in the midst of pervasive loss.

The Ongoing Process of Life

The only constant is change. In every moment of existence, we are influenced by the past and the possibilities available to us. The past includes our own individual past as well as that of the world around us. Using these factors, we become our own things. We sift through multiple experiences in order to decide or achieve or become one. As soon as we do this, our decision, action, or experience becomes part of the great world of experience. It is now available as a factor of influence in the world. We continually become part of the world, part of what influences others. This happens over and over again. We have new experiences moment to moment. There are ever-new possibilities available to us in each shifting circumstance. We can't stay exactly the same moment to moment. We are constantly changing.

The process of becoming happens on every level. Whether an atom, a plant, an animal, or a human being, we are composed of units of energy that are influenced both by the world around them and by available possibilities. We all undergo this process of becoming. There are, of course, levels of complexity. For example, the molecules in a chair do not vary greatly from one moment to the next. We expect this when we go to sit down in the chair. Imagine, however, that the chair is made of wood and placed out in the sun. With more factors influencing the chair, it may slowly change color. Some organisms have a central system that grants them more unity, complexity, and harmony—and hence, more stability in the midst of change. This is the case with some plants, animals, and human beings. But all aspects of reality have an experience of becoming. Not all entities are conscious of this, but we all experience the world and possibility with some degree of freedom and with the potential to change. This postmodern framework is compatible with many lessons of science.

Individual Ability to Exercise Power

Process theology takes our freedom seriously. When we decide what we are going to do, we freely make that decision. We can decide to continue as we have in the past. Or we may decide to do something new. The past can be a strong influence on future behavior. This allows for much of the continuity in the world. Still, there are always new opportunities available to us. There are, however, always possibilities available to us that do not emerge from our past alone. This is part of the process of becoming. We can sift through the inputs of the past and the future possibilities and become our own thing. We own that decision. In that moment, we *are* that decision. This freedom to choose ensures that all individuals have the ability to exercise power in their given situations. We always maintain a sense of agency.

These possibilities are relevant to our particular contexts. Not all possibilities in the world are available to us. Each moment's opportunities are conditioned by our past experiences and what is happening in the rest of the world. Sometimes the conditions of our past and our environment do not allow for many new options. It may seem that we don't have much to work with; there are not as many choices as we would like or feel that we need. Sometimes we are "choosing from the lesser of two evils." Other times we are surprised by the number and kinds of possibilities that are available. Sometimes there are more options than we could have imagined.

Because we are genuinely free, the future is not guaranteed. It is easy to assume that one may continue on as one has done in the past. Yet one can choose not to do so. Once we act, God works with what we have offered to God and to the world in order to influence us in the next moment. God is always working with what the world has to offer. Because we freely choose one thing or another, God does not know what we are going to do before we do it. Thus, the end is not guaranteed or foreordained. In this sense, process is an open system.

Internal Relationality

On all levels of reality, relationships are inevitable. As mentioned earlier, the world is radically interdependent. We are influenced by those around us, and we influence those around us. The same is true of our relationship with God. This is different from saying that relationships have a strong influence on us or that we realize that we need other people and other things for our own lives to work. The past and possibilities come together as we decide not just what to do, but who we become. They don't just *shape* who we are; these factors *constitute* who we are.

We are constituted by our relationships to other people, to our environment, our past, our ancestors, our limits, our hopes and anticipations for the future, our potential—seen, imagined, and unforeseen—and our God. We cannot be who we are without being shaped by things beyond ourselves. There is nothing outside of these relations. Relationality is not a choice. It *is*. Relationships are not just the glue that holds the world together. Relationships compose the world. They *are* the world. Relationships weave together our moral, cultural, religious, lived-in, believed-about, hoped-in world. Relationships are what keep us together.

This internal relationality makes divine incarnation universal. Because God is the one who offers us possibilities—indeed, offers Godself to us—in God's calling to the world, God is a part of who we are. In every moment, God breathes into us, helps to create who we are. There is something of God in everyone. Again, this is true of God's relationship with the nonhuman aspects of the world. God is calling, influencing, leading, guiding, and co-creating the entire world. Thus, we may say that when we see one another, we also see God. This is true not because God and the world are identical, as in pantheistic thought. In that system, God is identical to the world. This postmodern theological framework is panentheistic—God is *in* the entire world. Likewise, the entire world is in God. We are distinct from God—we are not God ourselves—but we are part of who and what God is, and God is a part of who and what we are. The entire world reveals God. When God appears in the world, God is not just present in human beings or even particular human beings. God is present in all dimensions of the world—the human and nonhuman components.

Because God is in every one of us, we are discouraged from valuing one part of the world over another. God's purposes are connected to God's ideal vision for the world, not the characteristics of the inhabitants in the world. In this postmodern theological framework, male is not superior to female or human beings to animals and nature. This is consonant with the ecological movement's insistence that the natural world and animals have intrinsic value. They are valuable not just because human beings are dependent on them for their lives, but because they have value in themselves. The natural world is partly divine—holy, sacred. This is also true of reason and emotion. All experiences have accompanying feelings. We experience facts and feelings together, and God is present throughout them all.

The Eternal Vision of God

God has hopes and preferences for the world. As we engage in the ongoing processes of life, God is actively involved. God offers us the possibilities that introduce newness into the world. Because of God, we are not destined to repeat our pasts. As God calls us to grow in new ways, God promotes certain ideals. In other words, God is not indifferent to the change in the world. God maintains an ideal vision for who and what the world can be. God calls us toward particular goals.

Affirming the goodness of God asserts that God's vision is for the common good of the world. After all, God is offering Godself to us in God's calling. God's vision is known by its principles, the ideals that God promotes within the world. This vision for the common good precedes any particular thing we say or do. It is informed, but not determined by, the events of the world. Because God does not know what we are going to do before we do it, we don't know ahead of time how God's ideals will look in the world. The actual form and details of God's vision will differ by context. Thus, what Whitehead calls "the kingdom of God" will play out differently in a small town in the southeastern United States than it will in a large city in South Africa. Each community's embrace of God's vision will look different.

This vision comes to the world in God's calling to each one of us. God orders the possibilities within each context according to God's ideals. This is not a strict ordering, though. God does not always offer five possibilities, ranking them in order of preference. There may be several equally "good" options. They simply lead in different directions. What we actually do is conditioned by our freedom. There is, however, no cause to assume that there is only one option that will embrace God's calling.

Opportunities for Immortality

In the midst of the ongoing processes of life, there will be loss, but there are ways to preserve life. As the events of the world become part of God's nature, we live on in God. We have a kind of eternal life within God. Yet we don't have to wait for the community of God outside of this world to experience any level of immortality. As we remember the past, we keep it alive within ourselves. When we become one of the factors that influence other parts of the world, we live on. Who we were in our last instance, last moment, last year, is gone. What we just did is indeed over. But as our impact is felt by others in the world and throughout the world, it is still alive. This kind of immortality gives our lives meaning. Our legacy matters. The facts of who we have been and what we have done can live on long after they have actually occurred.

Ultimately, this postmodern framework supports particular understandings of evil and its resolution. This theology acknowledges that the experience of evil, pain, and suffering has the ability to destroy our hope, our ability to make a difference in the world, and indeed our very faith in God and ourselves. Even when we survive these experiences, they have the capacity to make us into weaker, more fragile shells of who we once were. They can be our own personal and collective shipwrecks. So we must address them.

It's grasping for God in the midst of evil and pain and suffering that keeps us up at night. The manifestation of some evils—illness, poverty, war, violence, oppression, individual suffering—keeps us up at night. We are grasping in our own ways for words, thoughts, beliefs, and other people who will understand, explain, or comfort.

Do we simply accept that evil is a part of life? Should we wait for good to overcome evil in some realm outside of this world? Or do we resist evil here in the world? Yes, yes, and yes. This is what we live with. We live in a world not necessarily characterized by evil, but one that must contend with evil. And waiting for the resolution of evil and suffering is insufficient for us here and now. We must combat evil and try to overcome it. We can't, but we must.

We cannot overcome evil completely. There are some forms of evil that we cannot seem to eliminate alone. We can't get it out of the fabric of our society, out of the structure of our world—not without losing our freedom, and not without losing the aspects of life that we know are part of living in this world. Some evil, some loss can only be overcome in God, in the kingdom of God, in God's self, and in God's offering of Godself to the world.

And yet we must try. We must strive to enact God's ideal vision on earth even if we know we cannot see it in its fullness here. We still must heed the calling. As we heed God's calling, we can eliminate some evil in the world. That is, when we use our freedom in accordance with God's calling, we negate some aspects of the past that have created evil in the world. This is how we can avoid perpetuating some evils. This is how we can help to overcome evil. God's calling offers novelty or newness. Without it, we would be stuck repeating the past. While it sometimes hurts to lose some of the past, other times we rejoice when we can move beyond the past. Moving forward into newness—into what God desires for us and calls us to—can rid the world of some evils. It's a bit of a conundrum. The same freedom that destroys can be used to create. The same loss that causes us suffering can also leave evil behind and alleviate some of our suffering.

God's constant calling is to address, among other things, the evil of the world. God calls us, knowing who we are and what our situations are, and God tailors God's calling to us for our life situations. God calls us in every moment, so we always have the opportunity to do something new, to create again, to get rid of the bad, to be reborn. God does not give up on us, but calls each and every one of us to Godself, to relationship, to community and to God's ideal vision. And we, imbued with that kind of calling, have the power to change the world.

Womanist Challenges

A postmodern framework based on Alfred North Whitehead's philosophy must be able to speak to the realities of black women's lives. It will understand the religious and everyday experiences of black women as valid sources for information about the world. In so doing, it will address the issues of systemic oppression and injustice faced by black women in the United States. A postmodern theology will have to describe the ways in which God resists oppression. Conversation with womanist theology demands that a postmodern framework seek justice and wholeness for the world's inhabitants in this world. There must be ways to combat evil in the world in which we live. In order to speak to the experiences of black women, a postmodern theology must depict a God whose vision for the world resists oppression, and describe ways in which justice can be achieved in the world.

Modern Assumptions

A postmodern theology must account for what we currently know about the world. Applying Whitehead's philosophy to a postmodern context requires a criticism of Whitehead's modern assumptions. Both *Religion in the Making* and *Adventures of Ideas* reflect a social Darwinism that describes the evolution of religions and societies as moving from lower to higher. The civilizations and religions that he describes as tribal and social tend to be ones that we could call "indigenous" today. The civilizations and religions that are described as rational and civilized are associated with Europe (Christianity) and Asia (Buddhism). In Whitehead's scheme, African traditional religions are "lower," "social" religions that are merely a stage in the evolutionary process toward a "rational religion." Whitehead reveals a supersessionism that is partly attributable to his own background and the modern notions of his day. Using Whitehead for any postmodern discussion of evil and wholeness requires a rejection of these aspects of his discussion.

Second, Whitehead's naming of the consequent nature of God as "the kingdom of God" or "the kingdom of heaven" reveals a monarchical and Christocentric interpretation of the realm of God's reception and valuation of the world. Many Christians critique this naming and find alternative ways to describe God's ideal: "heaven," "the kin-dom of God," "the family of God," "the community of God," "the commonwealth of God," and so forth. A postmodern theological framework maintains the critique of "kingdom" language, while also considering how some non-Christian religions understand something variously described as the changing aspects of God, God's incorporation of the world, the realm of idealized values within God, God's feeling of the world, and God's valuation of the world. A postmodern theological framework searches for multiple creative ways of naming what has traditionally been called "the kingdom of God."

Whitehead also assumes that society or "civilization" will change into forms that are increasingly complex, harmonious, interesting, and, by implication, higher. This attitude is also a reflection of modernity's hope in itself and in the progress of civilization. Postmodernism does not assume that modernism will lead to the common good or the most creative societies. There are too many examples of violence and destruction in today's society for those unqualified beliefs. Thus, a postmodern theology cannot guarantee a happy ending. It hopes and strives for the common good as the world and God work together. Yet it is constantly aware of the ways that our freedom and evil can impede upon and undo the good that is possible in our world.

Whitehead's commitment to experience affirms postmodern adaptations of his philosophy. Whitehead believed that his philosophy of organism should be able to describe experiences in the world: "Our datum is the actual world, including ourselves; and this actual world spreads itself for observation in the guide of the topic of our immediate experiences. The elucidation of immediate experience is the sole justification for any thought; and the starting-point for thought is the analytic observation of components of this experience."[55] These experiences should serve as the foundation for the theory and philosophical description of the world. [56] In his oft-quoted analogy of the airplane, Whitehead describes his methodology as constantly experimental. Whitehead's metaphysics is formed in the following manner—it will start in one field of observation, make flight into the air of generalization, and land again for observation in another field where the generalization will be tested, adapted, and tried again in yet another field to which the airplane will fly: "The true method of discovery . . . starts from the ground of particular observation; it makes flight in the thin air of imaginative generalization; and it again lands for renewed observation rendered acute by rational interpretation."[57] A postmodern theology that is true to Whitehead's vision always contains an element of philosophical generalization, but this generalization is constantly tested by specific examples. These examples will emerge from today's postmodern understandings and commitments.

Whitehead also believed that the experiences of the world were the final test of any theory. Whitehead describes the relationship between theory and experience in this way: "Whatever is found in 'practice' must lie within the scope of the metaphysical description. When the description fails to include the 'practice,' the metaphysics is inadequate and requires revision."[58] Thus, the theory is secondary to what we know about the world. If there are differences between what experience tells us and what the theory says, we should adapt the theory to account for what we know. In this way, a postmodern theology describes a system for how the world works, but the system is not ultimate. Experience has the last word. We are encouraged to revise the theoretical system as necessary to reflect our knowledge of the world. This reveals a commonality with womanist theology, which begins with black women's experiences. This notion of testing generalities against experience also provides an opening for a conversation with womanist theologies, because our philosophical understandings can be adapted to include multiple religious experiences.

When religious scholars took Whitehead's airplane and landed in the field of religion, process theology was born. Process theologians have creatively and insightfully combined Whitehead's metaphysics with religion and theology. They have developed process interpretations of many religions—Protestant and Catholic Christianity, Judaism, Buddhism, Hinduism, and others. This plurality of religious interpretations points to the fact that Whitehead's philosophical framework is not bound to the explication of any single religion. As a speculative description of the entire world, the system itself does not require or presume a Christian starting point. Thus, a postmodern theological framework based on Whitehead's philosophy can be used to discuss various religious traditions, as well as their relation to one another within the world and the divine.

Oppression and Injustice

Whitehead's philosophy has been criticized for its inability to address unjust suffering and oppression. Black religious scholar William R. Jones believes that process theology neglects ethnic suffering. The reality of ethnic suffering, he says, "demands the accommodation of the maldistribution of suffering in particular groups."[59] A theology adequate for African Americans must acknowledge and explain how oppression is experienced on the basis of race and ethnicity. Oppression is unjustly distributed. Process theology is too neutral for Jones. African American philosopher of religion Thandeka agrees: "Process thought does not make a distinction between suffering endemic to the entire human race and suffering which is meted out by one ethnic group to another."[60] Although all people may suffer, there are systems of evil that target one set of people rather than another.

In *Adventures of Ideas*, Whitehead introduces systemic evil in his philosophy. He says that if a system inhibits more beauty than it creates, it is, on the whole, an evil system: "Thus any system of things which in any wide sense is beautiful is to that extent justified in its existence. It may however fail in another sense, by inhibiting more Beauty than it creates. Thus the system, though in a sense beautiful, is on the whole evil in that environment."[61] From this statement, one can argue that certain systems are evil. When combined with Whitehead's earlier assertion that evil is produced when the social environment experiences a loss, there is room for a construction of systemic evil. Take the example of American slavery. Although some beauty was created by the economic value of slavery and the development of the South, slavery inhibited the beauty of the freedom and flourishing of African Americans, and the wider society was also constrained because of its acceptance of racism. Slavery inhibited a much greater beauty than it created and was, therefore, an evil system.

Without modification, a Whiteheadian construction of systemic evil affirms God's aesthetic and rational vision for the world. The primordial vision outlined in *Adventures of Ideas* identifies God's ideals as truth, beauty, adventure, and art. This aesthetic vision speaks of artistic endeavors such as painting and theater. Whitehead did not intend to include religious and cultural expressions—such as dancing to Oya's rhythm—in his vision of "beauty" and "art." Similar to his belief that civilization progresses and religions become increasingly rational in Christianity and Buddhism, Whitehead concludes that God leads the world to higher heights through forms of reason. God's role "lies in the patient operation of the overpowering rationality of his conceptual harmonization."[62] Thandeka finds this rational God insufficient for addressing the oppression that many African Americans face. She writes, "Whitehead's God has the manners of an English gentleman. The God of the oppressed has the hard-edged rage of random injustice, awesome power, inexplicable suffering and steadfast love."[63] Indeed, concepts of beauty and reason seem inadequate to describe the racism, sexism, classism, and heterosexism many womanist theologians describe as part and parcel of black women's experiences. God must offer more than beauty and reason for their resolution: "Whitehead's vision does not touch the immediate lives and needs of the oppressed. Its reach only exceeds, but does not include the immediate material concerns of the oppressed."[64]

Whitehead's philosophy can be amended to account for the reality of oppression in the world. African American process theologian Henry Young acknowledges that Whitehead does not address systemic oppression, but he does believe that Whitehead's philosophy contains the necessary elements for the transformation of social structures. God's ability to share in the world's experiences affirms that God shares in our sufferings.[65] The interdependence of God and the world, which is affirmed in process metaphysics, also avoids the otherworldliness and dualism that characterize race relations in America.

A postmodern theological framework must assert that God resists oppression. The modern period is marked, as ethicist Theodore Walker Jr. points out, by the commodification of human bodies as cargo and slave labor in the transatlantic slave trade.[66] Walker agrees with Griffin and notes that modernity's propagation of the transatlantic slave trade means that a constructive postmodern framework must also speak to the legacy of slavery. In so doing, a constructive postmodern theology will, among other things, have to identify God as one who struggles against oppression.[67]

This postmodern theological framework must assert that one of God's ideals for the world is justice. God is not impartial or insensitive to experiences of suffering that result from systems of oppression and unjust power relations. As God desires the well-being of all of creation, God resists injustice wherever it is found. This is different from the black theological assertion that God is the God of the oppressed. God is, rather, the God of all. God is the God of all people, and the nonhuman communities of the world as well. God opposes injustice and oppression. This constructive move can account for the multivalency of oppression. For example, a black man in America is oppressed in a racist society. If God is the God of the oppressed, then God is on his side. But if this black man abuses his female partner, does God switch sides to be with her? What if she abuses her child? A God who resists oppression does not love or hate, accept or despise one person in this scenario more than another. God resists the oppressive activity and calls each party to justice in their future actions. God calls the world around these people to enact justice in their lives. A postmodern theological framework that takes seriously the experiences of black women will expand Whitehead's description of God's ideal vision. God's ideals include justice and quality of life.[68]

Addressing oppression requires a postmodern theological framework to speak to justice and quality of life for the world here in the land of the living. This will also involve adjustments to Whitehead's options for addressing evil. Whitehead offers salvation most explicitly through eternal life in God. A vision of heaven is offered to the world, and good only truly triumphs over evil outside of this world—in God. Thandeka finds this to be a problematic aspect of process theology: "What we end up with . . . is an 'in the by-and-by' theology. Freedom eventually but not now. But as Jesse Jackson has said, justice delayed is justice denied."[69] This postmodern theological framework does not disagree with Whitehead's description of a realm outside of this world where God finds good and value in every occurrence of the world, and where God's ideals are actualized. However, a postmodern theological framework emphasizes the activity of God in the world. It cares more deeply about the way life is lived in this world. A postmodern theological framework focuses on opportunities for wholeness, justice, quality of life, beauty, and adventure in this world.

I've focused on evil in this chapter because I think it is the issue that makes our religious lives, our theologies, so difficult. It is where we often find ourselves, our beliefs, and our lives in pieces among boulders in the sea. Ship-wrecked. That notwithstanding, this postmodern framework does not just tell us how to respond to the reality of our suffering and our experiences and observations of evil in the world. It tells us how we exist in today's world in relationship to God. It describes how we live, and it promotes a certain way of living in the world—a way that will lead to the common good. This postmod-ern framework should be just as true to our beautiful, life-giving, and creative experiences in the world as it is to our wrestling with evil.

Three

Creative Transformation
Teaching and Healing Communities of God

I had come into the city carrying life in my eyes amid rumors of death.—Sonia Sanchez[1]

A lot is lost in this world. This loss is a result of how the world operates. We cannot fully maintain the past in its immediacy. While this loss of the past allows us to overcome and negate evil, it also means that it is difficult to maintain and perpetuate what is good. Much of this loss is really loss in comparison to what might have been. We do not become in accordance with our highest capabilities or the greatest ideals. We often act as if we are not interrelated. We act in our own self-interest and in the interest of self-preservation. When we do so, we fight against the reality of our own processes. This type of behavior leads to personal, social, and systemic evils. Such manifestations of evil include racism, sexism, heterosexism, oppression, unnecessary involuntary suffering, servanthood, surrogacy, injustice, rape, prohibitions to equality and wholeness, and devaluation of actuality. These are transformations of the world in destructive, rather than constructive, directions.

A postmodern womanist theology strives to overcome this loss and isolated decision making. Not all evil can be overcome in this world, and yet a postmodern womanist theology maintains hope in the struggle to creatively and constructively respond to it. Sometimes feelings of discord are the result of the conflicts in the world. Sometimes liberation is not possible, but survival and quality of life are. All-encompassing health, wholeness, unity, and salvation are never fully attained in this world. As we constantly become, we are constantly vulnerable to evil and also constantly capable of overcoming it. So how do we live? How do we go on in the midst of such soul-numbing and crippling circumstances? How do we "carry life in our eyes amid rumors of death"?

Postmodern womanist theology promotes living in cooperation with God for the constructive social transformation of the world. This is a process—a normative way of living toward the realization of the good. In postmodern womanist theology, salvation is an activity. Each new moment brings possibilities in both directions. A postmodern womanist theology strives for tangible representations of the good. The good includes justice, equality, discipleship, quality of life, acceptance, and inclusion.

Postmodern womanist theology is a normative process of becoming, a particular way of living in the world. Both the postmodern theological framework and the womanist concept of salvation assert that the movement of life is constituted by the past, God and creaturely agency. In and of itself, this process of change can be either destructive or creative. Salvation includes the creative modes of change in the world. In a constructive womanist theology, salvation is "making a way out of no way." In process theology, this concept can be called *creative transformation*. Correlating and adapting these two concepts reveals the normative processes that a postmodern womanist theology describes.

Postmodern womanist theology focuses on creative transformation in the activities of teaching and healing. It draws from the womanist emphasis on the life and ministry of Jesus to highlight the ways in which teaching and healing positively bring about change in the world. Finally, a postmodern womanist concept of creative transformation insists that this process of living with loss, death, and evil occurs in and through communities. Because evil occurs in a relational world and sin is understood as social and systemic (as well as personal), salvation must respond to evil in an explicitly communal context. A postmodern theological framework explains and expands upon the community focus of the constructive womanist concept of salvation. In so doing, the attainment of wholeness and health is described as an activity that happens in particular contexts throughout the entire world. Ultimately, postmodern womanist theology aims at the creative transformation of the world in accordance with God's vision.

Creative Transformation

The philosophical language of the postmodern theological framework combines with the metaphorical language of "making a way out of no way." The process theological concept of "creative transformation" relates to my description of "making a way out of no way." Creative transformation talks about how we work with God to implement God's ideals in the world. Although this concept explains what we should do with the evil we encounter, it is much more. Creative transformation gives us a model for how to live. Drawing from the womanist focus on the ministry of Jesus and the pursuit of justice, a postmodern womanist theology embraces the action verbs of *teaching* and *healing* to describe the ways that communities live with God and the world.

Process theologian John B. Cobb Jr. has a unique understanding of creative transformation.[2] Creative transformation is Cobb's way of talking about a certain type of change and growth that occurs as a result of God's introduction of novelty. Although Cobb was not the first process thinker to write about creative transformation,[3] I select his articulation of the concept primarily because of the notoriety of his work in the field of process theology. Cobb asserts that God does *not* sanction the norms and institutions of the past, but calls us beyond the achievements of the past to a new future. Creative transformation is more "a way change occurs rather than the specific content at any given time."[4] The Logos, or the Word of God, is the source of novelty in each moment, and when it is incarnate in the world, it is called Christ.[5] Thus, he concludes, "[W]here Christ is effectively present, there is creative transformation."[6]

We see the first articulations of this concept in *God and the World*. For Cobb, this change, this "call forward," breaks the bonds of determinism and introduces new possibilities into the world:

> The ideal and normative possibility for our self-actualization stands in tension with the power of the past and seeks to lure us beyond what the past would otherwise determine for the present. It is this claim of the normative possibility upon us which I am naming the call forward, and this call forward is the aspect of human experience in relation to which we as Christians have reason to approach the question of God.[7]

The call forward describes the relationship between God and the world. For Cobb, this call forward is connected to God *and* to Jesus. Cobb believes that our understanding of Jesus should be connected with what is happening in our contemporary context: "We can only go forward in a way that somehow corresponds for our time to the meaning of [Jesus'] life and message for the [people] of his time. My proposal is that we can do this best by attending to what I am hereafter designating as the *call forward*."[8]

In *Christ in a Pluralistic Age*, Cobb outlines creative transformation as a way of articulating a Christology.[9] Drawing from the Gospel of John, Cobb's articulation of creative transformation follows in the tradition of Logos-Christologies, wherein Jesus is understood as the preexistent Word of God. In Whitehead's terms, the Logos is the primordial nature of God: "The Logos is the cosmic

principle of order, the ground of meaning, and the source of purpose. Whitehead has called this transcendent source of the aim at the new the principle
of concretion, the principle of limitation, the organ of novelty, the lure for
feeling, the eternal urge of desire, the divine Eros, and God in his Primordial Nature."[10] Just as God's primordial or unchanging nature comes into
the world through God's calling, the Logos becomes incarnate in the world.
When it does, it is called Christ.

Christ is that power of transformation, the process of change itself. But it
is a normative change. Cobb clearly asserts that not all change is good, and
therefore not all change can be called Christ. That is, most of what is called
change is a rearrangement, a return to or rejection of the past.[11] However,
Christ is positive change for the new: "To identify Christ with the new is to
see the new as unrealized potentiality for transforming the world without
destroying it. The new builds upon the old and transfuses it with meaning it
could not have apart from the new. The new not only frees us from the old
but also frees us for it."[12] Christ is not an objective rule that is followed, but an
image for this normative changing:

> But we need a unifying image to guide us in our hopeful open-
> ness to being transformed. We need an image of that kind of
> existence that is optimally open to this transformation and
> hence appropriate as an eschatological image of what human
> beings should be and may become. Christ provides such an
> image as well. And, indeed, a major reason for concern with the
> particular structure of Jesus' existence is that he may provide us
> as Christians with the needed image of hope.[13]

Although Cobb's Christ is a universal concept, it is connected to the historical Jesus and the (Chalcedonian) creedal formulations of the church traditions. Christ is not reducible to Jesus, but we can discern Christ in Jesus in a
unique way. Jesus reveals God to us in two ways. First, Jesus is different from
most human beings. Jesus was co-constituted by God's calling. That is, Jesus
conformed to the calling from God in such a way as to bring about a distinct
structure of existence in which we now participate.[14] Jesus is the same as
other humans metaphysically but different structurally.[15] Second, the real life,
crucifixion, and resurrection of Jesus created a "field of force" that people can
enter. Jesus is present through this field of force, and as we participate in the
field, we are conformed, to some degree, to him. We participate in this field
through Christian traditions such as the teachings of Jesus and the sacraments
of the church. As people focus on Jesus, they become more and more open to
creative transformation.[16] Cobb rejects identifying Jesus as God but links them

closely: "To know Jesus' presence in this field of force, to be conformed to him, was also to share in his openness to God's future and hence to the Logos. The presence of Christ as Jesus and of Christ as Logos was united."[17]

In summary, Cobb's creative transformation is the activity of the Logos seen in the Gospel of John. This Logos was with God and was God and is effective in the world, giving us hope and salvation. The Logos became flesh in Jesus, and this "enfleshment" gave new effectiveness to the everlasting creative work of the Logos in the world. This creative transformation is Christ.[18] Cobb's description of creative transformation can be articulated with four identifiable characteristics. Creative transformation is (1) contextual and particular, (2) challenging, (3) noncoercive, and (4) universal.[19]

Creative transformation is not a categorical imperative to which one adheres in every situation. Rather, creative transformation is particular for each context: "The need is to discern the call of Christ in each particular situation. That is not decided by appeal to any established principle. It is to be determined in openness to the meaning of Christ for that situation."[20] For that reason, creative transformation will look different in each context. Creative transformation is tailor-made for the exact context in which we find ourselves: "The Logos in its transcendence is timeless and infinite, but in its incarnation or immanence it is always a specific force for just that creative transformation which is possible and optimal in each situation."[21] Thus, the details of creative transformation will differ in every context.

Because creative transformation is contextual and seeks the best possible option in each situation, it is not always felt as good. In some instances, none of the options are good; the best possible option is the "lesser of the available evils." In other situations, the divine perspective has more information than we do, and hence may lead in a direction that is the best given the wider context that we are unable to see. In other circumstances, the aim is pushing us out of our comfort zones. For these reasons, Cobb concludes that creative transformation is not always *felt* as good: "This aim is at what would be best in each moment in terms of a wider view of the consequences than we ordinarily take; . . . Hence the divine presence is experienced as an other, sometimes recognized as gracious, often felt as judge."[22]

One reason that creative transformation is not always *felt* as good is because it challenges the status quo. As creative transformation leads us into the future, it necessarily challenges the world as we currently experience it: "Indeed the Logos is threatening to any given world, for it functions to transcend and transform it. . . . In short, the function of the Logos is to introduce tension between what has been and what might be and continuously to challenge and upset the established order for the sake of the new."[23] Creative transformation upsets the status quo and demands that we give up the things to which we are attached. But the challenge is for our own sake as it moves us beyond the stagnation of the past that would destroy us.[24] Again, Cobb connects creative transformation to Christ and Jesus: "Whitehead noted how [Jesus'] teaching, just because of its impracticability and purity, creates restlessness with every existing system. When the world one is inclined to take for granted is rendered questionable, one is open to creative transformation."[25] Hence, creative transformation is always a call to action: "Christ is a reality in terms of which one is called and empowered to act responsibly."[26] Creative transformation is manifest in the action that we take when we incarnate the Logos.

Creative transformation is never forced on the world. Although the Logos comes to us, we must make our own decisions about whether to embody it: "But if the aim is at realization of a creative and novel goal, then the decision as to whether, and to what degree, to embody that possibility has considerable latitude and importance. The initial aim is the immanence of the Logos. . . . The decision is the locus of freedom."[27] The Logos is not a law, but an offering to the world.[28] The Logos calls us, but we may choose not to respond: "We are called to be what in that moment would be fullness. But the calling is not a compulsion. Our actual decision often misses the mark—sometimes rebelliously."[29] Because we have the freedom to accept or reject the Logos, the efficacy of creative transformation is ultimately our decision.[30]

Creative transformation is as efficacious as it is in part because of our decisions and in part because of the universality of creative transformation. Christ is not identical to Jesus nor to any historical figure in particular. Creative transformation is operative throughout the world. Cobb writes, "Let me finally say directly what I mean by 'Christ.' I mean the incarnation of God in the world. That God is in the world, and the effect God's presence has in the world, we know in and through Jesus. That God was present in him was unique. But Christ is not limited to the one historical person."[31] Christ is the change that occurs in humanity, in art, in philosophy, everywhere.

Cobb declares that Christ is the source of all life: "Christ is the giver of life to all who live, of freedom to all who are free, of understanding to all who understand, of love to all who love. Apart from Christ, there could be no life, no reason, no imagination, no personal or social redemption."[32] In *Liberation of Life*, Cobb and coauthor Charles Birch talk about *Life* as the general increase of order against the backdrop of entropy. Life, the guiding principle in evolution, works creative transformation in the world.[33] Cobb identifies Life as God, Breath, Spirit, and Logos. Thus, in his last published work that deals explicitly with creative transformation, Cobb expands creative transformation from human life and ideas to nonhuman life:

Creative transformation has its clearest manifestation to us as
energizing and providential grace in personal life. But . . . it
is also the life in all living things. The living differs from the
inanimate in that it is not a mere product of its past. Life is also
always a transcending of the past. Creative transformation as the
immanence of God in the world is not only the way but life
itself, the life by which all that is alive lives. . . . Creative transformation is a constitutive element in every truly individual
event.[34]

Creative transformation is everywhere and in everything. It has a universal
quality to it.

The universality that Cobb asserts can make it appear as if there is no
normative criterion by which to evaluate whether or not a specific change
is creative transformation. Creative transformation is, after all, not *all* change.
It is particular to each situation. It is decided by the aim of the Logos *and* the
freedom of the event. It is change that upsets the status quo and moves toward
greater complexity. In a later work, Cobb specifically writes that creative
transformation is manifest in the world in a particular manner: "*Christ* must
be the life that struggles against the death-dealing powers that threaten us and
the way that leads through the chaos of personal and global life to just, participatory, and sustainable society in which personal wholeness is possible."[35]
Thus, when humans are called to respond to God, creative transformation is
the response that liberates humanity and the planet from "the forces of death
that now threaten it."[36]

Cobb's creative transformation is tied to his Christology. Cobb initially
calls creative transformation "Christ" in order to open Christians to religious
pluralism. A broad concept of Christ allows Christians to see Christ outside of specifically Christian contexts: "Yet Christians can name as Christ
the unrecognized or misunderstood working of the Logos in the world if
they mean to identify what they name with what they intend to serve. In
this sense Christians can name as Christ creative transformation in art, in
persons of other faiths, and in the planetary biosphere."[37] Without inten-
tion, this understanding can further alienate Christians from non-Christians.
Because the word "Christ" has assumed a specific connection to Jesus and
Christian exclusivism, the result of Cobb's assertions is that Christians can
identify Christian concepts in non-Christian contexts. In fact, Cobb asserts,
Christ is most fully effective when Christians name creative transformation as
"Christ": "Christ can be most fully present and effective where people believe

in creative transformation, understand it rightly, trust it, and open themselves to it. This is most likely to happen when the effective presence of the Logos is recognized as Christ."[38] The implication of such a statement is that Christians must name this normative change as "Christ" for it to be fully effective. This move, intentionally or not, elevates Christianity to a place above other world religious traditions.

There is no need to intertwine the concept of creative transformation with ideas about Jesus and Christ. Cobb admits that he calls creative transformation "Christ" because of his own personal experience and faith conviction: "The divine presence in all creatures, that was incarnate in Jesus, I experience as creative and transformative, and so I have called it creative transformation. This creative transformation I also call Christ."[39] Cobb acknowledges that there are limitations to his concept of Christ, and later in his career he extends his Christology beyond creative transformation to incorporate lessons he has learned from liberation and feminist theologians.[40] Yet he still identifies creative transformation as Christ. This isn't necessary for a postmodern womanist theology. Whitehead's metaphysics provides a concept of change that incorporates the past, unforeseen possibilities, and decision-making in the becoming of the world. Both Whitehead and faith convictions insist on connecting this change to an entity called God. God must have a role in this change that occurs as the world advances, but a Logos-Christology is not necessary to maintain the best that the concept of creative transformation has to offer.

Cobb's concept of creative transformation gives a normative valuation to the process of becoming articulated in the postmodern theological framework. Creative transformation is the change that occurs when God's aims toward novelty are accepted and incorporated. Creative transformation is contextual and particular, challenging, noncoercive, and found in human and nonhuman life. Creative transformation incorporates the past and moves beyond it in a way that we could not have imagined by ourselves. Cobb tells us that there is something in this world that should and indeed does struggle against the death-dealing powers that threaten us personally and globally. Cobb tells us that there is something that is moving us toward just, participatory, and sustainable societies in which personal wholeness is possible.

This is the best that the concept of creative transformation has to offer, but it does not bind us to Cobb's Logos-Christology. Yet we retain the nomenclature of "creative transformation." Doing so reminds us that this normative change does not just move us through time, but it transforms us as we become. It transforms the world. The term *creative* affirms the way in which we are created and self-creating in our change. It also reminds us that this change emerges from grasping that which the past alone does not suggest. It surprises us; it amazes us; it is something we might not have seen on our own. It is amazing and creative. If we hold on to *this* understanding of creative transformation, a de-Christ-ed version of creative transformation, creative transformation can open us up to new possibilities. One of these possibilities is dialogue with other religious and theological traditions, such as womanist theology.

"Making a Way Out of No Way" and Creative Transformation

The constructive womanist concept of "making a way out of no way" and the postmodern theological understanding of creative transformation complement and enrich one another. "Making a way out of no way" involves God's presentation of unforeseen possibilities; human agency; the goal of justice, survival, and quality of life; and a challenge to the existing order. Creative transformation is contextual and particular, challenging, noncoercive, and universal. Postmodern womanist theology de-centers Christ and Jesus in order to expand the notion of divine-creaturely cooperative change beyond the scope of particular Christologies and Christianity in general. Postmodern womanist theology affirms creative transformation with the metaphorical language of "making a way out of no way."

Like creative transformation, "making a way out of no way" is a type of change that transforms humanity and the wider world. This constructive womanist concept of salvation comes from the new vision that God provides to black women, who then have significant agency in moving the future toward a just and participatory society. It, too, challenges the status quo. By operating in situations that black women find life threatening, it actually does, to use Cobb's language, "struggle against the death dealing powers that threaten us." Like creative transformation, "making a way out of no way" is contextual, particular, noncoercive, and challenging.

Like "making a way out of no way," creative transformation offers a new vision that does not come completely out of the past. Creative transformation challenges the oppressive forces of society. The aims of creative transformation are particular to each situation, and God may not always lead us in ways that feel liberating. Sometimes the God of creative transformation will feel like a judge. But creative transformation is leading us to a way that will improve quality of life. Creative transformation involves God's presentation of unforeseen possibilities; human agency; a telos of justice, survival, and quality of life; and a challenge to the existing order.

A postmodern womanist theology understands "making a way out of no way" as a type of creative transformation. Doing so moves womanist theology in important directions. First, it gives womanist theology a metaphysical grounding to what has previously been empirically observed by examining the experiences of black women. Now we can say with greater strength that "making a way out of no way" is not just particular to the lives of black women or the black community. This concept gives normative dress to the change that always occurs in a world of change and becoming. "Making a way out of no way" asserts that the aim of God is always toward survival, quality of life, and justice in every context. Now womanist theologians, starting with the experiences of black women, can make a claim for all of creation—not just black women.

Second, "making a way out of no way" as creative transformation necessarily extends to nonhuman communities. Karen Baker-Fletcher's theology incorporates justice for nonhuman environments. A postmodern womanist theology goes several steps further. It states that the nonhuman environment is also guided by the aims of God. When Baker-Fletcher expresses the need to be concerned about the natural world, she describes this as an extension of concern for humanity—because of humanity's dependence on the earth. For Baker-Fletcher, womanist concern for the earth is motivated by the correlation of women, people of color, and poor people in areas of environmental toxicity and the mere fact that humanity needs a healthy earth to exist.[41] A postmodern womanist theology talks about divine and *creaturely* agency. It will alert African Americans to ecological crises and the notion that the natural world, too, is and must be transformed into a higher quality of its own life. With or without the presence of humanity, God is guiding and transforming the natural world to its best potential as well.

Postmodern womanist theology understands salvation as activity, as a kind of changing. The quest for wholeness, health, freedom, and justice involves a combination of God's activity in revealing possibilities that affirm God's vision for the world and the agency of the world. Our lives should challenge the status quo and yet not be coercive. Saving activity is not always experienced as good as it aims for justice, survival, and quality of life. Salvation is universal in that all human beings, living things, and nonliving things may experience it. Still, salvation is particular and contextual for each of us, each situation and each community in the world.

Teaching and Healing

A postmodern womanist theology sees creative transformation in acts of teaching and healing. Although a postmodern womanist theology de-centers

Christology from its concept of creative transformation, it expands upon womanist theories of salvation and Jesus to find a descriptive image of creative transformation. Such specificity is necessary because the previous discussion of creative transformation offers theoretical criteria with little reference to their manifestation in the real world.

In womanist discussions of salvation and Jesus, salvation comes from per- petuating the saving activity of Jesus. Whereas Jacquelyn Grant focuses on black women's ability to identify with Jesus because of their shared experi- ences of suffering, Kelly Brown Douglas focuses on black women's imitation of Jesus. Douglas's assertion that Christ can be found in the faces of the poor- est black women is not about the race, gender, or suffering of black women. Rather, Christ is found in black women when they are struggling for whole- ness for the black community. For Douglas, it is Jesus' activity, not his constitu- tion or particular experiences, that make him Savior and worthy of emulation by contemporary African American women. She writes, "[T]o portray Christ in the face of Black heroines and heroes signals that it was not who Jesus was, particularly as a male, that made him Christ, but what he did."[42]

Douglas places particular emphasis on Jesus' inclusion of all people, includ- ing the least of these. The Synoptic Gospels represent Jesus dining with sin- ners, healing lepers, and teaching women. These are all acts of welcoming the marginalized of society into fellowship. Jesus' inclusion and acts of hospitality are acts of healing. In the activity of welcoming and fellowship, Jesus heals the fragmented society of his time. Healing does not always refer to the transfor- mation of the physical body.[43] The activity of healing, while sometimes bodily, is the activity of restoring wholeness and community where there is exclu- sion, corruption, individualism, fragmentation, and brokenness. Thus, salvation is found in Jesus and in those who imitate Jesus in these acts of healing.

Similarly, Delores Williams's ministerial vision suggests that salvation is mediated through the activities of teaching and healing. When Williams focuses on the activities of Jesus, she describes activities that are instructive and healing: "Jesus showed humanity a vision of righting relations between body, mind and spirit through an ethical ministry of words ... through a heal- ing ministry of touch and being touched ... through a militant ministry of expelling evil forces ... through a ministry of prayer ... through a ministry of compassion and love."[44] The "ethical ministry of words" describes Jesus' teach- ing the community through the beatitudes, parables, and moral commands. Jesus' "ministry of prayer" can be seen as a learning process whereby Jesus took time to commune with God, nature, and his inner self in order to return to the larger community with greater wisdom and resources. The "healing ministry of touch" includes the instances when Jesus heals lepers, women, and the blind, to name a few. The "militant ministry of expelling evil forces" is also an act of healing individuals and oftentimes the communities that mistreat individuals who are different from the majority.

JoAnne Terrell and Karen Baker-Fletcher also refer to the dimensions of teaching and healing that contribute to salvation. In her search for the significance of the blood Jesus shed on the cross in the religious experiences of African American Christians, Terrell concludes that the present generation can learn from the crucifixions of those who have died unjustly and from the sacramental witnesses of those who died for the sake of righteousness. In this case, it is not the blood but the activity that led to the bloodshed that Terrell finds instructive:

> This is what I think it means to witness *sacramentally* to the character of God: loving one's own, *not* loving others uncritically and, most important, *not* being defined by one's victimization but by one's commitment. . . . God is, as revealed in Christ, loving and challenging, humane and sovereign, culturally engaged yet countercultural, personal, a healer and a mystic, a co-sufferer and a liberator.[45]

The activities of loving, maintaining convictions, challenging, healing, liberating, and praying are markers to the sacramental witness that Terrell proscribes in interpretations of the cross. Terrell gives the examples of the martyrs who learned from Jesus: "[T]he martyrs . . . sought to demonstrate bodily the utter feasibility of life in love and honor, as their association with Jesus had taught them."[46] Past acts of resistance and conviction teach the present generation how to strive for the goals of salvation.

Karen Baker-Fletcher's contribution to the activities of teaching and healing is revealed in her discussion of the role of the ancestors and the natural world in theological construction. The ancestors are important because of their ability to convey knowledge. Whether that knowledge comes by the present's memory of the ancestors or by the activity of the ancestors in the lives of the present generation through dreams, visions, possessions, and so forth, the ancestors have something to teach contemporary black women. Regarding the activity of healing, Baker-Fletcher asserts that the natural world must be healed and that the health of humanity, black women in particular, is tied up with the health of the planet.

Postmodern womanist theology focuses on creative transformation in certain types of activity. Creative transformation comes through teaching, learning, healing, loving, welcoming, remembering, and tuning into the voice of God. A postmodern womanist theology categorizes these activities into acts of teaching and healing. Just as womanist interpretations of salvation understand teaching and healing as the activities that lead to the ideals of discipleship, wholeness, justice, survival, and quality of life, a postmodern womanist theology focuses on the activities of teaching and healing to assert ways that creative transformation is both mediated to the world and represented in the world.

Communal Context

Postmodern womanist theology requires a communal context for salvation. A constructive womanist concept of salvation states that community is the vehicle and goal of salvation for black people. The postmodern theological framework requires that salvation occur in and through community. The activity of salvation cannot occur in isolation, but rather in the relationality of the world and God. That is, salvation aims at bringing communities together, and there is no salvation unless the entire community is saved. Postmodern womanist theology understands community as critical to the process of salvation.

"Making a way out of no way" insists that salvation be extended to the entire community. Although womanist concepts of salvation focus on the experiences of black women, they insist that salvation concern the entire community. In the most general sense, womanist theologians are referring to the well-being of the African American community. Yet in the development of womanist theology, the circle of concern has grown wider and wider. Jacquelyn Grant insists that womanists are concerned about the salvation of both black women and black men. Kelly Brown Douglas's inclusion of heterosexism as sinful exhibits this principle. If black lesbian women do not experience the same freedoms as their heterosexual counterparts, then no black woman is truly liberated.[47] Douglas also looks beyond the experiences of black women in America and highlights the need for African American women to make alliances with third world women of color around the globe:

> If we are truly committed to the struggles of our sisters, we must forge links with each other whether we are Third World women living in Third World countries or Third World women trapped in the First World. It is only together that we will be able to free our churches and society from the evils of race, class, gender and sexual oppression that keep our sisters in bondage.[48]

Douglas's focus on the collectivity of third-world women reiterates the point that salvation is not just *for* the community, but happens *through* community and through collaboration for the same goal. Karen Baker-Fletcher extends salvation beyond the scope of humanity to include the natural world. The natural world also needs to be saved—oftentimes from the ways humanity abuses it. She writes, "The entire earth cries out with humankind for justice. . . . The earth is described as fallen because of humankind's corruption in Genesis. It too is in need of the salvific power in the universe to 'make the wounded whole.'"[49] If the planet is not thriving, humanity cannot thrive. The health and well-being of humanity and the natural world are entwined. This is both an organic and an ethical statement. By focusing on more than human justice, womanists give new meaning to the well-known statement of Martin Luther King Jr.: "Injustice anywhere is a threat to justice everywhere."[50]

The postmodern theological framework asserts a communal dimension to the change that occurs in the processes of becoming. In the process of becoming, we combine the influences from our pasts with the possibilities offered by God to become our own unique selves. In becoming, we deal with more than just ourselves. We deal with the community of the past and future possibilities. When who and what we are become a part of the larger world around us, we become part of the many factors that will influence the future. Thus, we cannot live, change, or become in isolation. This does not mean that there is no sense of individuality for us. In fact, we do experience a type of solitude in our processes of becoming. The process of becoming that we undergo within ourselves is a kind of "breathing space" in time in which each one of us is alone in our decision-making process.[51] We really do self-create. But the process of creating ourselves involves sifting through the influences that we receive. Whether one decides to repeat one's past or change in a novel direction, one is always considering the past and the thrust for the future. The process of becoming cannot be an isolated one.

Thus, the postmodern theological framework suggests that salvation must happen in and through community. This is deduced from the fact that all change happens in and through community in a process world. Salvation is this change in accordance with certain ideals. We are always a part of a wider community. This fact is encompassed in Whitehead's summary statement that "the many become one and are increased by one."[52] Our lives outside of community can only be understood in abstraction. In the actual workings of the world, becoming is a cyclical process of synthesizing the community of the past and then rejoining the world community.

In both the postmodern theological framework and a constructive womanist concept of salvation, community is also the goal of salvation. Process theologian Marjorie Hewitt Suchocki states that God's calling will always aim for community. Suchocki bases this conclusion on the fact that God's very nature is communal. As God takes the world into God's self (in the consequent nature), God holds together events from the world. These events are held together in a complexity that includes the fact of their existence and how they experienced life.[53] They are then valued according to their highest qualities and related to God's ideal vision for the world. In this sense, God has a process of becoming, and this divine becoming is communal, and communal in a manner greater than that of any of us in the world. That is, within God's self, God can gather together more than can be gathered together in this world. God's unity comes to the world in God's calling and reflects the communal dimension of who God is:

> Thus the . . . effect of God's [unity], experienced by every standpoint in creation, must carry with it an echo of the divine reality in novel urges toward deeper and richer forms of well-being in finite community. . . . This means, then, that every [calling] from God will be toward that which builds up the richness of community, and that the structure of [the world's] redemption will be and must be essentially communal.[54]

Because God incorporates and evaluates the world communally, God's unity and calling are communal. Salvation must, therefore, be communal in its very essence.

The postmodern womanist insistence on community can also be seen as an outgrowth of womanist definitions of sin. The stated goals of "making a way out of no way"—discipleship, wholeness, right relationship—give specificity to the larger ideal of community. The sins of racism, sexism, classism, heterosexism, servanthood, and surrogacy share the common thread of being exclusivist practices and systems that divide communities of people. Likewise, environmental racism treats the natural world as if it is not a valid part of the same world community as humanity. If salvation aims at the eradication of these sins, then salvation necessarily aims for a greater and more genuine sense of community.

As a corollary, a postmodern womanist theology extends the concept of Savior beyond Jesus and looks for a savior in every theological community. From the example of Jesus, womanists find salvation in the activities of teaching and healing. Postmodern womanist theology focuses on the activity and suggests that it is not the person of Jesus, but rather the activities of teaching and healing that are exhibited in the life and death of Jesus that make Jesus a savior. The activities of a community leader who demonstrates salvation make for a savior. That is why Christian womanist theologians can encourage the present generation to see Christ in the faces of the poor, blacks, women, the elements, and the earth. In the same vein, postmodern womanist theology encourages the present generation to look for saviors in unlikely places. The least of these can be saviors. They are saviors, again, not because they are the least likely or because they are uniquely constituted, but because these people mediate salvation; they teach and they heal for the creative transformation of the world. They lead communities that "make a way out of no way."

In sum, postmodern womanist theology affirms that salvation is found in the activity of communities. Postmodern womanist theology does not reference individuals as being saved apart from the communities in which the individuals participate. After all, all individuals are communal by their very nature. Postmodern womanist theology speaks of theological communities. Theological communities are those communities that adopt and adapt God's calling and creatively transform the world in which they live. Suchocki even states that evil is so deep and broad that it can only be addressed with the collective power of individuals working together: "Societal evil is the responsibility of the whole society, but the specifically redemptive communities within the larger society have a unique role in holding forth the norm of a dynamic inclusiveness of well-being in community."[55] Combating evil, fighting injustice, resisting violence, questing for wholeness and health—these things are never about the actions of a single individual. Salvation is about the activity of communities. These communities are creatively transforming the world through the acts of teaching and healing.

Four

Learning from the Past
The Role of the Ancestors

Those who have died have never never left.—Birago Diop[1]

Postmodern womanist theology emphasizes the ways that we learn from the past in order to live in today's society. Womanist theologies reminds us that black women have histories with experiences of violence and destruction. Womanist theologies discuss the ways that black women find resources for survival and life in their spiritual and cultural pasts. The postmodern theological framework acknowledges that every move into the future entails some loss of what we once were and what we once experienced. Nevertheless, there are ways that the past remains alive to us today. We can creatively transform the past to decide how we should move into the future. We can also draw power from the lives of those who have come before us. As we learn from the past, our ancestors have their own kind of immortality. Postmodern womanist theology details the ways that we can learn from the past in order to make a way out of no way.

There are two ways of learning from the past that contribute to creative transformation. The process of "rememory" is one approach to keeping the past alive in the present and the future. We are called to remember our past and incorporate it into our process of becoming. As we do so, we can use past survival techniques to help ourselves live into the future. We can also remember the destructive death-dealing aspects of the past and vow not to repeat them as we move into the future. In keeping with the concept of creative transformation, we find that this conscious remembering is best done in community. When we are able to highlight the best of the past for our current becoming, we honor the past. Honoring the past helps us to make a way out of no way.

A second approach to learning from the past focuses on the role that the ancestors play in our lives. Black women often describe the past as more than a memory: "My grandmother came to me in a dream"; "Jesus speaks to my heart"; "I can feel the movement of the Holy Spirit"; "Oya rules my heart." These descriptions of the relationship between the past and the present center on individuals who are no longer living with us today; these are references to ancestors. The ancestors are a critical component of African traditional religious practices. This chapter discusses the role of African traditional religions in black religiosity, giving particular attention to the practice of the traditional religion of the Yoruba people and its expression in the United States. In this African traditional religion, the ancestors are closely related to the divine and are active in the everyday and ceremonial lives of practitioners.

A postmodern womanist theology describes how ancestors relate to today's world and help us to creatively transform. Whitehead discusses ways that the events of the past are alive within God and the world. Marjorie Suchocki expands upon Whitehead's philosophy to talk about the ways that God can share in the feelings of our experiences. To some extent, those of us in the world can feel the past as the past felt itself. Explaining the immortality of the ancestors requires another step. In a postmodern theological framework, those of us in the world have access to the knowledge and experiences of the ancestors, and we can use this knowledge to guide us into the future.

While a postmodern womanist theology is attentive to African traditional religions, this understanding of the immortality of the ancestors is also applicable outside of these religious traditions. Through a concept of ancestral immortality, we can understand the visions, dreams, charismatic embodiments of the Holy Spirit, and possession by African ancestors that are critical to the religious experiences of black women. We can also understand how the ancestors help us to creatively transform the world and leave it a better place than we found it.

Postmodern womanist theology will incorporate the historical experiences and theological reflections of black women with a theoretical attempt to describe the workings of today's societies. It will speak of teaching, healing communities of God, and the ways that we learn from the past to live into the future. It will be able to describe how and why small activities like braiding and dancing in white and purple lead to wholeness and divine acts of responding to violence.

Rememory

A postmodern womanist theology finds creative transformation in the memory of the positive value of the past. When womanist theologians describe the ways that black women strive for wholeness and quality of life, the past plays a significant role in their descriptions. This is consonant with the postmodern theological framework's description of how our memories help us to preserve life amid the loss that occurs in the world. Black women can take their past experiences and perpetuate them to assist in our contemporary quest for survival, life, and wholeness. We may also decide that there are aspects of the past that we should not imitate. As we repeat the life-giving aspects of our past, we can help to save ourselves and our communities.

Postmodern Theological Framework

A postmodern theological framework affirms that the present retains traces of the past. As who we have been and what we have done is lost as we live into the present and the future, our experiences become part of "the past." This past is available to us and to those around us to incorporate into the ongoing processes of life. After all, we constantly take in the past and the relevant possibilities ordered by God. Through a process of acceptance and elimination, we sift through all of these factors and become our own things. This is an internal activity. It is something we do within ourselves. When we embrace the influence of the past and incorporate that influence into our becoming, we can be said to "positively" incorporate it.

If, however, we decide not to repeat that aspect of the past, its imprint stays with us. Whitehead writes about it this way: "A feeling bears on itself the scars of its birth; it recollects as a subjective emotion its struggle for existence; it retains the impress of what it might have been, but is not. It is for this reason that what [we have] avoided as datum for feeling may yet be an important part of its equipment."[2] Even if we "negatively" incorporate our past, we still bear the traces of that aspect of the past. Just the consideration and rejection of the past give it a kind of life beyond itself. We are shaped by what we do not do just as much as we are shaped by what we do.

On a very fundamental level, the past is partially embodied in the present. For most of the world, the process of becoming is not conscious. There is a great deal of repetition in the world. This results from the fact that much of what we do involves repeating the past over and over again. Thus, a rock may appear rather static from moment to moment. In addition, we have a general awareness of the ways in which the present incorporates and contains the past. We acknowledge that there is a cyclical nature to life. Our existence bears the record of our past. The hills and valleys reveal the glaciers that were there centuries earlier. Fossils are evidence of extinct plants and animals. The tree decomposing in the woods gives life to the plants that grow there. The food that gives humanity energy, strength, and sustenance was once the life of vegetables rooted in the earth, or for some, of animals once roaming the grounds or swimming the waters. We have the physical attributes of our parents. The process of becoming declares that everything in the world is, to varying degrees, the product of what came before. The past is incarnate in the present, whether we are conscious of it or not. This is a kind of preconscious memory.

For the aspects of the world with a higher mentality, such as human beings, the past can be present in a process we normally think of as memory. The conscious remembering of the past contributes to the salvation of the world as we creatively transform the past, embracing its positive values and negating its negative influences. In the lives of human beings, the past achieves a level of immortality in our memories.

Constructive Womanist Theology

Womanist theologians focus on the role of memory in their concepts of salvation. Karen Baker-Fletcher believes that our memories can help bring wholeness, quality of life, and indeed salvation in the lives of black women. Baker-Fletcher believes that the past will assert itself in our lives whether we want to remember it or not. She recommends consciously remembering the past in order to learn from it. We must remember as much as we can so that we know the best path to take into the future.

Remembering is often a challenging task. The brutalities of the Middle Passage, slavery, segregation, and Jim Crow have caused many black people to lose conscious knowledge of their ancestral past. Baker-Fletcher asserts that the past can never be fully erased. She gives examples from Toni Morrison's novel *Beloved* to highlight African Americans' difficulties in accessing their past. *Beloved* takes place in the home of Sethe, a former female slave living in post–Civil War Ohio. The spirit of Sethe's murdered child, known only as "Beloved," breaks mirrors and makes life difficult for Sethe and her family. Although Sethe tries to forget the pain of her slave past, she cannot move on until she acknowledges Beloved's presence. "Morrison's work reminds us that we cannot erase histories we would like to forget . . . not even memory can be erased permanently."[3] Baker-Fletcher refers to this preconscious feeling and rejecting of the past as "disremembering." When we disremember the past, it does not die out, but it does fade from our consciousness. Only through consciously remembering the past can we resolve the difficulties and strengths that often lie within our past.

The process of "rememory" helps us to address the challenges of our past. "Rememory" is Baker-Fletcher's term (borrowed from Morrison) for how she thinks we should respond to "disremembering." Rememory "involves the power of reconnecting those memories that have been forcefully

disremembered from community consciousness."[4] It is the first step in drawing lessons of salvation from the past.

Communities should engage in particular activities to help remember the
past. Baker-Fletcher suggests that storytelling keeps our societal, spiritual, and
cultural past in the forefront of our minds. Indeed, we have ritual ways of
remembering the dead. When we visit grave sites, place flowers in the places
where someone has died, construct memorials, light candles, and pour libations, we are not just consoling the feelings of those who are still living.[5]
Rather, in stories, rituals, and liturgies, we tell what we remember and pass on
what was told to us. When we remember the ancestors—discussing, grieving,
and venerating them—we keep the past in our consciousness as a dominant
force in our becoming.

There is a difference between remembering the past and honoring the past.
There is always a selective incorporation of the past. For black women, the
memory of European, Native American, and African ancestry can bring conflict. Baker-Fletcher believes that most black women's experiences with their
European heritage are experiences of rape and betrayal. On the other hand,
Native American heritage is often unacknowledged even though it is a part
of the constitution of many black women and is one of the sources of black
women's connectedness with the land. Black women and men have forgotten many of their memories of their African ancestral past as well. Drawing
on Alice Walker's writings, Baker-Fletcher states that all ancestors need to be
remembered—European, Native American, and African—but we should not
imitate all of their activities.

Destructive acts need to be remembered so that their evil effects are not
perpetuated into the present and future. How do we decide what to repeat
and what to reject? Here Baker-Fletcher distinguishes between the general
practice of remembering the past and honoring the past. We should consciously remember as much as possible, but we should not honor all of it:

> It is necessary to tell the stories of as many ancestors as pos-
> sible in order to better discern the good and evil acts we might
> learn from. While it is important to *remember* as many ancestors
> as possible, I would suggest that it is not helpful to *honor* all
> of them. We choose who we would honor according to their
> contributions of healing and wholeness to our historical and
> contemporary communities.[6]

We should pay attention to those things that lead to health and wholeness. We
should be concerned about more than just our individual health and wholeness; we should focus on that which has brought health and wholeness to

communities. We only need to honor the aspects of the past that can help us to creatively transform the world. Our measuring stick should be the ability to assist in the work of "making a way out of no way."

Postmodern Womanist Theology

A postmodern womanist theology emphasizes Baker-Fletcher's "honoring" of the ancestors. JoAnne Terrell makes a similar argument when she locates salvation in the lessons gleaned from the sufferings of Jesus, the martyrs, and abused black women. Both Terrell and Baker-Fletcher are careful to note that salvation comes from remembering and imitating the *best features* of the past. Baker-Fletcher writes, "We can believe because we can remember the times when our ancestors overcame evil and suffering through faith in God."[7] In our remembering of the past, we must learn from the past. As we remember the past, it becomes a part of us. It shapes who we are. But in our learning from the past, we can reject or choose not to propagate the activities of the past that led to oppression, destruction, suffering, and pain. On the other hand, we can use the same survival strategies as those who came before us. In different ways, the positive values of the past can help us to make a way out of no way.

The process of rememory is best done in community. Otherwise, Baker-Fletcher argues, rememory may be too painful. Referencing *Beloved* again, she suggests that remembering necessitates community: "How could an individual remember the terror of the bodily and psychic abuse of millions without suffering the kind of insanity Sethe [the protagonist] endured? Perhaps the solution is not exorcism, but recollection of the past in community, holding one another together with tar-like power of community building."[8] Again, Baker-Fletcher does not recommend ignoring the past or trying to remove the influence of the ancestor, Beloved. Metaphysically, it's not possible. The past stays with us, whether we acknowledge it or not. It is, Baker-Fletcher implies, healthier to consciously remember our past and to do so in community. Oftentimes, people need the support of others in order to manage the memories of their past. When we are left alone[9] with some of the most difficult aspects of our past, we can feel overwhelmed. We may emerge from such encounters with the past as weaker and more fragile beings. Without community connectedness, rememory can be destructive. Like creative transformation, remembering should be done in a communal context.

We often practice rememory in community. When we seek the assistance of a therapist or support group to process difficult aspects of our past, we engage in communal rememory. When we gather around the table repeating Jesus' words "Do this in remembrance of me," we engage in communal rememory. When we tell our children about our childhoods and how things were when we were younger, we engage in communal rememory. When we publicly celebrate Martin Luther King Jr.'s birthday, we engage in communal rememory. When we whisper our scariest experiences into our daughter's ears with the hope that she will learn from our mistakes and take another path, we engage in communal rememory.

Postmodern womanist theology insists that we remember the past to better inform our present activities. The understanding of immortality from the post-modern theological framework describes how this process can occur within the structure of the world. Womanist concepts of salvation acknowledge that wholeness and survival come by remembering the past and learning from it. Ancestral immortality is a community process of honoring the ancestors that involves ritual activities such as storytelling. When we honor the past, we learn what kinds of activities we should avoid and what we should continue to do. "Making a way out of no way" is not just the memory and repetition of the past. We make our way forward in creative ways by remembering and repeat-ing the best aspects of the past. "Making a way out of no way" focuses on the ways that we *honor* the past.

Spirit Possession

Learning from the past also involves the active role that the ancestors play in our contemporary processes of becoming. A postmodern womanist the-ology seeks to affirm African traditional religions and their concepts about the ancestors. This affirmation extends the concept of immortality to include the activity of ancestors. I focus on the most complex activity of the ances-tors in this world—spirit possession. In the act of spirit possession, ancestors convey their knowledge to the present generation and influence its future activity. Whitehead's metaphysics contains the framework for a philosophical understanding of spirit possession. I combine Whitehead's concept of objec-tive immortality and Marjorie Suchocki's concept of subjective immortality to discuss the ways in which an ancestor can be fully present in God with knowledge and agency and then influence the present.

Constructive Womanist Theology

African Traditional Religions

As African traditional religions came to the Americas in the memories of enslaved Africans, enslaved Africans helped to birth African American reli-gions. Although sociologists and anthropologists continue to debate the degree to which African cultures influenced the birth of African American culture,[10] most scholars agree that some type of transformation occurred as African traditional religions encountered other traditions. In his landmark book *Slave Religion*, Albert Raboteau describes African traditional religions in the Americas as living religions:

> It is important to realize, however, that in the Americas the religions of Africa have not been merely preserved as static "Africanisms" or as archaic "retentions." The fact is that they have continued to develop as living traditions putting down new roots in new soil, bearing new fruit as unique hybrids of American origin. African styles of worship, forms of ritual, systems of belief, and fundamental perspectives have remained vital on this side of the Atlantic, not because they were preserved in a "pure" orthodoxy but because they were transformed.[11]

In the Caribbean, where the French, Spanish, and Portuguese dominated the slave trade, African traditional religions syncretized with Catholicism.[12] In the southeastern United States, enslaved Africans contended with the Protestant roots of British and American Christianity.

African traditional religions maintain an openness that allows them to adapt to the religious influence of other cultures. Although neighboring ethnic groups in Africa often have distinctly different traditional religions, it is not uncommon to see some of the same deities in two different religions—especially if there was an unusually friendly or hostile (enslavement) relationship between the two groups. Similarly, some Africans were exposed to Islam and Western Christianity prior to the Atlantic slave trade. Yet Raboteau also notes that Africans often mixed Islam and Christianity with traditional African beliefs, carrying verses of the Qur'an [Preferred over Koran] inside the amulets and charms of their traditional religions.[13] Nevertheless, Raboteau continues, most of the enslaved Africans held the traditional beliefs of their ethnic groups.

The missionary patterns of the Caribbean enslavers amplified the retention of African religions in the Caribbean. In British Jamaica, the Christianization of the slaves was a low priority: "The Church in the British slave colonies denied the Africans religious instruction for well over 200 years."[14] Among the French and Spanish colonies, African religions found similarities with the Catholic saints and thrived under the syncretic blending of the two religious systems: "The syncretism between Orisha [Worship] and Catholicism developed in part because of the multiplicity of saints who could be identified with Orisha deities."[15] Catholicism was particularly, though unknowingly, predisposed to adaptation by African traditional religions. Catholicism's emphasis on ritual, belief in the saints, and the use of icons complemented the ways in which African traditional religions engaged their lesser deities.

Through both the triangular slave trade and contemporary reversionist attempts at recapturing traditional religions, the religion of the Yoruba people (of current-day Nigeria) has constituted a base for African-derived religious practices throughout the Caribbean, South America, and the United States. Although all these different manifestations of Yoruba-based religions share a similar cosmology and key religious concepts, they differ in ritual detail and linguistic referrals due to the different historical and religious contexts of the encounter between Yoruba religion and various New World situations. As Yoruba traditional religion travels through space, time, and circumstance, it syncretizes, or blends, with other religious and cultural traditions—most particularly Western Christianity and other African traditional religions.

Traditional Yoruba religion can be described as the worship of a supreme deity, Olódùmarè/Olórun,[16] under various forces or deities, the òrìṣà. There is no adequate description for the òrìṣà outside of the Yoruba universe. They have been variously described as ministers of Olódùmarè, forces of nature, angelic forces, lower gods, and sub-deities. According to Yoruba lore, the òrìṣà are ancestors who did not return to earth because their *iwà* (human character or human consciousness) was so closely aligned with the character of Olódùmarè. While Olódùmarè is neither male nor female, nor embodied, the òrìṣà have genders, stories, and geographical and natural associations. The òrìṣà have their own characteristics, herbs, personalities, and devotees. Veneration of the òrìṣà is such an important part of Yoruba religion that the entire religion is often referred to as "òrìṣà worship." The telos of Yoruba religion is *iwà pele*. Yoruba religion identifies 401 òrìṣà, with five to ten òrìṣà having more importance and appearing more than the others. The wisdom and content of Yoruba is traditionally transmitted orally in the wisdom contained in myths, songs, and the odù, verses of wisdom and divination.

In Yoruba-based religions, Catholic saints often correlated with different òrìṣà. At times, the association was based on a similarity of power. In Bahia, Brazil, St. Barbara, the protector against thunder and lightning, was identified with Ṣango, the òrìṣà of thunder. Other times, the association was emblematic. In Cuba, St. Francis, traditionally pictured with a rosary that resembles the *opele* chain used in Ifa divination, was associated with Orunmila, the òrìṣà of divination. Other times, traditional Yoruba rituals were held at the same time as Catholic feast days, allowing for even more syncretism. The pattern of the slave trade and the method and type of Christian evangelism allowed African traditional religions to remain a vital part of many Caribbean religions.

Thus, Caribbean communities retain a shared African religious heritage. Many Caribbean religions seem to be distinctly connected to traditional Yoruba religions—Haiti's Vodun, Cuba's Santería, Brazil's Candomblé, and Trinidad's

Shango and Orisha worship. Still, the religious elements from Akan, Fon/ Dahomey, and Kongo also appear in the African religious landscape of the Caribbean, because the majority of enslaved Africans came from these tribes.[17] These various traditions share similar understandings about a supreme being, lesser deities, and ancestors. These common themes are also found in Cuba's Lucumi (Lukumi); Jamaica's Kumina (Cumina), Myalism, Pocomania,[18] and Revival Zionism; Brazil's Nagô and Umbanda; St. Lucia's Kele; Grenada's Big Drum and African Feast; the French-speaking Caribbean's (especially Guadeloupe and Martinique) Quimbois; and even the masquerade carnivals[19] of several Caribbean countries.

As individuals who are raised in the Caribbean travel and relocate, the diaspora reflects this syncretism of African-derived religions, which often change further in new contexts. The best example of this phenomenon is found in obeah. The term obeah denotes a pan-Caribbean understanding of African-derived spiritual practices. Womanist Caribbean theologian Dianne Stewart refers to obeah as "the most common and popularly referenced African-derived [religious] practice in the Caribbean."[20] Obeah is a term used throughout the English-speaking Caribbean to express belief in "the power of spiritually endowed individuals, on behalf of the self or another, to manipulate spiritual forces to procure good or to activate evil or to counter evil."[21] Obeah is not a religion with devotees and adherents. Obeah is "a set of hybrid or creolized beliefs dependent on ritual invocation, fetishes, and charms."[22] Obeah itself is a blend of African religious elements: "It now appears quite clear from the records that rather early in the period of Caribbean slavery there occurred a fusion of the various African tribes and the new groups centered around the religious specialists."[23] There are two categories of practice in obeah. The first involves casting spells for numerous purposes—protecting self, property, or family; attaining love, employment, or other personal goals; or harming enemies. The second category of obeah involves using knowledge of herbal and animal properties for the healing of illnesses.[24]

Caribbean governments made no distinction between the creative and destructive uses of obeah and outlawed its practice, severely persecuting its practitioners.[25] As a result, the practice of obeah went underground. Through an underground secret network, obeah survived in the Caribbean and its diaspora: "Practitioners are numerous across the Caribbean, the United States, England, and Canada, many of them working out of storefront consultation rooms in urban settings or discreetly out of their houses."[26] Outside of the Caribbean, practitioners often could not find the herbs to which they were accustomed, adapting local (often cold-climate) herbs to their remedies and potions. In the diaspora, practitioners of these different religions often ignored their differences to create a kind of pan-Caribbean African-derived religion that set them apart from the wider context in which they lived. Writing of the Caribbean community in Toronto, sociologist Daniel Yon writes, "Thus we see Caribbean black subjectivities and identities being forged as a reaction to marginality, exclusion, racism and Eurocentricism and to differential incorporation to the Canadian 'multi-cultural ethnic mosaic.'"[27] Thus, the religion is creolizing once again.

In the United States, African religious and cultural elements fared quite differently. There, the slave trade ended nearly a hundred years before it did in parts of the Caribbean. Thus, most slaves were American-born. In addition, there was a much lower ratio of slaves to masters in America, thereby increasing the contact between slave and enslaver. Tribal unity was not encouraged for fear of rebellion. Last, Protestantism's emphasis on the Bible and conversion experiences did not readily allow for the kind of religious and cultural blending found in the Caribbean. Although scholars have still found "substantial instances of Africanisms in diet, dress, language, music, styles of labor, thought patterns and religious belief and practice" among African Americans, the appearance of African traditional religious elements was much more subtle.[28]

African religious elements appeared in the African American Christian and cultural practices of singing, dancing, spirit possession, and conjure.[29] Scholars have noted some similarities between traditional African religious practices and the Christian practices of baptism by immersion and ecstatic worship traditions such as the ring shout. It is, however, impossible to discern to what degree these practices were influenced by the African traditional religious heritage of the slaves or the evangelical Protestantism of the enslavers. Both traditions were mutually influential in the development of American Christianity. The uniquely African American development of spirituals and conjure beliefs are more easily identified with African traditional religious elements.[30] Still, these practices were syncretized with Protestantism, and were found most prominently among African American communities with a smaller degree of contact with European culture.[31]

When speaking of the presence of traditional Yoruba religion in the United States, one must also include contemporary reversionist attempts to reclaim cultural identity through an intentional revival of and return to ancient traditions. Practitioners will often refer to this system of belief and practices as "Ifá" or "Yoruba." In "African-Derived Religion in the African-American Community in the United States," Mary Cuthrell-Curry states that this manifestation of traditional Yoruba religion is much less obvious than in the Caribbean: "The dress of initiates and botanicas are the only two visible manifestations of the Yoruba Religion that a casual observer sees. The Religion (in most instances) does not have churches or buildings devoted to its practice."[32]

Although this Yoruba-derived traditional religion has been active in the United States since the 1960s, the Nation of Islam and the Christian fervor of the civil rights movement overshadowed it. Among native-born African Americans (and a smaller number of whites), this Yoruba religion is spread by conversion. African American practitioners of Yoruba religion are influenced in part by the Haitian and Cuban diaspora in the United States. For these African American practitioners, "conversion to the Yoruba Religion meant a rejection of Christianity and a searching for a religious perspective that would foster African-American identity."[33] Cuthrell-Curry estimates that there are probably Yoruba religious communities in every major city in the United States, while the most visible communities are in Dade County, Florida, and New York City.[34]

Yoruba religion has also adapted to the American context. In some cases, adaptation is necessary because of geographical differences. For example, kola nuts do not grow in the United States, so Yoruba devotees in North America will use coconuts where kola nuts were traditionally employed. In other instances, African American practitioners have maintained preslave trade traditions that practitioners in Yorubaland have not. For example, in the United States, only men are allowed to serve as *babalawos*, priests who specialize in divination; in Nigeria, both men and women can be babalawos.[35]

In conclusion, blended forms of traditional Yoruba religion exist throughout the Americas. The religion has been further syncretized in the diaspora of those practitioners. All of these things contribute to both the uniqueness and diversity of black religions. African American religion must always contend with its African traditional religious heritage, whether it has been retained to greater or lesser degrees within the practice of Christianity or is practiced outside any association with Christianity.

Ancestors

The ancestors play a critical role in the practice of traditional African religions. Although traditional religions differ significantly, they share common themes: a communal conception of the divine that includes the worship of a high God through various spiritual powers or entities; the belief that the spirit lives on after death in the form of spiritual knowledge; a belief in ancestors who should be honored, venerated, and consulted; the belief in divination—access to spiritual knowledge that will assist in solving problems in the world; the belief that offering food and animal sacrifices amplify prayers to the divine and the ancestors; belief in a neutral power—sometimes contained in herbs—that can be used for benevolent or malevolent purposes; and the belief that spirit possession and ritual song and dance are crucial forms of communication with the divine.[36]

The cosmology of traditional African religions does not fit into the Western philosophical and theological categories of monotheism and polytheism, mortal and immortal. African religions scholar Jacob K. Olupona describes four distinct types of deities in African religious systems.[37] First, there is a Supreme Being who is identified as the creator of the universe. Second, there are "lesser deities" who are messengers of the Supreme Being. They serve as intermediaries between the Supreme Being and the created temporal world. These "lesser deities" are the direct objects of worship. Third, there are "culture heroes" who are "mythic founders of communities and villages who go through an apotheosis after their heroic sojourn on earth."[38] Fourth, there are "ancestors," the deceased members of the lineage of the living.[39] Culture heroes are hard to classify because they seem to have some of the same characteristics of both the lesser deities in that "they are regarded as greater in importance and authority than the ancestors, whose sphere of influence is more or less limited to their lineage and their descendants."[40] In most African traditional religions, the Supreme Being is rather remote and rarely referenced outside of creation stories. It is the lesser deities and the culture heroes who have devotees; they perform activities such as spirit possession.

In African traditional religions, ancestors have a different role than the lesser deities and culture heroes. At death, one can become an ancestor; however, not all deceased persons are regarded as ancestors. In order to be an ancestor, one must have lived a morally exemplary life, lived to a very old age, died a "good death" (not by a disease such as smallpox or leprosy), and received a proper burial by one's family. There is a strong relationship between the ancestors and members of their lineage, as the ancestors' living family members must consciously remember them and honor them through storytelling and the building of shrines and altars. These ancestors are usually honored in the way previously described. This honoring of the ancestors is often referred to as "ancestor veneration" or "ancestor worship."[41] This focus on the ancestors causes many observers to interpret the activity as "worship." Postmodern womanist theology notes that ancestors are "kept alive" in the present in these activities, which are a kind of rememory.

Ancestors appear to be like humans in that one often assumes that they do the same things in the spiritual realm that they did while living in mortal bodies: "Like humans, they drink, eat and excrete."[42] Yet they are unlike humans in that the ancestors have a moral responsibility to the living. They serve to remind the living to live according to the norms of society, and acting against these norms is said to "anger the ancestors." Olupona describes this quality of the ancestors as significantly different from humanity: "In order to function [as guardians of morality], the ancestors are freed of the human weaknesses and conditions of pettiness, particularly common among living lineage members. They are, therefore, eminently qualified to act as the guardians of social and moral order in the world."[43] Thus, ancestors are not simply human beings who maintain activity after death. "Through the process of death, ancestors undergo a change in their ontological status that makes them into supernatural entities."[44] Ancestors are transformed in the afterlife; they have a divine quality to them. In summary, African traditional religions affirm that human beings can live on after death. The ancestors, along with lesser deities and culture heroes, have special knowledge that can be accessed by the living through rituals of remembrance, rites of divination, or spirit possession.

I use the term *ancestor* as a philosophical term to refer to a spiritual force or soul that is disembodied, at times because of the death of the mortal body, as in the case of the ancestors as they are described in the context of African traditional religions. This term also refers to the lesser deities and culture heroes who are more properly objects of worship and have a larger role in African traditional religions. I acknowledge the differences between lesser deities, culture heroes, and ancestors that are maintained in African traditional religions. One would not consider most òrìṣà as having once been mortal, and the ancestors do not "possess" devotees. However, I also want to illustrate some of their similarities. There are culture heroes that seem to be regarded as òrìṣà. For example, among the Yoruba, Ṣango is the legendary king of the village of Oyo; yet his "death" was a disappearance into the ground, and he is now considered an òrìṣà by Yoruba devotees in both Africa and the Western hemisphere.

Grouping òrìṣà, culture heroes, and ancestors together stresses the ways that they are similar kinds of beings. Olupona seeks to challenge the idea that ancestors are elders who are ontologically different from the supernatural lesser deities (òrìṣà) and spirits. He acknowledges that some understandings of African religions draw a clear line between the sacred and the profane, but he argues that this is not the case in the African setting.[45] My confluence of terms is not merely convenient and philosophical; it is also illustrative of the similarities between distinct forces and the fluidity between the spiritual world and the world in which we live. My terminology is also reflective of the kind of syncretism that has occurred as African traditional religions have been adapted and practiced in the Americas. This is yet another reason why the practice of African traditional religions appears to many as ancestor worship. The close relationship between the "ancestors" and the "supernatural" or "divine" easily conflates whether the object of worship is simply the memory of one who has died or one who is divine. The following discussion of spirit possession will offer an explanation of how the ancestors and God are connected, and why it can be so difficult to distinguish the two.

Spirit Possession

In African traditional religions, spirit possession is an important resource for the interaction between the ancestors and the present generation.[46] Social anthropologist I. M. Lewis defines spirit possession as a "mystical exaltation in which [one's] whole being seems to fuse in a glorious communion with the divinity."[47] Carl Becker defines spirit possession as "the phenomenon in which persons suddenly and inexplicably lose their normal set of memories, mental dispositions, and skills, and exhibit entirely new and different sets of memories, dispositions, and skills."[48] Spirit possession leads to such phenomena as speaking in tongues, the transmission of messages from the dead, and other mystical gifts. Spirit possession occurs when an ancestor's spirit strongly influences the living person in order to communicate to and through this person, displacing his or her normal sense of consciousness.

My concept of ancestral immortality accounts for the process by which the human past can access and fill the present in such a way as to produce the experience of spirit possession. A metaphysical concept of spirit possession must allow for (1) the possibility of life after death and the existence of the ancestors, (2) action and perception on the part of those ancestors, (3) a way for those ancestors to "return to" the present world, and (4) a way for the present to access those ancestors and conform to their influence.

Postmodern Theological Framework

The concept of the ancestors rests on a general concept of immortality. Whitehead's concept of immortality explains that what has died to the world is indeed accessible to the present. What has died to the world is present and alive in God and the world, but only objectively. That means that the world and God have access to the fact of what has happened but cannot feel the past in its experience of itself. God and the world can sympathize with what has happened in the world, but they don't know us as we feel within ourselves. The present can feel the past with a high level of sympathy, but the present cannot feel the past completely. Likewise, God can sympathize with the world, but we cannot be known as we knew ourselves. No one, not even God, can feel us from the inside out. Neither God nor those in the world can feel the past "subjectively."

A traditional African religious understanding of spirit possession believes that the living have access to more than just the fact of the ancestors' existence.

The living must also be able to access the experience of the ancestors. This necessitates a kind of subjective immortality.

Marjorie Suchocki develops a concept of subjective immortality using White-head's metaphysics.[49] She argues that in the process of becoming, there is a moment between when we become something new and when we cease being the old person where we can "enjoy" ourselves. By "enjoy," I mean that we can have a sense of who we are and offer that self to the world and to God. If there are feelings and experiences of self in this intermediate or transitory place, then those feelings and experiences are available to those we influence. Our feelings and experiences are only partially available to the rest of the world. The world can never know us as we know ourselves. But our feelings and experiences are fully available to God. God feels us, know us, takes us into God's self. And God does not just know us by the fact of who we were and who we are, but by how we experience ourselves. That is, God knows us from the inside out. Thus, God can feel our feelings. God does really suffer with us and rejoice with us.

While there is a distinction between having access to what happened in the past and having access to how those in the past felt, it is not as big a difference as may it originally appear to be. The concept of "subjective immortality" enlarges the scope of how we feel the influence of the past and how God feels and incorporates the world into God's self. Suchocki describes subjective immortality as "a difference of degree rather than kind."[50] Subjective immortality is significant inasmuch as it is important to most of us that, even while others in the world cannot completely know us, God should be able to know and feel us both in terms of what has happened to us and in terms of how we feel.

We can enjoy ourselves or "experience" ourselves even as we are becoming something new. This enjoyment continues when we die to the world and continue on in God. Because we—our spirits, our souls, now the ancestors—retain experience within God, the ancestors experience the world as God experiences it. Thus, within God, the ancestors can (1) experience themselves as themselves, (2) experience themselves in God, and (3) experience the way that God relates them to God's vision. The ancestors have access to what is happening in the world because God is taking in the events of the world into God's self. Here, there is a genuine life after death—life in God. For Suchocki, this is the kingdom or community of heaven. In our context, this is the ancestral realm where ancestors commune with one another and with God while "looking in" on the activity of the world. That is why we say that the ancestors have access to more knowledge than the living. We only know our part of the world, what is happening within our corner of the world. The ancestors, now a part of God, have access to the entire world. Thus, we are broader in death and in God than we are in life.

Postmodern Womanist Theology

The possibilities that we consider when we make decisions come from God. God orders these possibilities, calling us to choose those options that lead to a vision of the common good. This movement of God is shaped by what happens in the world and how God relates that to God's vision. Now that we consider the ancestors to be a part of God and think of them as having knowledge and experience as they participate in God, we can see that they influence what God offers to the world. As God integrates all these inputs with God's vision, the ancestors are available to those of us in the land of the living—through God. They are available not just in the fact of who they were, the fact that they existed, but at least in part in their knowledge and experience. Thus, as we in the land of the living are influenced by God, we can also feel or incorporate the ancestors—with their expanded knowledge— into ourselves. For this reason, African traditional religions portray ancestors as uniquely connected to the divine. Baker-Fletcher affirms this divine quality of the ancestors: "[Ancestors] are considered part of present, past, and future reality [or 'possibility']."[51] The concept of ancestral immortality acknowledges that one of the ways that the world experiences the past is in the call from God. We have access to the ancestors in God's calling to the world.

In what I have described in terms of spirit possession and African traditional religions, the agency of spirit possession belongs to those of us in the present, in the land of the living. Whether or not an ancestor's spirit "possesses" an individual depends on how we take in the influence from God. In this sense, spirit possession is more aptly described thusly: When a human being dies, she becomes an ancestor. Inside God, this ancestor has actuality, experience (objectivity and subjectivity), and a broader knowledge of the world than she did when she died. Here, the ancestor can be said to "commune" with other ancestors. Hence, the consequent nature of God could rightly be referred to as an "ancestral realm" or "spiritual realm." Since the events (and now feel-ings) of the world are evaluated within God's nature according to their value and the best that can be found and then related to the possibilities available to the world, the ancestors are present in God's calling to the world. When we embrace the new possibilities offered to us in God's calling, we may be "pos-sessed" with a spirit of an ancestor.

There are still questions: Does God passively contain the ancestors in God's offering of possibilities to the world, or does the ancestor have knowledge *and* agency as it is available to the living? Does the ancestor know that he or she is available to the present world? Does the ancestor want to be incorporated into the living? And if so, for what purpose?

There is still a problem in what I have described. In the concept of God I have outlined, God is constantly integrating the world with what's possible and the divine vision. When the ancestors are present in God, they are being integrated and woven into the mix. So, when the ancestors are presented to the world through the movement of God, they are not presented in their individual forms. Rather, they are "swirled together" with all these possibilities. Still, we are not overcome by all of this. How is this possible?

As we are influenced by the past and what is possible, we are pretty selective. We aren't even aware of how selective we are. It is "preconscious." Some people may be predisposed to selecting particular ancestors. For example, being born into a particular lineage may predispose one—consciously or not—to selecting a particular ancestor. Perhaps we know that our ancestors focused on one particular òrìṣà, and we choose to honor that same ancestor. Or perhaps we aren't even aware of this, but we seem to be drawn to particular colors and idiosyncrasies and personalities, and we later learn that an ancestor honored the òrìṣà with those qualities. Likewise, practices that are said to "induce possession" such as participating in certain rituals or the beating of certain rhythms also influence the selecting of particular ancestors. Thus, one might say that there are factors, conscious and preconscious, that can be said to structure or influence an individual's process of how she incorporates certain ancestors.

Spirit possession can be described in this way: When a human being (the body) dies, the spirit lives on. This disembodied spirit is an ancestor. As she participates in God, this ancestor spirit can still know what is happening in the world. Here, she is also woven together with all the other aspects that influence God. This is the expanded knowledge of the ancestor. As this ancestor is related to God's vision and incorporated into what God will offer to the world, she maintains her knowledge and agency, while her purposes align with those of God. This ancestor is now included (along with many other possibilities available to the living) in the movement of God in the world. Those of us in the land of the living never lose our ability to make our own decisions. For possession to occur, an individual must select and conform to the influence of the ancestor. The individual can always reject the lure of the ancestor as it is contained in the influence from God. Yet the ancestor may even be felt and incorporated when the individual is particularly receptive to influence, for example, during sleep. Thus, we may say the ancestor "came to me in a dream." When the individual selects and conforms to the influence of this ancestor, the spirit "possesses" the receptive individual.

Many African traditional religions acknowledge this kind of activity. Thus, devotees may engage in meditations, altar construction, worship, and so on in order to position themselves to "hear the voices of the ancestors." Likewise, people will also participate in sweat lodges, festivals, masquerades, drumming, dancing, and other "rituals of remembrance" in order to draw the ancestors, or a particular ancestor, to influence the present. We may beat out a distinct rhythm or display certain objects, believing that the ancestor can perceive these actions and that they will get the ancestor's attention. The living want to receive some type of communion with the ancestor.

Metaphysically, of course, these acts really influence the ways we incorporate the variety of inputs that are available to us. Similarly, the ancestor may "cause" an individual to dance in a specific manner. The individual may recall a dream with the imagery or names of the ancestors. As the individual dances a particular dance or exhibits certain behavior, the presence of that ancestor is acknowledged. The influence of the ancestor is known in its specificity. Even though the ancestors are said to "come to" the living, the living individual "calls" and "selects" the ancestors from the multiplicity of available possibilities in God's offer to the world.

Final questions remain: Why does an ancestor influence the world? For what purpose does an ancestor "come" to the present? A full concept of spirit possession states that spirit possession is often the result of an ancestor asserting herself into the temporal world. That is, the ancestor herself desires to possess the present occasion. In *Varieties of African American Religious Experience,* Anthony B. Pinn refers to spirit possession in Haitian Vodun as a way in which the ancestors "manifest and provide information for various persons gathered, reveal their flaws and suggest alterations in behavior or attitude."[52] Pinn's description attributes activity and purpose to the ancestors. Likewise, Baker-Fletcher believes that some ancestors have particular reasons for wanting to influence the temporal world. From her reading of *Beloved,* she concludes that disrememberment brings "angry haunting by the ancestors."[53] She believes that the people who have died unjustly seem to be more insistent about being recognized in the present. Baker-Fletcher asserts that some ancestors act powerfully because they want the present world to acknowledge them, know something, and/or do something on their behalf.

African traditional religions express the ancestors' influence in the world as an ancestor who "wants to come back" to the present. The ancestor may have unfinished business, wisdom to convey, steps to dance, or stories to tell that will help the present generation choose the best path in their current decision-making process. That is, there appears to be some kind of purpose in the act of spirit possession.

Traditional African religions suggest that there can be a normative motivation for spirit possession. African traditional religions often describe the ancestors as guiding individuals into right relationship with the sacred and each other. For example, in traditional Yoruba religion, the ancestors are there to guide the believer into the development of good character, or ìwà pele. Iwà pele is achieved by consistent righteous actions through complex processes of divination with a priest and possession by the ancestral spirits.[54] Those pursuing ìwà pele ascribe to high moral character, maintain composure in all situations, have unblemished reputations, conduct philanthropic deeds, and practice internal and external cleanliness. In other words, the ancestors want to help the present generation to be the best that it can be. They want their knowledge and experiences to be used for the achievement of creative transformation. Through spirit possession, the ancestors strive to guide the present generation toward creative transformation. This is the purpose of possession.

In this philosophical system, can an ancestor have a hope or a longing for how the ancestor might be incorporated by the present? Both Whitehead and Suchocki suggest a move in this direction, but they don't go all the way.[55] Whitehead believes that, in the process of becoming, we have hopes for how we will be in the next moment. Whitehead acknowledges that those of us in the present can influence our futures. What we contribute to the world as we become our own thing includes a thrust for our future: "[T]he future has *objective* reality in the present, but no *formal* actuality. For it is inherent in the constitution of the immediate, present actuality that a future will supersede it. . . . Thus each [aspect of the world] . . . experiences a future which must be actual, although the completed actualities of that future are undetermined."[56] In other words, the details are undetermined, but we do consider the future. Our hopes for the future are implied, and therefore in some way present, in what we have done.

Suchocki refers to a human being's vision for the future as *imagination*. When we make decisions about what we are going to do now, we have a sense of our future: "Through imagination, one transcends one's present circumstances and envisions a future. . . . Through this vision of the future, the self participates in the transformation of the present; . . . [T]ranscendence through imagination calls upon the novelty of that which may yet be, the future."[57] We often evaluate how we will impact the future. Whitehead and Suchocki agree that as we make decisions and continue on in life, we can and often do consider how we may impact the future. I believe that this is also true of the ancestors. Because the ancestors are related to God's vision for the world, they hope or imagine that their impact in the world will be in alignment with the purposes of God. Like God, the ancestor aims at the ideals of truth, beauty, art, adventure, peace, and justice. That is, ancestors also aim at creative transformation. As the ancestor is incorporated by those of us in the world, his or her knowledge and experience are also guiding the world toward this vision of creative transformation. The power of the ancestors is available to the world through God's calling.

Although the ancestors want to provide information to the living to guide us toward a vision of the common good or, as in the earlier example, ìwà pele, how and whether or not this information is accessed depends on the agency of the living. The ancestors are not coercive. The ability to incorporate the ancestor lies within the living individual, and the individual has true freedom and agency in determining how and in what direction she will become. Thus, the knowledge and agency of the ancestor, while purposive and directed toward God's vision, can be used and transformed by an individual creatively *or* destructively.

In a postmodern theological framework, we are always partly self-determining, and we may or may not become in accordance with God's vision for us. David Ray Griffin affirms such a possibility when he writes, "[T]he soul's power can be exerted directly on actualities beyond one's own body, both 'physical' things and other souls. This power can, in relation to living matter, either promote or discourage growth, either bless or curse."[58] Likewise, African traditional religions continually affirm that the power that comes from or through the divine—whether we are referring to the ancestors, herbal knowledge, or a force such as àṣé—is morally neutral. Evil, "demon-possession," or "witchcraft" are results of its manipulation by those with evil intentions and destructive purposes. Likewise, ìwà pele, to use that earlier example, comes from those who are intentionally "seeking blessings" or who purposively try to become in such a way as to promote the vision of God. A postmodern womanist theology encourages us to use our access to the knowledge and experiences of the ancestors for creative transformation.

This understanding of spirit possession may be applicable outside of African traditional religious experiences. For example, charismatic Christians may find some resonance with this concept. The Gospel of John describes the Holy Spirit as the ancestral spirit of Jesus. Jesus speaks to the disciples and tells them, "Nevertheless I tell you the truth: it is to your advantage that I go away, for if I do not go away, the Comforter will not come to you; but if I go, I will send him to you" (John 16:7). In the way that I have used the term *ancestor*, the Holy Spirit can be understood as an ancestor. Thus, a postmodern theology can also explain what some Christians call "getting happy," "feeling the spirit," "speaking in tongues," and/or "holy dancing." It can also account for what some Christian women in the South Carolina low country call "tulking to de dead," an "ongoing exchange between the living and the dead—prevalent in their song traditions, worship services, and daily activities of church work, storytelling and sweetgrass basketry."[59] This theology both explains those experiences as valid within a contemporary worldview and affirms them as healthy.

Conclusion

A postmodern womanist theology believes that the past is a critical dimension in "making a way out of no way." This theology asserts that "those who have died have never left." The past shapes who and how we are in the world. We are encouraged to remember the past and to do so in the context of community. We are working toward wholeness when we remember the past, lift up the most creative and life-giving activities, and carry those activities on into our current forms of becoming. A postmodern womanist theology also acknowledges the ancestors' constructive role in the process of salvation. The ancestors can creatively transform us as they teach and heal us—helping us to be the best individuals and communities that we can be. The ancestors can also assist us as we transform the world. When the ancestors guide us toward creative transformation, they not only represent the vision of God but also become part of the transformed community itself.

The processes of rememory and spirit possession can produce destructive or creative effects within the world. Remembering and embracing the past does not always help us to move creatively into the future. A postmodern womanist theology insists that we *learn* from the past and then use what we have learned, what we have experienced, toward God's ideals of truth, beauty, adventure, art, peace, justice, and quality of life. Creative transformation remains the process, goal, and measure for "making a way out of no way."

There is an ethical imperative in postmodern womanist theology and its understanding of how we learn from the past. It insists that contemporary humans remember the past. Honoring, embracing, and repeating the creative dimensions of the past allow human beings to transform the temporal world creatively with the unique knowledge of the past. We must, therefore, be about the business of rememory. We should pour libations, light candles, tell stories, and pursue ideals. We should try to attune ourselves to the activity of the ancestors, pay attention to our dreams and visions, and allow ourselves to be possessed. We should be open to the lessons from the ancestors that creatively transform us to creatively transform the world. We increase our consciousness of the past and our own resources for attaining health, wholeness, and quality of life when we regularly and ritually acknowledge the past and conform according to God's calling. Thus, we open ourselves to "being possessed by the spirits of the ancestors." We can, as suggested in the introduction, remember the ancestors and dance with ourselves and our communities in wholeness. Metaphysically, we can discipline our own souls, selectively incorporate particular ancestors, and use their knowledge and agency to augment our own ability to creatively transform the world.

Five

A Communal Theology
Two Communities

A way out of no way
It's too much to ask
It's too much of a task for any one woman.—June Jordan[1]

Twenty-first-century African American women can still describe their God as one who helps to "make a way out of no way." We make a way out of no way as we live in and through communities that seek to creatively transform the world in which we live. We teach. We heal. And we do it all over again. In so doing, we transform our souls, our communities, and ultimately the whole world. We "make a way out of no way" as we draw upon the best of the past to positively change our world.

Postmodern womanist theology focuses on the teaching and healing communities that learn from the past in order to creatively transform the world. These theological communities perpetuate the survival techniques of the past to creatively transform their contemporary contexts. In this chapter, I offer portraits of two communities that "make a way out of no way." Following in the womanist tradition of engaging black women's literature, the first community is found in *Parable of the Sower* (1993)[2] by black female science fiction writer Octavia E. Butler. The other is a particular community in the contemporary United States. GSN (God, Self, and Neighbor) Ministries in Atlanta offers religious community to individuals who experience racism and heterosexism in both Christian communities and the wider society. They intentionally incorporate community education into their mission. These communities embody postmodern womanist theology and demonstrate how teaching and healing communities not only transform the lives of the members of the communities, but can actually save the world.

These communities may not be immediately recognized as theological communities. These communities are often marginalized among the marginalized. They represent the challenges that today's context poses to the theological enterprise. Members of these communities live out their interaction with change, dynamism, and oppression while maintaining a relationship with God.

The first example is a community represented in Butler's novel *Parable of the Sower*. Womanist religious scholars have often looked to black women's literature as a source for theology. Thus, *Parable* can serve as prophetic literature that both warns the current world of the dangers that lie ahead and offers proposals for how we can "make a way out of no way." *Parable* offers a religion that draws heavily on traditional Yoruba religious traditions and the ancestors that represent change and flux. These ancestors guide the characters into a community that can sustain itself in the midst of a violent world.

Black Women's Science Fiction

Womanist theologians and ethicists have diversified the sources for theological study through their use of literature. Womanist religious scholarship often uses black women's literature as a source for understanding black women's experiences. One example is Emilie Townes's second book, *In a Blaze of Glory: Womanist Spirituality as Social Witness*, in which she uses Toni Morrison's *Beloved*, Alice Walker's *The Color Purple*, and Paule Marshall's *Praisesong for the Widow* as revealers of womanist spirituality.[3] Womanist ethicist Katie G. Cannon forthrightly describes black women's literature as an ideal source for understanding the experiences of black women. She writes that the African American women's literary tradition is "the best available literary repository for understanding the ethical values Black women have created and cultivated in their participation in this society."[4] Even within the womanist concepts of salvation examined here, slave narratives, nineteenth-century autobiographical narratives, *Beloved*, and Julie Dash's *Daughters of the Dust* have served as repositories for accessing the experiences of past and contemporary black women. Womanist theologians use nineteenth-century slave narratives and autobiographies as well as twentieth-century authors from the Harlem Renaissance and the 1970s, 1980s, and 1990s.

A postmodern womanist theology expands this use of literature by investigating black women's science fiction for an image of its theological images. In "Why Women Can't Write," feminist science fiction writer Joanna Russ offers science fiction as a liberating genre for women—one that welcomes the display of alternative attitudes and cultures. According to Russ, "the science fiction arena is particularly appropriate for introducing figures that challenge traditional literary representations of women."[5] In looking at black women's science fiction as a reflection or illustration of its theology, postmodern womanist theology uses black women's literature to provide visions of a possible society. It critiques the current society and offers proposals for "what could be," "what should be," and possibly "what will be." Black women's science fiction talks about salvation.

Black women's science fiction is uniquely positioned to disclose postmodern womanist theology. It has the potential to give specificity to the previous theoretical discussion of postmodern womanist theology. Situating black women's science fiction within the genres of utopian writing, science fiction, feminist literature, and African American literary traditions demonstrates that it is exceptionally capable of providing imaginative models of creative transformation and ancestral immortality.

Creative Transformation

Black women's science fiction is a syncretic combination of the various genres of utopian writing, science fiction, and feminist literature. There are four key aspects of black women's science fiction: (1) it is a critique of current society, (2) it is concerned with issues of social justice, (3) it offers possibilities for the future, and (4) it aims to change its readers. These characteristics are consonant with "making a way out of no way" as creative transformation.

Black women's science fiction offers a critique of contemporary society. Science fiction can be described as utopian literature that draws upon the resources of science and technology. In its most basic sense, utopian literature depicts the author's ideal society. Literary critic Dingbo Wu defines utopian literature as "literary speculation about nonexistent worlds as a critique of the contemporary human society."[6] In his work on utopias, Peyton Richter claims that every author of a utopia pronounces a moral judgment upon the society in which she or he lives.[7] In other words, describing an ideal society involves an evaluation of the shortcomings of the present society. As a utopian genre, science fiction is constructed, in part, out of dissatisfaction with the world as it is.

Utopias do more than reject the author's inherited world; they also offer solutions for ways to make that world better. In rather strong language, literary critic Joseph Wellbank states that justice is a requirement of utopias: "Having an adequate conception of social justice should be of the first importance to every serious utopian thinker and practitioner."[8] Wellbank identifies four criteria of justice that utopian visions must include: a definition of genuine justice, a theoretical frame for the social accomplishment of the demands of justice, a fair schematic for the social structure, and impartiality in these accomplishments.[9] A utopia is useless if, in its critique of society, it does not imply or provide a picture of justice.

Black utopias are particularly interested in social justice. "Blacks certainly envisioned a better future for themselves and America. . . . Utopian visions must have entered their thought, buoyed up their hopes and nourished their efforts at social change."[10] Combining freedom, justice, and religious ethics, black utopias are also characterized by their communal nature: "The hope is always for an altered status of blacks as a group and not simply as single persons."[11]

Feminists also focus on issues of justice in their utopian constructions. In *Women in Search of Utopia*, Ruby Rohrlich compares feminist utopian literature to that of men: "For men, utopia is the ideal state; for most women, utopia is stateless and the overcoming of hierarchy and the traditional splits between human beings and nature, subject and other, man and woman, parent and child."[12] Rohrlich states that feminist utopian literature is distinct from its male counterpart in its portrayal of the journey to freedom and destruction of hierarchical norms. Feminist utopian literature represents more egalitarian communities. All in all, utopias offer ideal visions for public consideration. Feminist utopias help us to envision an ideal social order.[13] That is, feminist utopian literature helps its readers to dream and imagine a better life.

Black women's science fiction also offers possibilities for the future social world. Rather than positing one idea, feminist science fiction writers often write in thought-experiments. Their writing says, "What if . . ." or "Let's try . . ." or "what would we get if . . ." or "I wished I could live like . . ." Literary critic Marleen Barr emphasizes this speculative nature of women's science fiction so much that she prefers the term *feminist speculative fiction*.[14] The female protagonists of feminist speculative fiction destroy patriarchal ideas of femininity: "Women who form communities, become heroes, and take charge of their sexuality and behave in a manner which is alien to the established concept of femininity—they show women with mastery and competence."[15] Barr distinguishes a separate category of black women's science fiction that she calls *womanist speculative fiction*. Womanist speculative fiction creates societies where "women co-exist with men, retain their female characteristics, and function as powerful individuals."[16] In so doing, the protagonists of black women's science fiction embrace part of Alice Walker's original definition of *womanist*: "they are committed to the survival of an entire people."[17]

Black women's science fiction can change the world. It offers something that women are often denied in the real world—the possibility for women to receive support from men.[18] First, it provides pictures of new relationships between men and women. The protagonists in black women's science fiction change the imperfect world of the novel and strive to create new societies with new values. Second, these protagonists change their worlds not by sacrificing love for power, but by combining special powers with commitments to others.[19] For Barr, this is a call to the readers of womanist speculative fiction: "[The authors'] visions summon us to rebuild society and make it possible for female heroes to experience both love and public importance."[20]

This quick overview of genre influences suggests that there are definable characteristics of black women's science fiction. Like all science fiction, black women's science fiction refers to future contexts, scientific possibilities, and advancements in technology that do not currently exist. Like utopian writing, black women's science fiction offers an ideal society that does not currently exist. These works of fiction also critique current society—including its patriarchy and limiting of roles for men and women. They are interested in freedom, justice, and ethics for the entire community. But black women's science fiction does not just offer one perfect idea—it is speculative. Black women's science fiction offers possibilities and alternatives for the future. In so doing, it encourages change in its readers—to rebuild society into the kind of place it can be, or to prevent it from being the kind of place it could be if we are not careful. Because of these functions, there is a connection between utopian literature and theology: "Utopian literature serves as spiritual guides demonstrating values and experiences of alternative societies that are in some ways better or worse than the readers' world."[21]

To quickly summarize, black women's science fiction offers its readers numerous resources—it critiques current society and offers an alternative vision of society. It shows the value of imagination in the process of creative transformation. The society it portrays includes portraits of justice, community, feminism, and gender and sexual equality. Black women's science fiction addresses some of the problems of the day and creatively suggests solutions. Black women's science fiction offers descriptions of creative transformation.

Ancestral Immortality

African American literary theory argues that African Diasporic literatures distinctly portray traditional African religious imagery in the plot development. As part of this literary corpus, black women's science fiction overtly references the ancestors and their activity in the context of the novel. This suggests that black women's science fiction can represent the postmodern womanist concept of ancestral immortality.

African Diasporic literature often reflects traditional African religions in its story world. Nigerian author Wole Soyinka writes of the appearance of traditional African deities in the literature of African Diasporic writers.[22] Soyinka asserts that European colonialism unwittingly spread Yoruba theology around the world. Yoruba theology and its "deities" are evident in the literature of African, Caribbean, and African American writers. African American literary critic Henry Louis Gates is even more direct in a similar argument. In *The Signifying Monkey*, Gates asserts that Pan-African (African American, African, Caribbean, and Latin American) writing contains evidence of traditional African belief systems: "There can be little doubt that certain fundamental terms for order that the black enslaved brought with them from Africa, and maintained through the mnemonic devices peculiar to oral literature, continued to function both as meaningful units for New World belief systems and as traces of their origins.[23] Together, Soyinka and Gates assert that Yoruba cosmology and its òrìṣà are evident in the literature of African, Caribbean, and African American writers.

When Gates and Soyinka refer to traditional Yoruba religious elements within African Diasporic literature, they are most likely referring to Yoruba-based religions in the various syncretic forms in which they are known in the Americas. Scholar of African religions Jacob K. Olupona notes that African literature often embraces ancestral imagery from traditional African religions: "Ancestor imagery has also become the instrument with which African literary figures have expressed anger at colonialism, political domination, and the subtle racism they come across in foreign lands."[24] Olupona notes that imagery of "the ancestors" helps authors to make statements about how they believe the world should be transformed. Because of the syncretism of African religions in the Americas, representation of the ancestors will probably blend together or use interchangeably the roles and activities of the òrìṣà, the culture heroes, and the ancestors who are distinguished in the context of traditional Yoruba religion.

The Yoruba òrìṣà continue to appear in African American literature and beg an interpretation that reflects the characteristics of the òrìṣà within the life of the protagonists. Gates argues that the òrìṣà constitute distinctive languages, or tropes, because they appear repeatedly in Pan-African literature.[25] Indebted to the work of Soyinka and Gates, literary scholar Alexis Brooks DeVita develops the concept of òrìṣà functioning as literary tropes into the concept of "mythatypes." Looking particularly at Pan-African women's literature, DeVita asserts that Pan-African women writers, consciously or unconsciously, invoke symbols that reflect African goddesses, including the female òrìṣà of traditional Yoruba religion:"[T]he fact that Pan-African women writers regularly invoke certain symbols such as trees, rain, and wind in the metaphorical depiction of their protagonists' dilemmas and decisions becomes abundantly clear as one reads these women's writings from a variety of cultures and in multiple languages."[26] The images of trees, rain, and wind, for example, form a coded language that signifies an associated òrìṣà.

DeVita believes that ancestors help the protagonists of African Diasporic literature to achieve their own forms of fulfillment. She uses the term *mythatype* for the literary appearance of "ancestresses-becoming-historical-figures-becoming-legends-becoming-deities."[27] DeVita argues that the influence or intervention of a mythatype indicates a heroine's access to divine power and assistance. Even when the protagonist appears defeated, a mythatypical reading reveals that a heroine has successfully completed a quest or attained her goal. Thus, when an òrìṣà appears in black women's fiction, readers should expect to see this ancestor guide the protagonist toward health, wholeness, and freedom.

Soyinka, Gates, and DeVita call for a literary interpretation that isolates the symbols and divinities of traditional Yoruba religion in black women's writing. Postmodern womanist theology draws upon this literary theory in its examination of black women's science fiction. Postmodern womanist theology looks for overt and subtle references to syncretized traditional Yoruba religion in black women's science fiction. It notes the mythatypes and the ways in which they mediate the activity of salvation within the story world of the novels. In summary, this literary interpretation echoes the concept of ancestral immortality as it looks toward the ancestors of traditional African religions for assistance in achieving salvation.

Using black women's science fiction as a theological resource stretches both womanist theology and postmodern metaphysics in new directions. Because black women's science fiction includes elements of traditional African religions, it helps womanist theology to include the non-Christian religious dimensions of black religion in its scope. Black women's literature can also have a prophetic function in theology. Black women's science fiction can provide concrete images, models, and proposals for what *could* happen or what *should* happen.

Black women's science fiction can offer examples of postmodern womanist theology. These works suggest models of salvation by portraying characters and scenarios that bring life to what has been stated in the metaphysical and theological language of postmodern womanist theology. Postmodern womanist theology recognizes the syncretized mythatypes of traditional Yoruba religion that help the characters in black women's science fiction to creatively transform their contexts. Thus, we will see *Parable of the Sower* critique its context through a picture of destructive transformation. Then it will provide concrete images of a new vision of salvation.

Walking the Way

Parable of the Sower provides an imaginative model of a postmodern womanist theology. In *Parable of the Sower*, the Yoruba òrìşà Oya functions as the immortal ancestor who protects the protagonist and her friends, guiding them to higher modes of creative transformation. Creative transformation occurs through an inclusive teaching and learning community that seeks to survive in a dangerous world while sharing a belief in the symbiotic relationship between God and the world. The community is juxtaposed against a picture of destructive transformation where other communities try to isolate themselves from the reality of the larger world in which they live, supported by an understanding of a nonrelational God who cares nothing for what happens in the world. These communities remember the past, but they do not honor it. *Parable* depicts a savior who might ordinarily be overlooked in the quest for salvation. The leader of this theological community is a black teenage girl living with the side effects of her mother's drug addiction.

Plot

Parable of the Sower portrays a twenty-first-century California of decay and chaos through the eyes of African American teenage protagonist Lauren Oya Olamina. Written in diary format, the novel unfolds through Lauren's record of her thoughts and life events from age fifteen in 2024 to age eighteen in 2027. When we enter the story, Lauren and her family live in a walled neighborhood in Robledo, California, a fictional suburb of Los Angeles. There has been a major breakdown in U.S. infrastructure: police and firefighters charge fines and harass and rob citizens; labor laws are so relaxed that there is no minimum wage, and slavery has been revived through "company store" corporations; state borders are closed to out-of-state residents; and drugs, poverty, and rape are so commonplace that people carry guns to leave their own neighborhoods and are not surprised at the sight of human corpses in their midst. Everyone except the poor and homeless live in walled neighborhoods. Outside, people are poor, illiterate, jobless, and without water.

When Lauren's neighborhood is invaded and destroyed, she begins to walk north toward Oregon, where jobs pay money (as compared to room and board or company script) and water is more accessible. In the process, she meets people who join her in her journey. New members join the community when the surrounding environment impinges on their journey: after an earthquake, when they intervene in an attempted robbery, after a night of gun-fighting. When they begin their walk, they are a group of ragtag survivors trying to stay alive and get to a better place. In the process, the travelers adhere to an ethic of inclusion and mutual care. Interwoven in Lauren's diary is a philosophical theology she has "discovered." She calls this "God-is-Change" theology "Earthseed." As more people join her in the journey northward, she teaches "Earthseed." At the end of the novel, the "Earthseed community" settles on the remnants of an old farm belonging to one of the travelers. They call their new community "Acorn."

Ancestral Immortality

Parable presents the Yoruba-based òrìṣà Oya as an example of an ancestor with knowledge and power available to world. Oya's knowledge and power is neutral and can be used by the members of the present generation for good or evil. Although syncretized African religions portray the òrìṣà as wanting to help people lead ethical lives, their knowledge and agency can be used for creative or destructive ends.

The context of *Parable* is framed by the presence and role of Oya. Oya permeates the story through the natural elements that confuse, destroy, and protect the characters. The name of *Parable*'s protagonist—Lauren Oya Olamina—indicates the presence of traditional Yoruba culture. Lauren does not make any mention of her name until late in the novel when she meets a new traveler who will become her lover:

> I talked to him, introduced myself and learned that his name was Bankole—Taylor Franklin Bankole. Our last names were an instant bond between us. We're both descended from men who assumed African surnames back during the 1960s. His father and my grandfather had had their names legally changed, and both had chosen Yoruba replacement names.[28]

The Yoruba heritage of the names is significant; as Bankole notes, "Most people chose Swahili names in the '60s."[29] Neither Bankole nor Lauren know the rationale behind their names, but the names become a source of intimacy for Lauren—Bankole never calls her "Lauren"; always "Olamina." The Yoruba surname Olamina strengthens the signification present in the middle name Oya.

In traditional Yoruba religion, Oya is the òrìṣà of change. In her work *Oya: In Praise of an African Goddess,* Judith Gleason refers to Oya as the òrìṣà of change represented in radical weather conditions. Oya manifests herself in several natural forms—wind, especially tornadoes, fire, the river, and the African buffalo. Oya is represented in the lightning that is partnered with the elements of thunder and rain. Oya is also the mother of Egungun, the masquerade of masks that honor the ancestors. Thus, Oya is another guardian to the realm of the ancestors: "It is *Oya* who brings the voice of those ancestors who preserved the wisdom that leads to the development of good character."[30] Oya is the most powerful female òrìṣà,[31] and is well known for her sense of justice and her intolerance of the abuse and oppression of women.

The elemental aspects of Oya form the backdrop for the story world of *Parable.* Some of the death and destruction of *Parable* is caused by the natural elements of wind, storm, and fire, which are closely associated with Oya. When the novel opens, Oya is present in the storms and rain that Lauren both laments and enjoys. There is a tornado that is destroying the eastern and southern United States. These storms occur throughout the United States as the novel progresses. Traditional Yoruba religion most commonly identifies Oya as a strong wind, a destructive storm.[32] Oya is present not only in the background, but also in Lauren's own context. Despite the incredible aridity of Southern California, it begins to rain, the first rainstorm that residents of Southern California have seen in six years.

The presence of lightning, wind, and tornadoes foreshadows Oya's central role in the story. Ṣango[33] is the Yoruba òrìṣà of thunder and rain, and Oya is considered the senior of Ṣango's three wives. One story about Ṣango describes Oya's association with lightning and thunder. While Ṣango was a mortal king, several factions challenged his leadership. In order to consolidate his power, Ṣango asked the king of a neighboring land for a medicinal preparation that, when placed under the tongue, would allow its owner to spit thunderstones with enough voltage to knock out entire armies. Ṣango sent Oya to the land to obtain the medicine. Oya did, but before she returned, she kept some of the medicinal power so that she could have some lightning for herself. While experimenting with his powers from a mountain, Ṣango accidentally threw a bolt of lightning towards his own palace, killing nearly everyone in the vicinity. Overcome by what he had done, Ṣango fled his kingdom and hung himself. Ṣango disappeared into the ground and Oya, overwhelmed with grief, also disappeared.

Thus, Ṣango and Oya are said to rule the storms in the sky together. "Oya's winds precede thunderstorms. Ṣango's rain seeds fertilize the earth. In between is the problematic of lightning."[34] Ṣango is thunder, but the lightning belongs to Oya. Although she initially appears in *Parable* as wind, tornado, rain, and lightning, Oya is also manifest in the fires that form, threaten, and shape the narrative. Oya's wind is a warm tropical wind that can cause fires. "Although wind is [Oya's] primary vehicle, Oya is perforce a fiery element as well."[35] One Yoruba song about Oya includes the verse, "Oya, strong wind who gave birth to fire while traversing the mountain."[36] Oya's fire is "both generative and all-enveloping."[37] Together, the wind and lightning dimensions of Oya render her a "divine pyromaniac [who] takes charge of post-lightning strikes."[38]

In *Parable*, there is a new drug known as "blaze, fuego, flash, sunfire . . . the most popular name is pyro—short for pyromania," which causes people to want to set fires.[39] Its abusers shave their heads and paint their bodies and burn anything and everything they can—including each other. The drug-induced state makes watching fire "better than sex."[40] In the dry climate of Southern California, the fires spread wildly, and Oya moves to the foreground.

Oya's presence can be destructive or creative, depending on whether humans honor or ignore her. When honored, she produces creative changes in the world. When ignored, she is angered and may manifest herself destructively. According to one Yoruba priest, neglect is a result of society's embrace of greed, individualism, and failure to propitiate the ancient spirits.[41] When honored, Oya can provide the fires that nourish and the winds that cleanse and establish the meteorological climates, and guide one in the transition from mortal to ancestor and from ancestor to veneration in the Egungun rituals. Oya reminds us that not only do we live within whirlwinds of changing conditions, but that the divine itself can be both an author and recipient of change.

Devotees of Santería also associate Caribbean hurricanes with Oya and the slave trade. Cuban devotees of Oya describe tropical storms with a particular travel pattern that begins on the western coast of Africa and moves over the Atlantic Ocean.[42] Gleason interprets this stormy pattern as an attempt to resolve the evils of slavery:

> Now storms along the seam, at their most violent . . . [drift] southwest over the Atlantic with ever-increasing amplitude, suddenly strike the Caribbean. Thus, by grace of atmospheric forces beyond human control, the tornadoes of west Africa, following the slave-trade routes along which those who first named them were hauled to the hurricane-prone islands of their diaspora, achieve in the New World their apotheosis.[43]

Devotees of Santería identify Oya in the storm. Oya is a witness to both the presence of Africans in America and the unique ways in which black religions blend traditional African religions with Christianity.

Destructive Transformation

All the characters of *Parable* strive to survive and find quality of life in the dangerous world in which they live. They form communities, develop a code of ethics, and sometimes adhere to a belief in God. Yet attempts to anesthetize or isolate oneself from the changing conditions of the world are destructive forms of transformation. *Parable* identifies problems with the communities that offer these responses and the theology that supports these false and ineffective attempts.

Overcome by the problems of twenty-first-century California, the pyro users numb themselves to the reality of the world through their addiction to the drug. They form their own traveling community of pyromanics. Lauren writes that the fires are an expression of the frustration that people feel: "People are setting fires to get rid of whomever they dislike from personal enemies to anyone who looks or sounds foreign or racially different. People are setting fires because they're frustrated, angry, hopeless. They have no power to improve their lives, but they have the power to make others ever more miserable."[44] The pyro addicts use Oya's power destructively.

Lauren's walled neighborhood also represents a destructive response to poverty and desperation. People live in the walled communities, believing them to be their best alternative to living in the dangerous world. There is a clear boundary between the inside and the outside, and the inside is decidedly a safer place to be. By choosing to live within the walls, people try to isolate themselves from the larger world outside of the walls. The neighborhood provides some sense of community as its residents protect each other from the threats of the outside world. Lauren's father explains the community ethic: "We help each other, and we don't steal."[45] Although the community establishes ethical rules of conduct for itself, the community exists out of its fear of living outside the walls. Aware of the threat of criminals, Lauren's father's idea of salvation is violent: "If they come . . . Freeze, aim, and fire. That will save you. Nothing else will."[46] In this context, salvation consists of a violent protection of one's possessions. The members of the walled community try to fight the changes that are occurring around them. The walled community tries to preserves its way of life, keeping the negativity of the outside world in the back of its mind.

The city of Olivar represents another kind of destructive community. As public services decline and cities feel threatened, a small coastal city sells itself to a multinational corporation named Olivar. This company offers jobs in exchange for security, room, and board. The salaries are low, the rooms are small, and the payment comes in company script, but the company will protect its residents from the declining economy and the danger of the outside world.

Debt to the company is inevitable. Olivar claims to counteract the threat of the current world, but in reality it reinforces the threat. It, too, perpetuates an insider-outsider mentality, and continues to erode the economy by forcing its inhabitants into what will soon become company debt. Although Olivar appears to offer a novel approach to helping people to live amid poverty and crime, in actuality it represents a return to a remote past of indentured servitude and decreased prosperity.

The walled neighborhood and Olivar do not honor the past, even though they cling to it. These communities represent attempts at exclusivity and isolation. Memory of the past either increases exclusivity and violence or imitates oppressive aspects of the past. The encroaching outside world destroys the walled neighborhood, and Olivar can only lead to a newfangled version of sharecropping. The pyros' fires are harmful ways of wrestling with the desperation of poverty. The way of destruction does not embrace change, and thus does not honor Oya.

Lauren also critiques the theology that the walled community embraces. She lists the different beliefs about God that she has heard about: "A lot of people seem to believe in a big-daddy-God or a big-cop-God or a big-king-God. They believe in a kind of super-person. A few believe God is another word for nature. And nature turns out to mean just about anything that they happen not to understand or feel in control of."[47] Lauren rejects an authoritarian kind of theism as well as pantheism. She concludes that most people use God to help them to cope with the exigencies of the world: "So what is God? Just another name for whatever makes you feel special and protected?"[48] For Lauren, this is insufficient.

Lauren critiques Christianity and the Bible for its impracticability. She sees the God of the Bible as an unfeeling actor in history: "But that God sounds a lot like Zeus—a super-powerful man, playing with his toys the way my youngest brothers play with toy soldiers. Bang, bang! Seven toys fall dead. If they're yours, you make the rules. Who cares what the toys think. Wipe out a toy's family, then give it a brand-new family. Toy children, like Job's children, are interchangeable."[49] Ultimately, Lauren rejects any God who is an "unmoved mover," a God who can make things happen but does not feel or care for the effects of what happens. Lauren finds a classical theism that asserts God's omnipotent authoritative power insufficient for her questions about the world. Classical theism deemphasizes the agency of the world. Thus, its adherents experience the divine as one who does not support the life or liberation of the world.

The walled neighborhood and Olivar do not embrace ancestral immortality. These communities represent attempts at exclusivity and isolation. Their memory of the past either is indiscriminate, as in the case of the walled community, or resurrects oppressive aspects of the past. This refusal to move forward does not deal with the pervasiveness of change. Classical theology cannot provide creative options for a better way of life, either. Rather than seeking ways to live prosperously in the world they are given, these communities use their faith to keep them stuck in one time and in one place. These communities cannot creatively transform the world in which they exist.

Creative Transformation

Parable never shows us a world without the problems that are described. Searching for salvation is making a way in the midst of unhealthy and destructive ways. In the midst of the chaos of her world, Lauren insists that there is another way. She doesn't want to escape or deny the world in which she lives. She wants to do something creative about it. The community "walks the way" to creatively transform the world. In so doing, they honor the past, teach one another, affirm a theology of change and process, and build community. Although *Parable* does not portray the fulfillment of this theological community, the reader can see that the community has the potential for growth and continued creative transformation. Without the full realization of this community, the reader is reminded that salvation is found primarily in the process.

In *Parable*, Lauren and her fellow travelers are trying to survive in a world of poverty and crime. As they walk north, they embrace a theology that can affirm the constant flux of the world. They learn that their salvation also requires an inclusive ethical community that has hope for the future and is willing to work together to improve the quality of life for its members. The Earthseed community honors Oya, and Oya helps them in their process of creative transformation.

As Lauren walks northward, her most immediate priority is survival. Lauren believes that survival can only come through a willingness to learn. While in the walled neighborhood, Lauren researches as much as she can to learn about survival skills in northern California. According to Lauren, learning is the only path to survival. Once Lauren is outside the walls, she plans to learn from everyone: "Everyone who's surviving out here knows things that I need to know . . . I'll learn from them. If I don't, I'll be killed. And like I said, I intend to survive."[50] Lauren is willing to learn from anyone she can in order to survive.

Survival is a two-way street of learning and teaching. Wondering what kind of job she will be able to obtain outside the walled community, Lauren believes that her ability to teach others to read and write will help her find a job once she gets to the north. As she travels, Lauren keeps a journal that contains her observations about the world. Her fellow travelers often look on and ask her to teach them to read what she is writing.

Lauren teaches Earthseed theology to her fellow travelers. Lauren knows that teaching will build community: "I can teach. If I do well, it will draw people to me—to Earthseed."[51] Whenever the travelers stop for a day or two to refuel their supplies, regain their strength, and communicate with each other, Lauren talks about Earthseed. After a while, long-standing members of the community begin to teach the new members about Lauren's philosophy. When a new traveler joins the group, the other travelers explain Earthseed. As Lauren and her students teach, Earthseed theology takes on a life of its own. The cycle of learning and teaching is necessary for both physical and spiritual survival. It helps to build community.

On the walk north, Lauren realizes that survival comes in and through the Earthseed community. Lauren begins walking with two other survivors from the walled neighborhood. They build a community of travelers through a policy of inclusion. Lauren embraces a diversity that others reject: "On the street, people are expected to fear and hate everyone but their own."[52] The mixed composition of this community is a literal testament to diversity. Members are black, white, Mexican, Japanese, and several combinations thereof. The youngest member is still feeding from the breast, and the oldest member is fifty-seven years old. Diversity is a principle of the community. Oya helps generate the diversity of the Earthseed community. One scholar believes that Oya is responsible for the diversity in the world: "If it were not for the random element of change represented by *Oya*, everything that existed in the universe would have the same texture, structure and appearance."[53]

Like the walled community, the traveling community is held together by a code of ethics. The ethics, however, have changed. Outside the walls, killing and stealing are sometimes necessary to avoid being killed or starving to death. The Earthseed community lives by an ethic to which all new members must agree before they join: "We don't kill unless someone threatens us. . . . We don't hunt people. We don't eat human flesh. We fight together against enemies. If one of us is in need, the rest help out. And we don't steal from one another, *ever*."[54] In a world where justice and solidarity are scarce, the Earthseed community still demands it. The ethic binds the community together and allows them to survive.

In her quest for new theology, Lauren begins to describe the workings of the world around her. She analyzes other people, herself, everything she can read, hear, and see, and all the history she can learn. She calls her new theology Earthseed, a "God-is-Change" belief system: "I've never felt that [Earthseed] was anything other than real: discovery rather than invention, exploration rather than creation."[55] When people accuse her of making up or creating her own philosophy, Lauren refutes them, stating, "All I do is observe and take notes, trying to put things down in ways that are as powerful, as simple, and as direct as I feel them."[56] Lauren is trying to describe how the entire world works. She does her own speculative metaphysics.

Lauren's metaphysics is based on the constancy of change in the world and a symbiotic relationship between God and the world. She expresses the core of Earthseed in verse:

> All that you touch,
> You change.
> All that you Change,
> Changes you.
> The only lasting truth
> Is Change.
> God
> is Change.[57]

For Lauren, change is the one common denominator in everything in the world. Earthseed teaches that God influences the world and that the world influences God. The central verse of Earthseed reads:

> Why is the universe?
> To shape God.
> Why is God?
> To shape the universe.[58]

Earthseed's God is constantly influencing the world: "Yet God has been here all along, shaping us and being shaped by us in no particular way or in too many ways at once like an amoeba—or like a cancer."[59] God's influence and shaping occur with or without the acknowledgment of the temporal world. It is just part of how the world works. Lauren acknowledges Oya's elemental qualities of change in Earthseed theology:

> As wind,
> As water. As fire
> as life,
> God
> Is both creative and destructive,
> Demanding and yielding,
> Sculptor and clay,
> God is Infinite Potential:
> God is change.[60]

Oya protects the Earthseed community because its theology acknowledges her.

Lauren's God-is-change philosophy reflects the presence of Oya. Oya represents change in the temporal world. Oya's embodiment in the wind and tornadoes identify her as the òrìṣà that induces change: "To call an Orisha the Spirit of the Wind is to make a symbolic reference to constant motion that exists in Nature."[61] Oya's ability to cause change extends beyond the creative and destructive power of her elemental nature. When Oya appears, society itself is encouraged to change. Oya's presence indicates a need for a change in human consciousness: "The unique function of *Oya* . . . is to provide those changing conditions that force consciousness to grow, expand and transcend its limitations."[62] Like Lauren, Oya wants to cause a shift in the way people see the world and themselves in the world. Lauren believes that a shift in consciousness will lead people to conclude that God is change. Thus, when Lauren describes God as change, she invokes the presence of Oya.

Lauren believes that the best approach to living in the world is to shape God consciously: "But we can rig the game in our own favor if we understand that God exists to be shaped, and will be shaped, with or without our forethought, with or without our intent."[63] Earthseed theology encourages people to be conscious about how they influence God. In positively shaping God, one can find creative aspects of change. Shaping God gives humanity agency in "the whens and the whys and the hows" of the change that is inevitable.[64] Likewise, God influences the world. Lauren writes about how the world understands God:

> We do not worship God.
> We perceive and attend God.
> We learn from God.[65]

Together, God and creation contribute to the workings of the world. Lauren speaks of agency as a co-creating with God: "God is better partnered than fought."[66]

Wholeness and well-being are found in a description of God and the world that can account for and respond to change. Earthseed describes a symbiotic relationship between God and the world. This God-is-Change philosophy focuses on the agency that humans have to influence and change the world. Talking to her friend, Lauren says, "This world is falling apart; you could help me begin something purposeful and constructive."[67] Earthseed theology is something that can adapt and persist; it is something purposeful and constructive.

Oya protects the Earthseed community from the dangerous fire created by the pyros' destructive transformation of her powers. Near the end of the novel,

Lauren notices a fire burning close behind the community's path. The fire continues to burn until it almost consumes them. They try to outrun the fire. Although the fire kills many people, the Earthseed community appears to be protected. Oya possesses the fire. Lauren refers to the fire as if it is a living person: "It teased like a living, malevolent thing, intent on causing pain and terror. It drove us before it like dogs chasing a rabbit. Yet it didn't eat us. It could have, but it didn't. In the end, the worst of it roared off to the northwest."[68] Bankole refers to the fire in language strikingly similar to a description of Oya: "Firestorm, Bankole called it later. Yes. Like a tornado of fire, roaring around us, just missing us, playing with us, then letting us live."[69] Oya, the tornado of fire that can destroy and kill, protects the Earthseed community, luring them closer to the place where they will finally settle. Oya guides the community to its first home.

Oya's creativity appears for the last time when the Earthseed community honors the dead as part of its first task in Acorn. Lauren suggests a ritual to help mourn the loved ones that everyone has lost. They gather in a circle, plant acorn seeds, and recite Bible verses, Earthseed verses, and poems to honor those who have died. Immersed in the acknowledgment that there is always death, they declare that community continues. Oya again! Oya is the òrìṣà responsible for honoring the dead and emphasizing the cycle of life. Oya is always present at funerals: "wherever and however the link with those who have gone before is established, there you will find *Oya*."[70] Oya's Egungun rituals honor the dead *and* celebrate the role of the ancestors in the present. At Acorn, the Earthseed community begins their own ritual to honor the dead. They are also able to derive life from their memory. The acorns will grow into oaks that will help feed them the acorn bread that is now a staple of their diet. This ritual is the last scene of *Parable*, and the reader can conclude that life and the community will transform and go on.

Saviors

This literary illustration of postmodern womanist theology also provides new images of "the Saviors." The Saviors are the ones who lead the theological communities. Although *Parable* describes Lauren as possessing a unique constitution, it also shows the different activity of other characters that have the same qualities. Lauren emerges as a Savior because she courageously uses her abilities to creatively transform. We know a Savior by what she does.

As the protagonist of *Parable*, Lauren is the Savior. Lauren survives the destruction of her walled neighborhood and leads a group of people into community and a viable future. Nevertheless, Lauren is an unlikely Savior. Because Lauren is young, black, and female, her leadership is questioned by the larger world. In addition, Lauren lives with a condition that gives her a radical form of relationality. Lauren is a Savior because she uses these qualities to build a postmodern womanist theological community.

Lauren's age and gender prevent her from being considered seriously by people around her. When Lauren tells her father about preparing to live outside of the walls, he demeans her youth. Lauren knows that her age prevents many people from taking her seriously, and she also worries that her gender will make surviving more difficult. Walking north with her neighbors—another black female and a white male—Lauren is concerned about how she will appear to others. She knows that people do not expect a woman to be strong enough to ward off potential attackers.

Thus, Lauren decides to disguise herself as a man while traveling. She cuts her hair and uses her height and androgynous-sounding name to try to avoid threats. Lauren's cross-dressing reflects assistance from Oya. Oya is the mother of the Egungun tradition in which Yoruba men cover themselves in masks and several layers of cloth. Yet Oya is also known to masquerade herself as a man to accomplish important tasks. Gleason describes the Cuban Oya as a woman who dresses as a man when necessary. In postmodern womanist literary interpretation, Oya "anoints" Lauren a Savior through the act of masquerade.

Oya also protects Lauren as part of her role in protecting the rights of women in general. Oya is the "patron of feminine leadership."[71] Oya resisted being a battered wife and sought justice for women throughout Yorubaland. In stories, Oya is initially married to the warrior òrìṣà of iron, Ogun. Ogun insists on Oya's role as a submissive wife and beats her whenever he finds her to be too feisty. Oya refuses to accept such treatment and has an affair with Ṣango. In one story, Ogun finds them and Ṣango runs away in fear of Ogun. Oya then battles Ogun until they reach a stalemate. Oya is now free to become Ṣango's wife and possess some of his powers. Another narrative also states that Oya initiated the Egungun rituals to protect the rights of women.[72] Even though the practice was later usurped by men, Oya is known throughout Yoruba as the defender of women: "Many secular songs used by women in solidarity rallies still look back and derive inspiration from *Oya's* original narrative."[73] Like Oya, Lauren also refuses to "stay out of the enclaves of ideology and social control long, long ago preempted by men."[74] Lauren believes that her message is strong enough to overcome the discrimination she receives because of her gender and age.

More importantly, Lauren manages a condition called "hyperempathy syndrome," which causes her to consciously experience radical relationality with those around her. While pregnant, Lauren's mother abused a prescription drug that was originally designed to fight against Alzheimer's disease. As a result, Lauren shares the pain and pleasure of other people. She shares the feelings of all living beings—squirrels, rats, birds, dogs, and people. She calls her condition "sharing." Lauren can share pleasure—usually in the form of sex. Most of the time, her sharing is very painful because there is so much pain in the world.

Lauren uses her sharing to bond with others in a unique way. When one traveler dies in a self-defensive gunfight, Lauren walks with the traveler's sister to share her pain and feel closer to her. Lauren allows her ability to share to become a point of interpersonal bonding and transformation. Lauren's unusual condition allows her to maintain her own self in the experience of radical relationality while incorporating the world around her and transforming it into a community.

Radical relationality does not come without its vulnerabilities and exploitations. Lauren later realizes that four of her co-journeyers are also sharers and ex-slaves. These sharers are described as refusing to be touched, having an "odd tentativeness," and maintaining "a posture of protection and submission both at once."[75] At the slightest fear, they drop to the ground and curl into a ball to protect themselves. Their vulnerability was exploited, and hence they encounter the world with suspicion and trepidation. It is not the ability to share that makes a Savior. Lauren is a Savior because of what she does with her sharing.

Radical relationality operates as a norm for how members of the postmodern womanist theological community should relate to each other and the world around them. Lauren wonders if her condition wouldn't make the world a better place: "If hyperempathy syndrome were a more common complaint, people couldn't [torture other people terribly]. They could kill if they had to, and bear the pain of it or be destroyed by it. But if everyone could feel everyone else's pain, who would torture?"[76] What if hyperempathy was normative? What if it was the goal we all strive to achieve? We would all be tied together. The relational self would survive. This unsuspecting teenage girl, the equivalent of today's black American crack baby all grown up, is the one who holds a vision of salvation. A postmodern womanist theology echoes the response of one member of the Earthseed community: "You ain't got nothing wrong with you, Lauren."[77]

Young, female, and disabled, Lauren does not appear to have the characteristics of a Savior. Yet as a theologian, teacher, leader, and sharer, Lauren proves herself to be a worthy Savior. Lauren's teaching and vision develop a community of disciples. With Oya's help, Lauren is able to offer an image of postmodern womanist theology. As in postmodern womanist theology, *Parable* understands the Savior as one who puts forth a theology of change while teaching and building community.

Salvation is Challenging

Neither the Earthseed community nor Lauren enjoys smooth or flawless journeys to salvation. While the postmodern womanist reading of *Parable* emphasizes the creative transformation of community and theology, the novel also
reveals that the intended goal is not always achieved and that community can
often center too heavily on its leader.

Lauren's vision for a physical place goes beyond her desire to move northward. The Earthseed verse states:

> The Destiny of Earthseed
> is to take root among the stars.[78]

Lauren believes in the space program and that life on another planet is the
best alternative to life in the dying world she currently knows. Lauren begins
to think about the promise of the space program while she is still living in the
walled community. While Lauren is excited about the idea of living on Mars,
she realizes that it will be difficult for people to understand. When her fellow
travelers reject the idea of going to the stars, Lauren retorts that her idea is
better than classical notions of heaven: "After all, my heaven really exists, and
you don't have to die to reach it."[79] As far as Lauren is concerned, heaven and
hell are real places, and the Destiny in outer space is the best hope that future
generations can have.

Likewise, Lauren believes that traveling northward is not her true goal.
Traveling northward is the vehicle to her true goal—Earthseed. In believing
that the land in the north was the solution to the problem, Lauren commits
a "fallacy of misplaced concreteness." The "fallacy of misplaced concreteness"
is Whitehead's term for "the accidental error of mistaking the abstract for the
concrete."[80] Lauren's goal of going north or to the stars is a misplaced abstract
goal. Lauren thinks salvation is found in a locale rather than in the process
of walking to that locale. Salvation is not found in a northern paradise or in
achieving the Destiny. Salvation is not the goal; rather, it is the journey itself.

Lauren is also ambivalent about whether her leadership is critical to the
development of Earthseed. On the one hand, she wants the focus to be on
her message rather than her person. Lauren anticipates a time when people
won't be deterred by her young age: "Then, someday when people are able
to pay more attention to what I say than to how old I am, I'll use these verses
to pry them loose from the rotting past, and maybe push them into saving
themselves and building a future that makes sense."[81] Lauren believes that it is
Earthseed theology that saves. Lauren is a savior because she teaches a theology

of change and because she is able to build a community of people who trust and respect one another.

On the other hand, Lauren doesn't like the idea of Earthseed developing without her influence. Bankole tells her that people will take Earthseed and reinterpret it and make it more complicated, mystical, and comforting. Lauren retorts, "Not around me they won't!" When Bankole reminds her of how other religions changed after their leaders died, Lauren replies, "I mean to guide and shape Earthseed into what it should be."[82] Lauren wants to have control over the development of Earthseed. Although Lauren does not want to be dismissed for her age or gender, she still seems to think that there is something about her that makes salvation possible.

Salvation is often a difficult task. In *Parable*, there is nothing easy about the process of survival, teaching, or building community. Lauren knows that attaining her goals will be difficult. She realizes that salvation is a far-reaching plan and that it will require a lot of work: "There's so much to do before [the Destiny] can even begin. I guess that's to be expected. There's always a lot to do before you go to heaven."[83] Lauren also discovers that the challenge of attaining her goals is literally painful: "Walking hurts. I've never done enough walking to learn that before, but I know it now. It isn't only the blisters and sore feet, although we've got those. After a while, everything hurts."[84] Despite its pain and difficulty, walking the way is the only way to survive.

The way of survival, Earthseed community, and theology is imperfect and difficult. Within the story world of *Parable*, the Destiny and space travel are never actualized. Lauren's focus on the Destiny and the northern location where Acorn is founded can detract from seeing salvation where it does occur—in the process of walking the way. Lauren's human fallibility means that there are times when she wants to do more than lead Earthseed; she wants to control it. Even when functioning at its best, a theology of change—walking the way in a diverse community that teaches and learns together—is hard work.

In *Parable*, creative transformation is, quite literally, a way that is walked. Lauren finally realizes that her goal of teaching Earthseed theology and building an Earthseed community is attained in the process of walking north. She writes, "Earthseed is being born right here on Highway 101."[85] When another person considers joining the traveling community, she asks what Earthseed is. Lauren replies, "We share some ideas. We intend to settle up north, and found a community."[86] The essentials of Earthseed are simply stated: "[T]o learn to shape God with forethought, care and work; to educate and benefit their community, their families, and themselves."[87] Earthseed is creative transformation—the theology, the community, and the process of teaching and learning that occur on the journey.

A postmodern womanist interpretation of Octavia E. Butler's *Parable of the Sower* describes salvation as "walking a way out of no way." Salvation is found in the process of building a community of diverse, disenfranchised people with a common yearning for a better life. In walking north, a way is made out of no way. The disenfranchised, mournful, and lost find community. The illiterate learn to read. People find ways of understanding that affirm both a compassionate God and their own ability to change the world. Desperate people find an ethic of care such that the problems and successes of others are their own. It is not a static community, but one that will continue to grow over time. While still living in the walled neighborhood, Lauren writes, "I am Earthseed. Anyone can be. Someday, I think there will be a lot of us."[88]

The Earthseed community survives by honoring the spirit of Oya. With the assistance of Oya, the Earthseed community survives threatening fires, honors the dead, and embraces feminine leadership. As it honors the dead with the planting of acorns, the Earthseed community acknowledges the cycle of life and the objective immortality of the community's deceased loved ones. When they embrace God as change, they summon the creative aspects of Oya. Creative transformation is found in a theology that is strikingly similar to both traditional Yoruba-based religions and the postmodern theological framework. As Lauren and the Earthseed community walk north, Oya travels with them.

Loving the Way

GSN (God, Self, and Neighbor) Ministries offers another portrait of postmodern womanist theology. GSN Ministries finds inspiration and support in African American and Christian heritage. GSN Ministries invokes African American sacred music, the activism of African American church communities and leaders, Jesus' message of liberation, and social justice traditions. These sources guide GSN into higher modes of creative transformation. Creative transformation occurs through a teaching and learning community that offers inclusive faith community in a context of condemnation and prejudice while emphasizing a belief in the loving relationship between God and the world. The community is juxtaposed against destructive transformation in other communities that neglect the holistic needs of their members and reject wider contexts. These communities disremember the past through their selective or pejorative use of the past. GSN Ministries boasts a Savior who might ordinarily be overlooked in the quest for salvation. The leader of this community is a black lesbian woman living with mental and physical health challenges.

Context

GSN Ministries is a United Church of Christ (UCC)–affiliated ministry in Atlanta, Georgia. Founded by Rev. Dr. Kathi Elaine Martin in 1999, GSN Ministries was established in response to the homophobia in African American churches. Atlanta is the home to the largest population of gay and lesbian African Americans in the South and is often referred to as a "black gay mecca." In recent years, the city's black gay pride celebration has drawn approximately forty thousand people.[89] Atlanta is also home to a growing number of conservative black megachurches that do not welcome gays and lesbians. Thus, the relationship between Atlanta's black gay and lesbian population and many black churches is strained.

This strained relationship is complicated by the fact that African Americans represent the fastest-growing population of HIV-infected people in the United States. According to the Centers for Disease Control, the leading cause of infection for both black women and men is sexual contact.[90] Although black churches have historically responded proactively to social, political, and economic crises in black communities, the close association between HIV/AIDS and homosexual contact inhibits many black churches from developing ministries that take action on HIV/AIDS.

The daughter of a minister in the African Methodist Episcopal (AME) Church, Martin founded GSN Ministries after serving as pastor of an AME Church for three years. Although 30 percent of her local parish was gay and lesbian, Martin left the AME Church denomination after being reprimanded by her supervisors for blessing a same-gender union in the local parish. With eighty to ninety people in weekly worship, the majority of the members of GSN Ministries are gay and lesbian African American Christians. GSN Ministries encourages its members to love God, themselves, and their neighbors—in that order. GSN Ministries engages in social outreach and educates people about gay and lesbian concerns as well as HIV/AIDS.

Ancestral Immortality

GSN Ministries draws on the best aspects of the past in order to reach out to its members and the wider Atlanta community. As a Christian community, GSN draws on the lessons of Jesus as articulated in the Bible as a source of power and support in its everyday practices. As a black church, GSN also draws on the worship and activist traditions of black churches and historic African American figures in its own religious and social practices. These same sources can be used to create and sustain religious community that is inclusive of all people or to justify the exclusion of some individuals and constituencies.

Christian communities generally affirm Jesus as being central to their faith. Since the Bible is a primary source that describes the birth, ministry, death, and resurrection of Jesus, Christian communities often hold the biblical witness as an authoritative source for theology and ethical practice. As a UCC-affiliated ministry, GSN Ministries upholds the UCC statement of faith: "We believe in God, the Eternal Spirit, who is made known to us in Jesus our brother, and to whose deeds we testify."[91] There are also Christian communities that refer to the same gospel to condemn homosexuality. For example, Exodus Ministries is an interdenominational Christian organization that "promot[es] the message of freedom *from* homosexuality through the power of Jesus Christ."[92] Thus, the gospel of Jesus can inspire Christian communities that welcome gays and lesbians as well as those that do not.

Many black Protestant churches utilize the worship and traditions of African American church culture. While there is a variety of liturgical and worship styles among African American Christian churches, many worshipers and scholars agree that there is something distinctive about the music in African American Christian worship: "African American sacred music traditions are rooted in the primal worldviews of African traditional religions."[93] The religiosity of enslaved Africans encountered the historical contexts of slavery, emancipation, and twentieth-century America. The unique product is evident in African American spirituals, hymnody, gospel music, and instrumental music.

Martin believes that this particular worship style is part of what draws African Americans to Christian worship experiences. When working with a predominantly white church to attract more African American members, Martin requested a budget for musicians who could help lead worship in an African American style. The church was already quite effective in including persons of diverse sexual orientation and class; they wanted to become more racially diverse. Martin states, "I took over an evening worship service and tried to bring that flavor. . . . I told them I couldn't just have a piano. I needed someone who could lead the worship and songs."[94] The church constituency grew to approximately 30 percent African American.

The activist tradition of many African American churches also shapes GSN Ministries. As noted above, Martin was raised and ordained in the African Methodist Episcopal (AME) Church, where she also served a parish. Founded in 1787 by a small number of free blacks in protest against the racism in St. George's Methodist Episcopal Church in Philadelphia, the AME Church is considered one of the first African American denominations in the United States. White church leaders at St. George's removed black worshipers from their kneeling positions, insisting that they pray after the white members of the church. When these black worshipers walked out of the church, they formed the Free African Society, the founding organization of the AME Church. Martin was undoubtedly influenced by this commitment to resisting discrimination that she experienced in her church of origin. This resistance is not unique to the AME Church, however; religious scholars have widely recognized that "African American Christianity provided . . . a political language to engage American slavery and racism."[95]

This black church activist tradition takes on more significance in the Atlanta context because of its connection to Rev. Martin Luther King Jr. One black gay man states that Atlanta's reputation as the "cradle of the civil rights movement" is inspiration for it eventually to provide a haven of justice for its black gay and lesbian citizens.[96] Noting that he often drives by Martin Luther's King Jr.'s tomb and birth home, he states, "This is a city that effected so much change around the country. . . . You feel it's a city that still wants to effect change."[97] This black Atlantan invokes Martin Luther King Jr. as an ancestor who strove for justice and equality. This remembrance of King, proximity to places where King's life began, and being situated in the city that houses the Martin Luther King Jr. Center for Nonviolent Social Change suggest that Martin Luther King is an important ancestor for black Atlantans who desire justice. The work of GSN Ministries and other black churches in Atlanta is framed by the legacy of Martin Luther King. While King serves as an important ancestor for many Americans and individuals around the world, his rememory may be particularly noteworthy among black Christians in Atlanta.

Many black churches in Atlanta and elsewhere affirm the centrality of Jesus, an African American style of worship, and inspiration from Martin Luther King Jr. These historical figures, traditions, and legacies can function to creatively or destructively transform the world. The creativity of these sources from the past depends on how contemporary communities remember and invoke them. When honored, these sources will strengthen and motivate the formation of inclusive communities that strive to produce justice and wholeness in the world through teaching and healing. These traditions and ancestors can also be used by religious communities to draw lines between who is acceptable and who is not. Jesus, black church traditions, and historic African American figures can also help to form the basis for destructive transformation.

Destructive Transformation

Many black churches in Atlanta engage the world around them as they offer a Christian message and aim for social transformation in the contemporary American landscape. They engage the music and worship style of African American church cultures, preach messages based on the Bible, and often engage in acts of social, economic, and political relevance. Yet attempts to condemn homosexuality or fight HIV/AIDS without an honest conversation about homosexuality are destructive forms of transformation. Postmodern womanist theology identifies problems with communities that offer these responses and the theology that supports these attempts as destructive transformation.

Atlanta's significant black gay and lesbian population is an ideal context for conversation about the black Christian understanding of homosexuality. Atlanta's black gay and lesbian residents reflect the popularity that Atlanta holds for many African Americans regardless of sexual orientation. One local newspaper notes that "around the country" Atlanta is viewed as a "mecca, a magnet or . . . newfound hometown," for gay, lesbian, and straight African Americans.[98] It's common to hear black gays and lesbians celebrating Atlanta's unique opportunities resplendent with black gay bars, black gay book clubs, and so on.[99] The 2000 U.S. Census ranks Atlanta third among cities with a population of more than 100,000 in the number of same-sex households, and second in the number of African American same-sex households (behind the Washington, D.C.-Baltimore area).

The increased number of openly gay and lesbian African Americans in Atlanta does not lead to acceptance in all sectors of the community. In a national Gallup Poll, only 40 percent of black respondents felt that homosexuality was an acceptable lifestyle, whereas more than half of white respondents accepted homosexuality as socially acceptable.[100] This lack of acceptance is greater in church culture. Fifty-four percent of black gays and lesbians say that their faith community views homosexuality as wrong and sinful.[101] Almost no mainstream predominantly black churches welcome and affirm gays and lesbians.[102] In *Their Own Receive Them Not*, Horace L. Griffin summarizes the treatment of gays and lesbians in black churches:

> Lesbians and gays in most black churches are subjected to being silent about their partners, vague or deceptive about marriage interests, or dishonest about their relationships for fear of repercussion. Gay relationships are not recognized publicly along with those of heterosexuals, and, in order to pastor or serve in the black church, gays and lesbians must learn to stay in their place and shut up about "it."[103]

There are several common reactions to the condemnation of homosexuality in black churches. One response is to stay in these black churches and filter, or "sift through what [is] being taught or said."[104] Other black gays or lesbians engage in "searching," where they try out various faiths, churches, or denominations. Other black gays and lesbians leave Christianity altogether. Still others reject their own homosexuality in favor of the teachings that consider homo-sexuality sinful. Each of these reactions has enough participation that they constitute various communities.

For many black gays and lesbians, predominantly white churches are not a viable option when looking for inclusive faith community. Churchgoing white gays and lesbians "generally have more options than their black coun-terparts in finding an acceptable church."[105] A black gay member of GSN describes it this way: "The white faith community didn't speak to me as a whole. It spoke to me theologically, but it didn't speak to me as a whole. It was an option, but it wasn't an option per se."[106] Griffin affirms this: "For many [black gays and lesbians] the risk of encountering racism by a group of strang-ers is not worth leaving the familiar, albeit homophobic black church worship experience."[107] For some black gays and lesbians, the racism in white churches is a deterrent. For others, the unfamiliar worship style repels them from join-ing white churches. "African American gay Christians who value the black worship experience, however, often feel they must stay in [homophobic] black churches . . . since most Christian churches that affirm same-sex relationships are predominantly white."[108]

Separation from the black church of one's childhood is, for many black gays and lesbians, a separation from one's African traditions. A field organizer for the Human Rights Campaign, a national gay rights advocacy organiza-tion, affirms this: "To separate from [black churches], and just try to be gay, means you're into a whole 'nother world that you're not familiar with, the white gay world. It's so different, you'd rather go back and hold on to your African traditions."[109] Many black churches rather unintentionally draw upon this African American tradition for destructive ends. Their black church wor-ship styles attract black gays and lesbians, while their teachings and theology reject homosexuality.

Thus, many black gays and lesbians remain in black churches that do not welcome or affirm them. Some black gays and lesbians disguise or deny their sexual orientation in their churches.[110] These black gays and lesbians follow a "don't ask, don't tell" policy. When asked if she feels judged or condemned in her mainstream black church, one black lesbian replies, "I don't feel con-demned, because they don't know."[111]

Horace Griffin uses the typology of "passing" in the African American tradition to discuss the ways that African American gays and lesbians conceal their sexual orientation in black churches.[112] He parallels this to the often-decried practice of racial passing of light-skinned blacks into white society:

> Since African Americans generally did not accept passing of
> light-skinned African Americans, in spite of their ability to

understand why African Americans passed, there is some irony in expecting gays to pass as heterosexual. African Americans generally felt that blacks should have racial pride and resist passing, avoiding any hint of being ashamed or denying their racial identity as colored people, even if it meant immense suffering.[113]

Thus, the passing of black gays and lesbians recalls and repeats a destructive aspect of African American history. Even worse, Griffin argues, many black heterosexual churchgoers expect their gay and lesbians colleagues to engage in this destructive kind of rememory.

Few black gays and lesbians who remain in nonaffirming churches are active in church organizations or leadership.[114] Some individuals even describe open denial in some black churches that hold funerals and memorial services for gays and lesbians. On these occasions, the deceased is "heterosexualized," or spoken of as if they are heterosexual, and AIDS-related deaths are renamed as "cancer."[115] These acts of disremembrance do not embody ancestral immortality. Rather, these church communities reconstruct and recount the past to hide the areas where they feel shame.

The black churches that declare homosexuality a sin represent a destructive response to the presence of openly black gays and lesbians. Some black churches resist being labeled "homophobic" because they condemn homosexuality. One pastor of a black church states, "It is a serious mistake for some African American intellectuals, gay rights activists and liberal politicians to brand the [b]lack church as Victorian and homophobic because we lift up a different standard on the issue of sexuality."[116] He believes that churches have the right to "define issues of sexual morality, sexual preferences and safe sex for its members in a way that is consistent with the congregation's understanding of the scripture."[117] This is not, Kathi Martin preaches, "the liberating Good News of Jesus" that embraces "the poor, the outcast, the abused, the left-out, and the put-out."[118] Both Martin and these black churches draw inspiration from Jesus and the Bible, but they come to different conclusions.

For the black churches that condemn homosexuality, the rejection of homosexuality is a matter of sexual ethics. A pastor of a socially and politically active AME church feels that this is a matter of Christian ethics: "If the church is going to be true to its biblical roots, it cannot endorse the [homosexual] lifestyle and cannot endorse same-sex marriage."[119] Martin believes that these ethics are questionable because they are based on biblical passages with other teachings to which few people adhere. She retorts, "For those who are practitioners of the law or followers of Leviticus, you should not leave your house on Sunday morning without checking yourself for polyester, tattoos, piercings—as in earrings, and for those who seek to honor the words of Paul, women should never enter a church without a covering on their heads."[120] She also states that the same people who condemn homosexuality as a sexual sin are often guilty of other sexual sins: "If I had a dollar for the many times I have been approached by very married reverends . . . I'd be a rich woman today. Many of them justified their actions by saying, 'Well, David did it and he was a man of God.'"[121] Martin has disdain for the double standard in language about sexual ethics. It is clear that biblical passages can be used for the justification of conflicting messages about appropriate sexual behavior.

At their best, nonaffirming black church communities preach tolerance. The comments of Rev. Al Sharpton, a nationally known black minister and civil rights leader, are a good example of this approach. Regarding the acceptance of gays and lesbians in black churches, he asks, "If we can forgive adulterers, why do we allow the right wing to attack homosexuals?"[122] This approach to homosexuality in the church does not create inclusive community. It still considers homosexuality a sexual sin, like other sins, and purports a "hate the sin, love the sinner" mentality that still denies justice to gays and lesbians.

Theologies of condemnation and tolerance often push gays and lesbians into an exilic relationship with black churches where they leave church community altogether. For some black gays and lesbians, the filtering or searching process is too cumbersome. Craig Washington, a black gay activist in Atlanta, asks, "Why should we go in [to a black church that condemns homosexuality], then try to fish out of that experience what is affirming?"[123] Best-selling black gay fiction writer E. Lynn Harris doesn't go to church anymore because he's "heard enough hell sermons."[124] This kind of theology destroys community as it requires people to choose between their faith and being their authentic selves. Martin recounts how this theology kept her from attending black churches: "The thought was that I would never make anything of myself and I would never grow spiritually or in relation to God because of this whole sexual orientation thing. I started doing drugs and I wasn't going to church."[125] She describes herself as an exile: "I see myself as a person in exile from the African-American church experience. And like all exiles, I hope to return home someday."[126] Yet Martin will remain outside of predominantly black churches if there is no justice there.

Some black churches believe that the quest for social and political justice for African American communities does not include the struggle against heterosexism. In December of 2004, Rev. Eddie Long, the pastor of the largest black church in the Atlanta area (with twenty-five thousand members), led a march calling for various social and political stances—including a constitutional ban on same-sex marriage.[127] With almost ten thousand participants, the march began at the birthplace of Martin Luther King, Jr. and was co-led by Rev. Bernice King, King's youngest child. Eddie Long named the march "Reigniting the Legacy" as a direct reference to his belief that his social and political positions align with King's vision. Other civil rights leaders, such as King's widow, Coretta Scott King, Congressman John Lewis of Georgia, and Julian Bond, the chair of the NAACP, have supported same-sex marriages. These people have divergent understandings of King's legacy of justice for all. Events such as the "Reigniting the Legacy" march do not honor the historic African American freedom fighters like Martin Luther King, Jr. They use the memory of the past to deny equal rights to a segment of the black community. These communities bring some of the destructive aspects of the past into the present.

The ex-gay movement in Christianity represents another type of destructive community. Some black gays and lesbians reject their sexual orientation because of their understanding of Christian theology. One contemporary example is Charlene Cothran, an African American lesbian activist who founded *Venus Magazine*, a magazine for black gays and lesbians named after her friend Venus Landin, a black lesbian activist in Atlanta who died as a result of domestic violence. Cothran discusses her religious calling to change her sexual orientation on the television show *The 700 Club*, which is hosted by conservative Christian evangelical Pat Robertson. Cothran states, "Something spoke in my spirit: this [being lesbian] is that road that leads to destruction, and [I'm] on it."[128] Cothran notes that she is now celibate because she is "so focused on spirit, [she has] no urges for anyone, man or woman." One critic of Cothran and others in the ex-gay movement states that these experiences are only a change of behavior.

In fact, this kind of ex-gay movement prevents individuals from living holistically. One critic states, "It's not intellectually honest to call yourself delivered from homosexuality when what you have actually achieved, by [one's] own admission, is celibacy."[129] These individuals often reject the black gay and lesbian community that "offered them ... genuine love and support." Martin responds to Cothran on a YouTube.com video, stating, "It's not about who you love but how you love: Are you loving honestly? Are you being just? Are you being kind? That's what matters. That's what Jesus taught us to do."[130] Rejecting one's own sexual orientation in order to live within a destructive theology injures creative community, denies one's entire self, and, for Martin, detracts from what Jesus actually taught.

The difference between those who condemn homosexuality as sin and those who affirm the equal worth of gays and lesbians often lies in their understanding of sexuality. Black gays and lesbians and their heterosexual allies do not interpret the black church rejection of homosexuality as a rejection of particular activities. Anti-homosexual theology still states that "who [black gays and lesbians] are and who [black gays and lesbians] love are against the word of God."[131] Womanist ethicist Emilie Townes also rejects the reduction of sexuality to sexual activity: "Our sexuality is who we are as thinking, feeling, and caring human beings. It is our ability to love and nurture. To express warmth and compassion. It is not only our gonads."[132] Reducing sexual orientation to sexual activity is another "fallacy of misplaced concreteness." When churches focus on sexual acts, they misplace their focus. Living a holistic and authentic Christian life entails caring more about the quality and tenor of the relationships between individuals. Wholeness is found not in whom we love, but in how we love.

To be black and gay or lesbian in a black church that condemns homosexuality is unhealthy. It is unhealthy for the black gay and lesbian membership. When discussing her reasons for leaving the AME denomination, Martin says that she refused to lie about her life: "Don't ask me to pretend to be something other than what I am."[133] She recalls her statements to the church's laity during the controversy over her leadership as an openly lesbian woman: "This isn't feeding anybody's spirit. . . . It's not healthy for you and it's not healthy for me, so I'm going."[134] Hiding her sexual orientation, "living in the closet," and fighting with local church and denominational leadership over her right to serve as a leader was unhealthy for Martin. This way of dealing with homosexuality does not support the health of church members.

Black church condemnation of homosexuality also inhibits many black churches from educating their members about HIV and AIDS. Sylvia Rhue, the religious affairs and constituency development director for the National Black Justice Coalition, a gay rights group, states that "HIV and AIDS is a major concern in the black community, and churches can't deal with it if they can't deal with human sexuality."[135] The pastor of an AME church with a ministry that fights against AIDS in the United States and in West Africa acknowledges that some black churches are slow to fight against AIDS because of "a general skittishness toward sexuality rather than outright disdain for gays."[136] Whether it is a discomfort with sexuality in general (as this pastor maintains) or the more specific religious condemnation of homosexuality, these churches are unable to address a critical health crisis in black communities.

Martin even connects anti-homosexuality theology with the spread of HIV/AIDS. When individuals are condemned as sinners, they are not inspired to treat themselves or others with respect. She says: "Once we [gays and lesbians] think we are sinners [who are] condemned anyway, we live any old kind of way, and this ties back to AIDS prevention. If you don't value yourself and think you are condemned to hell anyway, then you don't . . . care about protecting yourself and other people."[137] When black churches condemn homosexuality, they erode the self-esteem of black gay and lesbian Christians. Martin connects this low self-esteem to unsafe sexual practices. These churches represent a way of destruction that does not affirm a vision of justice, health, inclusion, or diversity.

Communities that affirm the religious acceptance of black gays and lesbians can function as destructive communities if they reject other types of sexual diversity. Like other areas of American society, gay and lesbian communities can be divided by race, class, gender, ability, sexual identity, and so on. Referring to transgender and intersex[138] individuals, Martin addresses a primarily black lesbian audience with these words: "It often baffles me when those of us who are already on the margins continue to divide ourselves from one another rather than celebrate and support the diversity and freedom of expression that exists among us."[139] Martin believes that these prejudices "negate the opportunity for same-gender loving women to come together as the strong positive force we could be in our communities."[140] Martin critiques exclusivity and prejudice wherever it is found—even in black gay and lesbian circles. This is not just an affirmation of inclusion for inclusion's sake. Martin understands that prejudice and exclusivity prevent us from creatively transforming the world around us.

Black churches that condemn homosexuality or preach tolerance do not embrace ancestral immortality. These communities can represent exclusivity, biblical and ethical inconsistency, and disease. Their memory of the past is destructive, when encouraging gays and lesbians to "pass" as straight, or fallacious, as in the case of the churches that "heterosexualize" gay and lesbian members at funerals, or selective, claiming the aspects of scripture and ethical conduct that support their statements while ignoring other passages. These communities can cause ill-health for their gay and lesbian members and fail to effectively address one of the largest health crises in today's black American communities. This refusal to affirm healthy sexuality and ethics in all of its variations does not serve a postmodern context well. Its theology cannot provide creative options for a better way of life. It encourages many black gays and lesbians to live in silence without Christian community and/or without the African American religious practices of their upbringing. Rather than seeking ways to live holistically in the world they are given, these communities use their faith to create greater injustice in the world. They cannot creatively transform this world at their full potential.

Creative Transformation

Today's society suffers from homophobia, the rapid spread of HIV and AIDS, and other types of social problems. In the midst of the challenges in the greater Atlanta area, Kathi Martin and GSN Ministries insist that there is another way.

GSN Ministries "loves the way" to creatively transform the world. They honor the past, teach one another and the wider community, affirm a theology of inclusive love of God, self, and others, and help to fight against the spread of disease. This community is diverse and changing, and has the potential for being implemented in various contexts.

The vision statement of GSN Ministries is to be "a Christ-centered inclusive community of faith committed to love and justice for all of God's creation."[141] For GSN, love and justice is the essence of Christianity. GSN's theology of inclusive love begins with God's love of the world and the love that the world should have for God. Martin writes, "If we call ourselves Christians, this is what Scripture teaches us: loving God as we love thy neighbor . . . There's no list of people that are exempt from that."[142] GSN aims "to be a place where persons come to grow in their relationship to an awareness of God."[143] This is embodied holistically in what Martin refers to as the "God Matters" campaign. At GSN worship services, everyone present recites together, "God matters to me; I matter to me; you matter to me; and we all matter to God." Replete with hand movements, this motto affirms a reciprocal relationship between God and the world that affirms the worth of God's creation because of its rootedness in God. Engaging the voice, theology, and the body helps to emphasize the all-encompassing nature of this message.

This theology of inclusive love affirms a theology of change. David Smith, a member of GSN who was licensed to preach in a black Baptist church before attending GSN, recounts lessons about the ongoing revelation of God: "God is still speaking is a major theme at the church."[144] This theology is open to the fact that what we know about and hear from God may change into the future.

As a Christian community, GSN Ministries participates in the ancestral immortality of Jesus. The name of GSN Ministries itself is inspired by the biblical verse attributed to Jesus: "You shall love the Lord your God with all your heart, and with all your soul, and with all your mind. This is the greatest and first commandment. And a second is like it: You shall love your neighbor as yourself" (Matt. 22:37-39). Martin affirms this when she says, "I always feel led by the Spirit. We don't have Jesus in the flesh, we don't have pillars of fire and all that stuff; all we have is the Spirit that guides us. The Spirit is the comforter that Jesus said would come."[145] Here Martin discusses the Holy Spirit as the ancestral spirit of the historical Jesus. This spirit is very much alive and active in her leadership of GSN Ministries.

While GSN's theology of love is derived from the Bible and referred to in much of Christian culture, it has to be taught in order to build creative community. When homosexuality is condemned as sinful, it is all the more critical for black gays and lesbians "to claim their wholeness as persons created in the image of God."[146] Black gays and lesbians first need to nurture their relationship with God to be healed and empowered.[147] This is the most important lesson taught at GSN. Martin describes it thus: "I wanted people to have the tools to share with other people how to have this relationship that would help as a guide and companion in their [lives] instead of condemnation and fear. I knew that all this condemnation and foolishness is not right, that is not what God is about."[148]

Teaching about love also means teaching about sin. GSN does not believe that homosexuality is a sin. Martin states, "I'm trying to help people to see that we [gays and lesbians] are not sinful people because of our orientation, but we are people who are just as prone to do sinful things like everyone else."[149] This teaching about sin acknowledges the destructive tendencies of all people and thus creates a more inclusive Christian community for those who have been taught that their very beings are sinful.

Martin teaches biblical interpretation at GSN. She encourages GSN members to apply the same kind of interpretation that disregarded the Bible's affirmation of slavery to their understanding of homosexuality and the Bible. Martin says, "Part of what we have been taught [in the Bible about homosexuality] is wrong just like "slaves obey your masters" is wrong. So we talk about the context and what the texts were talking about. I would try to teach people how to see texts, themselves, their partners and other people in the community differently."[150] GSN asks individuals to draw upon the same biblical interpretation that African Americans used to argue against the biblical justification for slavery. GSN honors this aspect of African American biblical interpretation and brings it into the future by applying it to the context of homosexuality.

GSN also teaches its members so that they may teach this theology of love to others in the community. Helping "gay people to feel good about themselves" is just a first step in this educational process. GSN strives to equip people in the congregation with the words to share with others about God and God's love. Members of GSN know how to communicate their scriptural interpretation to others. Teaching the theology of inclusive love leads to activism in the Atlanta community. GSN often hosts educational sessions about homosexuality in the Bible and self-esteem.

Social justice and community activism are significant aspects of GSN. In one sermon, Martin connects this to theology: "People on the margins of society, those that the spiritually, politically, and socially elite have ignored, are . . . looking for equality, justice, and peace. They, we, are looking for the Good News of the Gospel. . . . It's our responsibility to respond to the issues that yield to the pain that we and all endure."[151] GSN has encouraged people to vote and participate in organ-donor programs. GSN has also done outreach with Common Ground, an Atlanta agency that provides support for people living with HIV/AIDS.

GSN's message of love is also a message of healing. That healing refers to the spiritual healing of those who have been taught that homosexuality is a sin. Martin encourages members to ask themselves this question: "How do I come to love myself, accept myself, identify and erase the viewpoints I've come to accept about myself, and how do I encourage other people to do the same?"[152] The message is to "heal yourself" first.[153] GSN's theology also promotes HIV/AIDS prevention. Once released from the belief that oneself and one's partner are sinful, individuals can be freed to practice safe sex as an act of love for self and neighbor. Martin states, "Helping people to see that the way God sees you is not just to say I love you and respect you, but to treat people that way—you can't do that if you think your partner is the object of your sin."[154] Thus, GSN's theology can lead to safe sexual practices.

The focus on justice is not only central to GSN Ministries; it was the first goal. Martin originally intended for Sunday worship to serve as a place to energize the outreach activities that would be central to GSN. "[Worship] would just be where we would come to center in on why we do what we do. The focus would be that we would focus on the community."[155] Her original vision was not for GSN to be a church, per se: "If it had to be a church, it would be a church without walls."[156]

The social activism of GSN is grounded in the heritage of both African Americans and the UCC. The UCC has a history of supporting social justice for African Americans. It supported Africans in the Amistad trial, educated freed slaves in the South, and was the first major denomination to be open to and affirming of gay and lesbian laity and clergy.[157] Martin also understands that GSN stands in the tradition of African Americans and women who asserted that their experience with God was more important than doctrine or traditional church teachings.[158] Again, GSN draws from liberating aspects of the African American and Christian past to make a way in the present and future.

GSN Ministries also utilizes the black worship tradition of many black Protestant churches. For Martin, this is an aspect of black church tradition that deserves rememory. Martin writes "Although many of the traditions of the patriarchal, sexist, heterosexist structures of some churches were the source of wounds for many . . . there are many aspects to African American worship that are very nourishing."[159] David Smith acknowledges how significant the black worship experience is for him: "I feel that the black church experience has always spoken to me—from a music point of view. The experience at GSN was familiar to me. The same kind of structure you would find in most [black] churches."[160] GSN shares with other black Protestant churches in a style of music and worship that emerges from and perpetuates the unique way that black descendents of American slavery practice Christianity. This is one of the aspects of black church tradition that is honored and retained as GSN creatively transforms church community.

While the worship style is an appeal to African Americans, GSN is a diverse community. Smith appreciates the diverse family structures represented at GSN: "It was the first time I actually saw people of color living their sexual lives out loud—in church. You saw women come in with their partners and children. . . . I saw black men as a couple or they would come in by themselves. You also had a balance of some heterosexual families."[161] Although GSN's constituency is predominantly African American, it also includes a Latino family, a white family, and people from various religious backgrounds—Buddhist, Protestant, Catholic, Muslim, and atheist. This was Martin's goal from the beginning: "I did not enter ministry thinking I would exclusively minister to LGBT persons. I believed (and still believe) there should be no separation since we are all created in the image of God."[162]

Martin attributes this religious diversity to her low Christology. She describes herself as more theocentric than Christocentric. Although her theology is rooted in Jesus' words in the New Testament, Martin remains open to the teachings of other traditions—especially New Thought religions, such as Unity, Christian Science, Religious Science and the churches of the Universal Federation for Better Living. In her Doctor of Ministry (D.Min.). dissertation, Martin notes that New Thought religion is attractive for many black gays and lesbians because of its theology. Citing a scholar of New Thought religion, Martin writes, "If you are willing to free yourself from the idea of a vengeful scorekeeper in the sky, you are a likely candidate to be a New Thought Christian. If you are willing to eliminate any idea from your mind that separates you from your invisible source, you are becoming a New Thought Christian."[163] Martin believes her inclusive Christology leads to inclusive faith community: "That was why people could come [to GSN] and feel comfortable from various religious and nonreligious perspectives, and I always appreciate that. I am Christian, but I don't think Jesus was an exclusive Christian."[164]

This kind of social and theological inclusion is inspired in part by the legacy of Martin Luther King Jr. After Coretta Scott King died, Kathi Martin gave words of healing at a memorial service held in Atlanta's GLBTQ community. Afterward she was approached by a woman who said, "Thank you. This is the first time I've come to a religious gathering, and even as a Wiccan person, I felt included and welcome in your prayer."[165] This story is an example of how Martin is able to create a community that includes persons of diverse races, religious backgrounds, and sexual orientations.

In Atlanta, creative transformation comes by loving the way. Smith describes the safety found with GSN Ministries: "GSN is a place and space that's very important for same-gender loving people . . . where it's safe, where we can be who we are, we can work out all of who we are in those places, unapologetically."[166] As black gays and lesbians accept God's love, they can better love themselves and their neighbors. This love leads to greater justice in the church and the wider Atlanta community. GSN Ministries offers an image of creative transformation—the theology, the community, and the process of teaching, healing, and loving.

Saviors

Claiming GSN Ministries as a portrait of postmodern womanist theology contributes to an innovative idea of "the savior." Although most Christians name Jesus as Savior, postmodern womanist theology argues that salvation must occur in particular contexts. Communities across place and time need ways of attaining health and wholeness and resisting the evil and loss in their midst. As GSN is one such community, Kathi Martin emerges as a savior. Martin left a destructive community and leads a group of people into creative theology and community. Nevertheless, Martin is an unlikely savior. Because she is black and lesbian and struggles with health challenges, Martin's leadership is neither expected nor perfect. Martin is a savior because she leads a community that is engaged in creative transformation.

Martin's sexual orientation has been a barrier in her life as a minister. Although preacher's children are often looked to as bearers of the ministerial legacy, Martin felt exempt from such selection. She felt a call to ministry early in her life, but she was told that being a lesbian disqualified her.[167] When pastoring the AME parish, Martin preached a theology of inclusion without discussing her sexual orientation. After she conducted a same-sex commitment ceremony, many heterosexual members of the church admitted that they knew there were gay people in the church but said that Martin "had gone too far." After that point, Martin was open about her sexual orientation and her romantic relationship. About 60 percent of the church members left.

Even after many heterosexual members of the church left, many lesbian church members did not want to have Bible study about homosexuality. "Eventually, it was revealed that lesbian members of the church wanted a heterosexual male pastor with a family, rather than an affirming and openly lesbian pastor."[168] This kind of internalized homophobia among gays and lesbians is not uncommon and augments the discrimination against openly gay and lesbian clergy. These rejections did not deter Martin. As a child she referred to God as her imaginary friend, and she continues to think of God as her closest companion. She believes that God has chosen her for ministry.

Martin draws upon her familial ancestors as a source of strength in her ministry. Martin tells the story of her great aunt who lived with a woman for most of her life. As they aged, the aunt and her companion stayed in the same home, although it was difficult to maintain because they could not move into senior citizen housing together. Martin also notes that few churches welcomed her aunts because of their racial difference (the companion was white) and suspicions that they were lesbians. When Martin's aunt died, she requested funeral services in the one church that welcomed them. Martin states that her aunt's memory encourages her to include the injustices committed against elderly gays and lesbians among her social concerns.

Martin also lives with health conditions, which she uses to strengthen her connection with other people. Martin has been diagnosed with multiple sclerosis and has experienced pain in walking and everyday movements for years. In early 2003, Martin's father died, and she felt overwhelmed with church, personal, and familial responsibilities. Martin overdosed on Tylenol 3. The rejection and betrayal that Martin experienced at the AME church had long-lasting effects on her. Although she continued in ministry, the separation from her community and church denomination had a negative impact on her health. Martin consulted with a therapist and psychiatrist and learned that she had been depressed for years, and that she needed medication.

Martin believes that God has helped her to live through these challenges, and she shares this in her pastoral care work. Recently Martin was walking while delivering a sermon, and she recalls a time when she could not do that. She states, "I try to show other people how they can [survive their challenges] too. I went through it, and I studied it and I lived it and here I am."[169] Martin uses her difficulties to bond with other people facing challenges; her journey functions as a testimony. Living with mental health challenges and multiple sclerosis does not make Martin a savior. Martin contributes to salvation because she uses these health challenges to honor God and create community.

Again, as an openly black lesbian woman with mental health challenges and multiple sclerosis, Martin does not appear to have the characteristics of a savior. Yet as a theologian, teacher, preacher, and activist, Martin proves to be a worthy savior. Martin's teaching and vision develop the community of GSN Ministries. Honoring the past, Martin is able to offer an image of postmodern womanist theology. Like postmodern womanist theology, GSN understands the Savior as one who puts forth a theology of love and justice while generating greater awareness and health in the community.

Salvation is Challenging

GSN Ministries is not a static example of salvation. The postmodern womanist interpretation of GSN Ministries emphasizes the creative transformation found in its community and theology. Nevertheless, time reveals that such a vision is difficult to implement and can rely too heavily on particular individuals.

In early 2005, GSN Ministries ceased to exist as a worshiping community. Martin led GSN for over a year after her overdose, but things were not going well at GSN. Some members and regional leaders in the UCC believed that Martin was too unstable to continue to lead GSN. About 50 percent of the members left the church. Eventually, Martin realized that she needed to stop leading GSN Ministries.

Martin believes GSN grew away from its original vision. She never intended for GSN to become a church. She intended for GSN to be a training ground for theological activism in the greater Atlanta community. She hoped for an evolving community. She says, "I wanted [GSN] to be organic and become and change based on the idea of the community and the people and the needs that people brought with them and the need that other people saw. I wanted it to grow into whatever it was God wanted it to be."[170] But, she admits laughingly, when you worship on Sundays, people start to think it is church. Had she thought GSN would evolve into a church, she would have done more training for officers and offered more structure.

Martin also believes that she was not healthy enough to lead GSN Ministries. She acknowledges that she tried to give other people a level of care and acceptance that she had not given herself. She believes that it took her years to get over the rejection she experienced at the AME church. She did not deal with those emotions at the time; instead, they festered within her. Calling herself "a stubborn little something," Martin confesses she might not have been the best pastor.

Martin fears that she was too central to GSN. Martin knew that there's always a danger in a community rising and falling around its leader. She says, "I didn't want [GSN] to become a church that Kathi built."[171] Members of GSN felt represented by Martin in her activism around Atlanta: "Where Reverend Kathi was on a panel or giving a speech, we felt like GSN was represented—politically and socially."[172] Although Martin was the leader of GSN Ministries, members of GSN felt that they were the same as she was. It was not uncommon to see Martin at a house party, club, or a fund-raiser. David Smith exclaims, "I love that she can dance! She's very social. . . . You didn't feel the sense that she was different from you. This was Reverend Kathi but she was me. She didn't walk around with that ministerial thing."[173] Martin is a dancing, socializing, theologian activist savior. Others can be as well.

What made Martin distinctive was her theology. Accustomed to women as pastors, Smith declares that "the theology was different. It was social responsibility connected with spirituality."[174] He suggests that the reason for the collapse of GSN Ministries was the challenging message that Martin preached.

Although it seems that Atlanta's black gay and lesbian community should flock to a place like GSN, few wanted to commit to the vision. He states, "A lot of us as black gay Christians struggling with so much weren't ready for that stuff—practical theology for our lives on a regular basis."[175] Loving the way is difficult. It requires that individuals love not only God and their neighbors, but also themselves. For some, Smith suggests, this is a lot to ask.

Martin is still involved in communities that love a way in the midst of a homophobic culture. About fifteen former members of GSN and the AME parish meet with Martin a couple times a year in a coffee shop or her living room. They share their life journeys with each other and offer one another support. After years away from active ministry and support from Bishop Yvette Flunder, an openly black lesbian pastor in San Francisco, Martin returned to leadership in religious communities. Martin is currently the director of Multicultural Ministries at a Metropolitan Community Church in the Atlanta area, a predominantly white denomination that has always affirmed gays and lesbians. She is also the minister of Pastoral Care and Counseling at Victory Church, a three-thousand-member black church in Atlanta that left its Baptist affiliation (and half of its membership) when the pastor began preaching affirmation of gays and lesbians. Despite the dissolution of GSN Ministries, communities that love the way still emerge around the greater Atlanta area.

The way of inclusive theology and community can be discouraging and challenging. It is often unpopular and can lead to a decline in church membership, finances, and energy. GSN Ministries did not survive the test of time. When a community changes, it sometimes ceases to be the community that was envisioned or a community that lasts. Martin is human, and the strength of her personal leadership may have contributed to the conclusion of GSN. Nevertheless, the theology and communal dimension of GSN survives in new forms and in new places around Atlanta. Martin still experiences joy, grace, and renewed health as she loves a way in this context.

In GSN Ministries, creative transformation comes from a way of loving. Martin realizes that her goal is teaching a theology that stresses Jesus' message to love God, self, and neighbor. She desires to teach this theology to all people, but especially the black gays and lesbians who desperately need to believe that they are made in the image of God. She hopes that as individuals come together in community and accept this love, they will share it in their personal relationships and in the wider world. This will lead to greater awareness and health for all. GSN Ministries is creative transformation—the theology, the community, and the process of loving, teaching, and healing.

A postmodern womanist interpretation of GSN Ministries describes salvation as "loving a way out of no way." Health and wholeness are found in the process of building a community of diverse, disenfranchised people with the common yearning for a faith community. Those who have felt rejected and condemned find community. Those who have tried to separate their sexualities from their spiritualities can live holistically. People have ways of understanding the world that affirms both a loving God and their own ability to change the world. This is not a static community, but one that is located in different places and spaces over time. When Martin was leading an AME church, she was often told she was ahead of her time. A member of GSN confirms this: "GSN was really twenty years ahead of its time for the black faith community."[176]

GSN came into existence by honoring the best of the Christian and African American past. Jesus' words of love inspired the theology. GSN found affiliation with a denomination with a history of social justice advocacy on behalf of African Americans. GSN drew upon the worship traditions of black churches and its historic faith leaders to encourage its members and promote its activism in the Atlanta community. Creative transformation was found in a theology that was both Christian and postmodern. As Martin and GSN loved a way, a great cloud of witnesses accompanied them.

Conclusion

Both Earthseed and GSN Ministries offer two portraits of postmodern womanist theology. In their own ways, these two communities draw upon their faith and the past to transform themselves and the world around them. They are alternative communities in contexts of violence, desperation, prejudice, and oppression. They find ways of gathering diverse people around a shared ethic. They embrace theological and communal change. They teach their respective theologies to members of their communities and to others around them. They heal their own wounds as well as the wounds of the larger society. They call upon the creative aspects of their ancestors and their heritage for inspiration and protection. They "make a way out of no way." They "walk a way out of no way." They "love a way out of no way." In so doing, they help to create the community of God here on earth.

A Savior emerges as the individual who leads a postmodern womanist theological community. She could be a black teenage girl or black lesbian woman. Although they have particular constitutions—the condition of "sharing" or mental and physical health challenges—the constitution does not guarantee the activity of salvation. Saviors are those who draw upon the immortality of the ancestors to creatively transform the world around them.

Salvation does not come to an individual. We cannot wrestle with loss, evil, and pain on our own. We cannot attain wholeness, health, peace, and justice as individuals. Although Saviors are the individuals who lead our communities of creative transformation, a way out of no way is too much for any one woman. Saviors can rest, retire, or participate in new communities. Or perhaps the communities will outlive them. Making a way out of no way is not the Savior's job or responsibility. The responsibility lies with all of us. At times it is challenging, but it is not without moments of joy, love, and dance. Salvation is found as we participate in teaching and healing communities that promote the social transformation of the world.

Conclusion

The quest for health and wholeness in the midst of violence, oppression, and evil is a lifelong cooperative process between God and those of us in the world that occurs in teaching-healing communities for the social transformation of the world. The movement of life is constituted by the past, God, and the agency of the world. God offers an ideal vision of justice, survival, and quality of life that is particular and relevant for each of us. Health, wholeness, and justice occur as we embrace these aims of God. The past is a critical resource for this activity. Through rememory and spirit possession, the past is an active participant in calling the present world toward creative transformation. Postmodern womanist theology is a metaphysical and metaphorical proposal that describes salvation as "making a way out of no way." Salvation fits into a unified view of the entire world, and yet it is also gritty, localized, and contextual. It is grounded in the concrete experiences of the world. It must always look, feel, and taste like something.

Postmodern womanist theology is an activity. It is a verb, a gerund. Health and wholeness come through teaching, healing, remembering, honoring, possessing, adopting, conforming, and creatively transforming. Saving. It is making a way. We are being saved over and over again, feeling God's continual calling toward survival, justice, and quality of life, using each opportunity to become in higher and more intense forms than we did in the last occasion.

We are not saved apart from the communities in which we participate. And yet we do not exist for the salvation of our own particular communities. We accept and reciprocate God's love so that we might love ourselves and our neighbors. We teach others to read, write, and love so that they can go on to teach others as well. We teach and heal so that our communities might be examples for the wider world. We want our actions to creatively transform the world outside of our own local contexts.

Postmodern womanist theology recognizes the leaders of these communities as Saviors. Although Saviors may have different characteristics from the average person, they are not Saviors because of their particular constitutions. There are many people born to drug-addicted mothers who do not lead communities. Some are undermined and made weaker through their experiences in society. Many of us are born into families with particular occupations and traditions that can improve the world, and yet we do not embrace or imitate them. Many people have mental and physical health challenges and do not use these experiences to testify to God's healing and to encourage others. Saviors use their perceived vulnerabilities and differences to create, strengthen, and creatively transform community.

A Savior is known by what she does. A Savior creatively transforms and draws upon the guidance of the ancestors. She leads a community that makes a way out of no way. Since every such community has a leader, there are multiple Saviors. One community can have different leaders, different Saviors, in different times; and there are often multiple communities with their own Saviors coexisting at the same time as well.

Saviors are often those whom wider society least suspects. Womanist theories of salvation state that Jesus Christ can be seen as a black woman. Postmodern womanist theology argues that a black woman is often Christ. The Savior may be a teenager, a person living with a disability, a lesbian woman. We have yet to see how "the least of these" can lead the way.

Wrestling with evil, loss, and violence is not simple. The quest for health and wholeness can seem difficult on a daily basis. This quest is not a belief. Nor is this path of salvation found in following a particular person. Salvation is participation in a community that "makes a way out of no way." Postmodern womanist theology takes salvation away from the exclusive domain of Jesus, Christianity, and institutions. There is no one-time salvation once and for all. Salvation is the cooperative working together of the divine and creation. A church may be a salvific community, but salvation does not need to occur through an institutional faith community. This community can be found in a dancing circle, a coffee house, a book group, or a nonprofit agency. But salvation is more than ethical social justice activity. Postmodern womanist theological communities acknowledge the ancestors and a higher power. They understand their activity as being co-created by the community and God.

This quest for health and wholeness focuses on social justice in local communities. Salvation is often found in grassroots activism. Postmodern womanist theology generates ethical activity and a normative theology. "Making a way out of no way" produces both concentrated acts of teaching and healing and political stances. "Making a way out of now way" generates a theology that does not conflict with the insights of science, a theology that affirms the symbiotic relationship between God and the world.

Thrust into a world of poverty and crime, an orphaned teenage girl decides to walk north to find a job and clean water. As she walks, she invites other homeless people to join her. She teaches her friends how to read and write, and they teach her how to survive in a dangerous world. She forms her observations about the world into a philosophy that can deal with the pervasive change around them. Over time, these travelers form a faith community that is committed to helping one another and building a better future.

A minister is condemned by her church for affirming the love of two faithful members. She uses this rejection to connect with others who have been disparaged by religious communities. A ministry begins where she teaches individuals to love God, themselves, and all of their neighbors. Together, this community shares this love around their city and helps to prevent the spread of disease in their midst.

These theological communities affirm salvation as a process of "making a way out of no way." In these snapshots, salvation is described as walking the way and loving the way. These communities acknowledge the presence of God and God's novelty in all of the happenings of the world and in every element of creation. It is a way of living in a dynamic and symbiotic world that has the power to create and destroy. It is "making a way out of no way."

The beating of a djembe drum still makes me want to rotate my hips and lift my knees high in a dance movement. The drum and dance still reverberate with Maria's words: "I don't know how this works, but it makes me feel whole."

Maria's statement inspires me. I remember each woman in the circle and our eclectic way of dressing in white knock-off Keds tennis shoes, 1980s-style white jeans, plain T-shirts, and home-sewn skirts with wide sashes. We ignored the techniques learned in dance class and surrendered ourselves to a combination of natural rhythm and the movement of spirit.

I don't think I gave any response to Maria that day, but I do know what I would say now. I would tell her that change is probably the one constant in life. That we all change from moment to moment, from day to day. In each moment, we have the opportunity to see the world anew and do something new. And yet some changes feel bigger than others. When we change, we lose something. We're not the same people we once were. Sometimes we lose security and stability as we reach out for a promising unknown. Other times, change brings a greater sense of safety and family. Sometimes we shake free from a past that is holding us back. And isn't that wonderful? Some change is the goal we have worked hard for. It's exactly what we hoped would happen. And some change just catches us by surprise. Some parts of change we welcome, some we dread . . . but most . . . we just manage. Most of the time, the same thing that brings a new opportunity also brings with it new challenges.

So it makes sense to honor and respect how much we change. Oya is a spirit who embodies change. She holds our hands as we experience life's changes. Sometimes she disrupts our situations in order to bring change. Sometimes she is part of the gentle whisper moving us forward. The drums and dance help us to hear and feel and experience Oya. As we dance, we welcome her, we invite her into our process. We do this because she seems to have more knowledge than we do; she seems to be broader and deeper than we are; we believe that she can help us. We dance because, amid our religious differences, we believe there's something holy and divine about all of this.

If I could talk to Maria today, I would tell her that there is no way to avoid the changes that life brings, but that there are many ways to live creatively into them. The new college graduate could be resentful of her family's poverty. She doesn't have to send a portion of her new salary home. She could choose to distance herself from them. Even Maria could have decided she would not date, let alone marry, someone who already had children. But they made different choices. One of our friends, the new single mother, could draw strength and inspiration from her own mother who had successfully raised her alone. She could also remember how unhealthy her marriage was when she thinks about going back. Our other friend, the mommy-to-be, could happily anticipate her new family by recreating some of her fond memories of growing up, while working to create a society without some of the prejudices she hopes her children will not have to experience.

I would tell Maria it is no accident that we dance in a space that also educates and cares for young children. It is no accident that we dance with women who are teachers and activists, mothers and journalists. We are part of a community of people who want to make a positive impact in this city. And it takes time to make all this happen.

In the meanwhile, we do justice to ourselves. We acknowledge who and where we are; we mourn our losses; we celebrate our victories. This is how we honor our heritage. This is how we maintain health and wholeness in a world that sometimes cares little about our bodies and souls. While we are here in this space, we will honor our lives in the raising of our limbs—by dancing in a circle; yes, by dancing a way out of no way.

That other evening many years ago still echoes with Lisa's questions: "What did I do to deserve this? Why is God letting this happen to me? What am I supposed to do now?"

Lisa's questions still loom large in front of me. I still remember the texture of her hair, the dark brown splotches of her scalp. I recall her shivering as if she is sitting in front of me now. The silent pats and questioning looks of the other women, victims of domestic violence, form a cloud of witnesses that I can never forget.

I can't remember what I said to Lisa then, but I do know what I would say now. I would tell her that what happened to her is terrible and evil. I would tell her that she has not overreacted, but that the violence was real and her suffering was real, and it is evil. She has lost a lot—not just in this instance of violence, but in this relationship. This relationship is not allowing her to be the strong, beautiful, free-thinking person that I've come to know of her in group.

I would tell her that this is not what God wants for her life. That God wants peace and truth and justice for her. But someone, namely, her partner, did not heed God's call of peace and justice and beauty. Instead, he hurt her, and this hurts her children and those of us who care about her. He even hurt himself—although he may not recognize it that way. He also hurt God. God feels this pain. God not only *knows* about Lisa's pain, but God *feels* her pain with her. For every tear she cries, God is crying even more. God can feel her pain and the pain of what another one of God's creations did to her. God is thoroughly undone.

But God wants something different for her, something new. God is calling her to another kind of relationship, another way of relating to herself, her loved ones, and her children. God is calling her to do a small part in creating a world that does not know this kind of violence and abuse. I would tell her that I know that it's hard to follow that call. I know that there are times when she barely feels the beatings because she's become so numb; times when she barely hears the yelling because she's tried to block it out. I would tell her that I understand that she is hurting and that her children are hurting, and that there are times when she just has to push it all down so she can get up and go to work. But there is a safe place here where she can break from the familiarity of this relationship, of the way she has been living. I would tell her that she has my support, the support of the organization, the volunteers, and the other women in the group. We will help her in whatever ways we can. We will mobilize the community, go to court, find her a place to stay, talk with her employers, talk with the social workers. Doing that is part of what God is calling us to do. Until we have a world without stories like hers.

In the meanwhile, may Lisa remember the bad things she has experienced and endeavor not to repeat them. Perhaps one day she will have the strength to tell her story from the other side and encourage other women who are in her situation. But today, while we're here in this space—she can cry in this community of the called. And we will answer our calling in small instances of grace—by braiding her hair and fitting her for a wig; yes, by braiding a way out of no way.

Notes

Introduction

1. Alfred North Whitehead, *Religion in the Making: Lowell Lectures, 1926* (New York: Macmillan, 1926; repr., New York: Fordham University Press, 1996), 77. Citations are to the reprint edition.

2. Karen Baker-Fletcher and Garth Kasimu Baker-Fletcher, *My Sister, My Brother: Womanist and Xodus God-Talk*, no. 12, Bishop Henry McNeal Turner/Sojourner Truth Series in Black Religion (Maryknoll, N.Y.: Orbis, 1997), 155.

3. I'm indebted to lectures by Sallie McFague at Vanderbilt University Divinity School for this concept of a "functional theology."

4. Alice Walker, *In Search of Our Mothers' Gardens: Womanist Prose* (San Diego: Harcourt Brace Jovanovich, 1983).

5. Linda E. Thomas, "Womanist Theology, Epistemology, and a New Anthropological Paradigm," *Cross Currents* 48 (1998–99): 489.

6. Delores S. Williams, "Womanist Theology: Black Women's Voices," in *Black Theology: A Documentary History, Volume 2: 1980–1992*, ed. James Cone and Gayraud S. Wilmore (Maryknoll, N.Y.: Orbis, 1993), 266.

7. See Theodore Walker Jr., "Hartshorne's Neoclassical Theism and Black Theology," *Process Studies* 18, no. 4 (Winter 1989): 240–58; and Henry Young, "Process Theology and Black Liberation: Testing the Metaphysical Foundations," *Process Studies* 18, no. 4 (Winter 1989): 259–67.

8. Ronald C. Potter, "A Comparison of the Conceptions of God in Process and Black Theologies," *The Journal of the Interdenominational Center* 12, nos. 1–2 (Fall 1984–Spring 1985): 50–61.

9. Gene Reeves, "Liberation: Process Theology and Black Experience," *Process Studies* 18, no. 4 (Winter 1989): 225–39.

Chapter One

1. I use the terms *black* and *African American* interchangeably to refer to persons of African descent living in the United States and with cultural heritage in the history of the United States. This cultural heritage includes the legacy of American slavery and its particularities. This seems to be the tendency of other womanist religious scholars. Arisika Razak describes womanism as an "African American

concept [that] speaks to African American concepts of embodiment" with perhaps limited applicability to the experiences of African women (for example). See Arisika Razak, "Response to 'Must I Be Womanist?'" *Journal of Feminist Studies in Religion* 22, no. 1 (Spring 2006): 107. I will write "black" and "white" with lowercase letters. If I am quoting an author who uses "Black" or "White," I will preserve her or his original nomenclature. It is worth noting that nonblack women identify as "womanist." One example is Lee Miena Skye's work on Australian aboriginal Christian women who identify as womanist, in "Response to 'Must I Be Womanist?'" *Journal of Feminist Studies in Religion* 22, no. 1 (Spring 2006): 119–23. Karen Baker-Fletcher also notes that some global womanists adopt the "womanist" nomenclature; she affirms such identification as long as they are "in authentic relationships of mutuality, equality, and respect with black women" in "A Womanist Journey," in *Deeper Shades of Purple: Womanism in Religion and Society*, no. 10, Religion, Race, and Ethnicity, ed. Stacey M. Floyd-Thomas (New York: New York University Press, 2006), 163. My notation here does not seek to define the scope or content of womanist religious scholarship or womanist identification; rather, I seek to reflect the African American context and content of the womanist theologians I survey here, my own experiences, and the experiences that serve as the grounding (although not necessarily to the exclusion of other experiences) of this postmodern womanist theology.

2. Frances Beale, "Double Jeopardy: To Be Black and Female," in *Black Theology: A Documentary History, 1966–1979*, ed. James H. Cone and Gayraud Wilmore (New York: Orbis, 1979), 284–92.

3. Theressa Hoover, "Black Women and the Churches: Triple Jeopardy," in *Black Theology*, ed. Cone and Wilmore, 227–88.

4. Jacquelyn Grant, *White Women's Christ and Black Women's Jesus: Feminist Christology and Womanist Response*, American Academy of Religion Series, no. 64 (Atlanta: Scholars Press, 1989), 202. Grant first articulates these thoughts in "Tasks of a Prophetic Church," in *Theology in the Americas: Detroit II Papers*, Probe Third World Studies, ed. Cornel West, Caridad Guidote, and Margaret Coakley (Maryknoll, N.Y.: Orbis, 1982), 136–42.

5. Grant, *White Women's Christ*, 212.

6. Ibid., 217.

7. Ibid.

8. Ibid., 219.

9. Ibid., 220.

10. Jacquelyn Grant, "The Sin of Servanthood and the Deliverance of Discipleship," in *A Troubling in My Soul: Womanist Perspectives on Evil and Suffering*, no. 8, Bishop Henry McNeal Studies in North American Black Religion, ed. Emilie M. Townes (Maryknoll, N.Y.: Orbis, 1993), 200.

11. Ibid., 213.

12. Ibid.

13. Ibid., 210. Grant notes the ways in which some feminist theologians have addressed the problematic of servanthood language. Whereas some feminist theologians reject servanthood language in favor of the language of friendship or partnership, other feminist theologians attempt to salvage the language by promoting service rather than servitude. She finds all of these inadequate.

14. Ibid., 214.

15. Ibid., 211.

16. Kelly Brown Douglas, *The Black Christ*, Bishop Henry McNeal Studies in North American Black Religion, no. 9 (Maryknoll, N.Y.: Orbis, 1994), 101.

17. Ibid., 98, quoting Alice Walker, ix.

18. Ibid., 104.

19. Ibid., 113.

20. Ibid., 107.

21. Ideas about the blackness of Christ typically refer to Jesus Christ as a brown person who would be classified as "black" in the United States' racial categories. This was a particularly popular concept among black nationalists and literary artists in the nineteenth century and into the 1960s and 1970s. Robert Alexander Young (*Ethiopian Manifesto*, 1829), Henry McNeal Turner (1898), Marcus Garvey, Countee Cullen (1928), John Henrik Clarke (1972), and Albert Cleage (1969) are notable representatives of this movement. See Douglas, *The Black Christ*, 9–34.

22. Ibid., 108.

23. Ibid., 109.

24. Kelly Brown Douglas, "Is Christ a Black Woman? A Womanist Understanding of Christ Is Rooted in Healing Fractured Communities," *The Other Side* 30 (1994): 11.

25. Ibid., 8.

26. Delores S. Williams, "A Womanist Perspective on Sin," in *A Troubling in My Soul*, 138.

27. Williams specifically names patriarchy and demonarchy. *Demonarchy* is Williams's term for the oppression that black women experience at the hands of white American social institutions. White men and white women inflict this oppression. Williams distinguishes demonarchy from patriarchy by noting that white women benefit from patriarchy inasmuch as it is designed to preserve the lives of their children, whereas these same social structures have no regard for the lives of black women or their children. See Delores S. Williams, "The Color of Feminism: Or Speaking the Black Woman's Tongue," *Journal of Religious Thought* 43 (Spring–Summer 1986): 164–65.

28. Williams, "A Womanist Perspective on Sin," 146.

29. Ibid., 147.

30. Ibid., 134.

31. Delores S. Williams, "Straight Talk, Plain Talk: Womanist Words about Salvation in a Social Context," in *Embracing the Spirit: Womanist Perspectives on Hope, Salvation and Transformation*, no. 13, Bishop Henry McNeal Turner/Sojourner Truth Series in Black Religion, ed. Emilie M. Townes (Maryknoll, N.Y.: Orbis, 1997), 98.

32. Ibid.

33. Delores S. Williams, "Black Women's Surrogacy Experiences and the Christian Notion of Redemption," in *After Patriarchy: Feminist Reconstructions of the World Religions*, ed. Paula M. Cooey, William R. Eakin, and Jay B. McDaniel (Maryknoll, N.Y.: Orbis, 1991), 1.

34. In voluntary surrogacy, there is an element of choice on black women's part. There are, however, economic and social restrictions such that the available positions were still surrogate roles.

35. A. Elaine Crawford, "Womanist Christology: Where Have We Come From and Where Are We Going?" *Review and Expositor* 95 (1998): 375.

36. Williams disagrees with the objective version of Christian atonement theories that render Jesus as a substitution for sinful humanity. Objective theories of atonement emphasize the intervention of a transcendent God who counteracts the destructive effects of sin. The classical form of the objective model is found in Anselm of Canterbury's *Cur Deus Homo* (1098).

37. Williams, "Black Women's Surrogacy," 9.

38. Delores S. Williams, *Sisters in the Wilderness: The Challenge of Womanist God-Talk* (Maryknoll, N.Y.: Orbis, 1993), 167.

39. Delores S. Williams, "Re-Imagining Jesus" (paper presented at the international gathering of women participating in the World Council of Churches' Ecumenical Decade in Solidarity with Women, Minneapolis, Minnesota, 5 November 1993), tape recording. Quoted in JoAnne Marie Terrell, *Power in the Blood? The Cross in the African American Experience*, no. 15, Bishop Henry McNeal Turner/Sojourner Truth Series in Black Religion (Maryknoll, N.Y.: Orbis, 1998), 121.

40. Williams, *Sisters in the Wilderness*, 167.

41. Williams, "Black Women's Surrogacy," 11.

42. Williams, *Sisters in the Wilderness*, 175.

43. Terrell, *Power in the Blood*, 23.

44. Ibid., 76.

45. Ibid., 124.

46. Ibid., 125.

47. Ibid., 18.

48. Subjective types of atonement place emphasis on the human response to the Christ-event. The classic model of the subjective form of the atonement is found in *Exposition of the Epistle to the Romans* (1137) by Peter Abelard, Anselm's younger

contemporary. The argument goes as follows: In God's love to humanity, God tries to convince human beings to love God as well. God's love will not even withhold God's own Son. God does not punish and condemn guilty sinners. Rather, God waits for humanity to return to God in repentance and to stop sinning and acquire forgiveness. All God requires of humanity is repentance in the sinner. Both the life and death of Jesus are important for the efficacy of redemption. Jesus becomes a "moral exemplar" for human beings, a pattern that we try to emulate. But he is also more than an ideal, because Jesus actually influences human beings to want to emulate him. Atonement occurs as human beings experience the depth of the love of God and are transformed by it. It is the knowledge and experience of the particularities of Jesus' life and death that awaken human beings to repentance and imitation of Christ.

49. Terrell, *Power in the Blood*, 127.

50. Ibid., 143.

51. Karen Baker-Fletcher and Garth Kasimu Baker-Fletcher, *My Sister, My Brother: Womanist and Xodus God-Talk*, no. 12, Bishop Henry McNeal Turner/Sojourner Truth Series in Black Religion (Maryknoll, N.Y.: Orbis, 1997), 7.

52. Ibid., 6.

53. Ibid.

54. Williams makes scant reference to the similar abuse of black women's bodies and the land in "Black Women's Surrogacy."

55. Baker-Fletcher, *My Sister, My Brother*, 30.

56. Ibid., 35.

57. Ibid., 40.

58. Ibid., 30.

59. Ibid., 29.

60. Ibid.

61. Ibid., 75.

62. Ibid., 80.

63. Ibid., 84.

64. This is developed more fully in Karen Baker-Fletcher, *Sisters of Dust, Sisters of Spirit: Womanist Wordings of God and Creation* (Minneapolis: Fortress Press, 1995).

65. Baker-Fletcher, *My Sister, My Brother*, 88.

66. Ibid., 89.

67. Ibid., 90.

68. Ibid., 90–91.

69. Ibid., 91.

70. Ibid., 89.

71. Ibid., 155.

72. Ibid.

73. Ibid., 156.

74. Ibid., 35.

75. Ibid., 29.

76. Williams, *Sisters in the Wilderness*, ix.

77. Ibid., 241. Williams notes that Alice Walker dedicates one of her books to her mother who "makes a way out of no way."

78. Baker-Fletcher, *My Sister, My Brother*, 156–57.

79. I also detail these four components of "making a way out of no way" in "An Exchange of Gifts: Process and Womanist Theologies," in *Handbook on Process Theology*, ed. Donna Bowman and Jay McDaniel (St. Louis: Chalice, 2006), 165–67.

80. Ibid., 198.

81. Emilie M. Townes, *In a Blaze of Glory: Womanist Spirituality as Social Witness* (Nashville: Abingdon, 1995), 140.

82. Baker-Fletcher, *Sisters of Dust*, 5–6.

83. Williams, *Sister in the Wilderness*, 5.

84. Ibid., 129.

85. Jacquelyn Grant, "Servanthood Revisited: Womanist Explorations of Servant-hood Theology," in *Black Faith and Public Talk: Critical Essays on James H. Cone's Black Theology and Black Power*, ed. Dwight N. Hopkins (Maryknoll, N.Y.: Orbis, 1999), 134.

86. Townes, *In a Blaze of Glory*, 140.

87. Williams, *Sisters in the Wilderness*, 113–20. This is where Williams extends her understanding of "liberation" to more than just freedom; it could also mean survival.

88. Renee Leslie Hill, "Disrupted/Disruptive Movements: Black Theology and Black Power 1969/1999," in *Black Theology: A Documentary History, Volume 2: 1980–1992*, ed. James H. Cone and Gayraud S. Wilmore (Maryknoll, N.Y.: Orbis, 1993), 148.

89. Williams, *Sisters in the Wilderness*, 136.

90. Ibid., 130.

91. Grant, *White Women's Christ*.

92. Only recently has the constitution of Jesus become important for woman-ist Christologies. In *Sisters of Dust, Sisters of Spirit*, Baker-Fletcher describes Jesus' constitution as dust and spirit, earthly and heavenly, divine and human. In her lecture "Jesus as Dust and Spirit: An Incarnational Theology" at the 2001 Annual Meeting of the American Academy of Religion, Baker-Fletcher admits that she is looking toward a process metaphysic to support this assertion. She does this in

her work on the Trinity in *Dancing with God: The Trinity in Womanist Perspective* (St. Louis: Chalice, 2006).

93. Grant, *White Women's Christ*, 213.

94. Ibid., 212.

95. Williams, *Sisters in the Wilderness*, 203.

96. Baker-Fletcher, *My Sister, My Brother*, 31.

97. Crawford, "Womanist Christology," 376.

98. Williams, "Straight Talk, Plain Talk," 118.

99. This argument can also be found in my article "An Exchange of Gifts: Process and Womanist Theologies," 167–68.

100. Melanie L. Harris, "Womanist Humanism: A New Hermeneutic," in Floyd-Thomas, ed., *Deeper Shades of Purple*, 214.

101. I have expounded upon this critique of womanist religious scholarship in my article "Must I Be Womanist?" *Journal of Feminist Studies in Religion* 22, no. 1 (Spring 2006): 85–96.

102. Debra Mubashir Majeed, "Womanism Encounters Islam: A Muslim Scholar Considers the Efficacy of a Method Rooted in the Academy and the Church," in Floyd-Thomas, ed., *Deeper Shades of Purple*, 45.

103. Harris, "Womanist Humanism," 221.

104. Gayraud S. Wilmore, *Black Religion and Radicalism: An Interpretation of the Religious History of African Americans*, 3rd ed. (Maryknoll, N.Y.: Orbis, 1998), 280.

105. Maulana Karenga, "Black Religion: The African Model," in *Down by the Riverside: Readings in African American Religion*, ed. Larry G. Murphy (New York: New York University Press, 2000), 41.

106. It is worth noting that some enslaved Africans were Muslims. See Richard Brent Turner, "Pre-Twentieth Century Islam," in *Down by the Riverside: Readings in African American Religion*, ed. Larry G. Murphy (New York: New York University Press, 2000), 69–80. Even these enslaved Africans were exposed to African traditional religions both in their respective African contexts and in the slave community in the United States.

107. Wilmore, *Black Religion and Radicalism*, 280.

108. Anthony B. Pinn makes a similar argument, albeit from a black humanist perspective, in *Varieties of African American Religious Experience* (Minneapolis: Fortress Press, 1998).

109. It is important to acknowledge the diversity of religious beliefs and identities for African American women. In "Womanist Humanism," Melanie L. Harris notes that womanist theological discourse should "include 'womanist wisdom' from a variety of religious, theistic, pantheistic, and nontheistic perspectives that are life-affirming and life-giving to black women" (214). I completely agree with Harris, but this work will focus on theistic faiths—both traditionally monotheistic

religious affiliations and African traditional religions with a different understanding of the singularity and plurality of the divine. The religious traditions to which I am referring are variously called polytheistic, "diffused monotheistic," and "communotheistic." I will address this is more detail in chapters 4 and 5. I believe that these non-Western systems are not easily or well-classified in Western language, and I will tend to use the terminology of the religious tradition itself rather than name the tradition in terms of monotheism or polytheism. In this vein, all scholars and practitioners can agree that African traditional religions are not traditionally monotheistic religions, as are the "Abrahamic faiths" of Judaism, Christianity, and Islam. I am also quite interested in Alice Walker's paganism, which she variously describes as pantheistic and panentheistic (see Baker-Fletcher's "Womanist Journey," 170–71, for references throughout Walker's work), womanist humanism, and womanist adherents to nontheistic faiths like Buddhism. Harris investigates Walker's womanist paganism in her doctoral dissertation, "Alice Walker's Ethics: An Analysis of Alice Walker's Non-Fiction Work as a Resource for Womanist Ethics" (Union Theological Seminary in the City of New York, 2006), and in her essay "Loving the Spirit: Expressions of Paganism in Alice Walker's Non-Fiction" (paper presented at the annual meeting of the American Academy of Religion, Washington, D.C., 20 November 2006). Carolyn Medine gives womanist religious interpretation to black women Buddhists as well in "Jan Willis's *Dreaming Me*: Constructing a Baptist-Buddhist Womanist Identity" (paper presented at the annual meeting of the American Academy of Religion, Washington, D.C., 20 November 2006). This book, however, focuses on theistic forms of black religion, asserts a panentheistic theology (in the second chapter), and highlights African traditional religions.

110. Shani Settles, "The Sweet Fire of Honey: Womanist Visions of Osun as a Methodology of Emancipation," in Floyd-Thomas, ed., *Deeper Shades of Purple*, 191.

111. Tracey E. Hucks, "'Burning with a Flame in America': African American Women in African-Derived Traditions," *Journal of Feminist Studies in Religion* 17, no. 2 (Fall 2001): 89–90.

112. For a definition of systematic theology along these lines, see Neil Ormerond, *Introducing Contemporary Theologies: The What and the Who of Theology Today* (Maryknoll, N.Y.: Orbis, 1997), 55.

113. John Macquarrie, "Systematic Theology," in *A New Handbook of Christian Theology*, ed. Donald W. Musser and Joseph L. Price (Nashville: Abingdon, 1992), 469.

114. Ibid., 470.

115. Ibid., 473.

116. David B. Burrell, "Metaphysics," in Musser and Price, eds., *A New Handbook of Christian Theology*, 308.

117. Ibid., 309.

118. William James, John Dewey, and Alfred North Whitehead refer to this empiricism with such terms as "radical empiricism," "immediate empiricism," and "causal efficacy," respectively; empirical theologians Henry Nelson Wieman and Bernard Meland refer to empiricism with such terms as "mysticism" and "appreciative awareness," respectively. William Dean, "Empirical Theology," in Musser and Price, eds., *A New Handbook of Christian Theology*, 248–49.

119. Alfred North Whitehead, *Process and Reality: An Essay in Cosmology*, Corrected Edition, ed. David Ray Griffin and Donald W. Sherburne (New York: Free Press, 1978), 3.

120. Ibid., 13.

121. Ibid., 8.

Chapter 2

1. This is not an exhaustive list. It should also be noted that postmodernism is often discussed quite differently in literary and linguistic circles. The interpretation of postmodernism given here is particular to its development in Western philosophy, with attention given to the aspects that support the argument for a postmodern theology that can and should enter into conversation with womanist theology.

2. Heath White, *Postmodernism 101: A First Course for the Curious Christian* (Grand Rapids: Brazos, 2006), 37.

3. I will generally use the terms *modernity* and *modernism* interchangeably to refer to the worldview and understandings generated by the modern period I describe.

4. White, *Postmodernism 101*, 44.

5. Ibid., 55.

6. David Ray Griffin, "Introduction to SUNY Series in Constructive Postmodern Thought," in *Parapsychology, Philosophy and Spirituality: A Postmodern Explanation*, SUNY Series in Constructive Postmodern Thought (Albany: State University of New York Press, 1997), xi.

7. Other responses to the limits of modernism include what Griffin identifies as attempts to return to a premodern way of life, and deconstructive or eliminative postmodernism. In the attempts to return to a premodern way of life, individuals often want to return to the belief in and practice of ancient, indigenous, or traditional practices that predated the advent of the modern period. This retreat to the premodern period seeks to ignore or invalidate all learning from the modern period. Deconstructive or eliminative postmodernism focuses on the problems with the modern worldview. Some deconstructive postmodern responses include nihilism, the belief that there is no right answer, with the often correlative belief that there is no ground for hope; and relativism, the idea that truth varies

from person to person, or from one society or culture to another. Pragmatism, the idea that truth can be found in what functions best for an individual or a society, is another form of postmodernism. While I have just painted significant philosophical movements in broad strokes, these aforementioned responses share a repudiation/rejection of a philosophical metaphysic and stand in stark contrast to the constructive postmodern theology offered by Griffin and adhered to in this work. Referring to the work of Jacques Derrida, Martin Heidegger, Ludwig Wittgenstein, and others, Griffin believes that this kind of postmodernism is an anti-modernism: "It overcomes the modern worldview through an anti-worldview: it deconstructs or eliminates the ingredients necessary for a worldview, such as god, self, purpose, meaning, a real world, and truth as correspondence" (ibid., xii).

8. Ibid.

9. Ibid., xiii.

10. Carol P. Christ, "We Are Nature: Environmental Ethics in a Different Key" (paper presented at the Sixth International Whitehead Conference, Salzburg, Austria, 5 July 2006).

11. Griffin, "Introduction to SUNY Series," xiii.

12. David Ray Griffin, William A. Beardslee, and Joe Holland, *Varieties of Postmodern Theology*, SUNY Series in Constructive Postmodern Thought (Albany: State University of New York Press, 1989).

13. Generally, those following in the tradition of Charles Hartshorne refer to this same thought as "neoclassical metaphysics" or "neoclassical theology." In so doing, they seek to emphasize the connections with premodern or classical thought. As a student of Whitehead, I will refer to the theological implications of Whitehead's thought as "process theology." While Hartshorne affirms most of the same principles as Whitehead, there is a significant difference in terms of the language used, and (more importantly) in the metaphysical description of God. These differences are minor compared to modern theology and other forms of postmodern theology; however, they lead to differences in the understanding of God's vision, the possibilities offered to the world, and immortality.

14. Nicholas Rescher, *Process Metaphysics: an Introduction to Process Philosophy*, SUNY Series in Philosophy (Albany: State University of New York Press, 1996), 1–26. Rescher cites G. W. F. Hegel, Gottfried Leibniz, Charles Pierce, and William James (among others). Whitehead acknowledges indebtedness to Plato, Leibniz, and James, in particular, in *Process and Reality* (see n. 21).

15. Alfred North Whitehead, *Religion in the Making: Lowell Lectures, 1926* (New York: Macmillan, 1926; repr., New York: Fordham University Press, 1996), 77. Citations are to the reprint edition.

16. Marjorie Hewitt Suchocki, *Fall to Violence: Original Sin in Relational Theology* (New York: Continuum, 1994), 60.

17. Whitehead, *Religion in the Making*, 61–62.

18. Whitehead puts it this way: "These concepts [at work in the process of becoming] are that of the values of an individual for itself, that of the value of the diverse

individuals of the world for each other, and that of the value of the objective world which is a community derivative from the interrelations of its component individuals, and also necessary for the existence of each of these individuals." Ibid., 59.

19. Ibid., 87.

20. Ibid.

21. Alfred North Whitehead, *Process and Reality: An Essay in Cosmology*, Corrected Edition, ed. David Ray Griffin and Donald W. Sherburne (New York: Free Press, 1978), 340.

22. Ibid.

23. Ibid., 223.

24. Alfred North Whitehead, *Adventures of Ideas* (New York: Simon and Schuster, 1933; repr., New York: Free Press, 1967), 255. Citations are to the reprint edition.

25. Whitehead affirms this in these words: "But there can be intense experience without harmony. In this event, there is destruction of the significant characters of individual objects. When the direct feeling of such destruction dominates the whole, there is the immediate feeling of evil, and the anticipation of destructive or weakened data for the future." Ibid., 264.

26. Whitehead, *Religion in the Making*, 156.

27. Ibid., 98.

28. Ibid., 155.

29. Whitehead, *Process and Reality,* 346.

30. Ibid.

31. Whitehead, *Process and Reality*, 346.

32. Ibid., 349–50.

33. In a general sense, God *becomes* in the same way that we do—working with the past and possibilities to come to a final decision, action, or call. In a more detailed sense, within this process of becoming, God *becomes* in an opposite manner than we do. This is called the "conceptual reversion of poles." It is unique to a Whiteheadian process theology, because God is considered to operate as a single actual entity—the basic units that compose the world. This is what is meant: In the world, we feel or are influenced by the past first (in what Whitehead calls the physical pole), and then consider them with the possibilities that are available to us (through the mental pole). God, on the other hand, knows or contains all possibilities for the world and then works with the events of the world as they are occurring and uses that information, correlates it with the ideals of God's vision, and issues a call to each of us. God begins with the mental pole (possibilities), whereas those of us in the world begin with the physical pole, or the past.

34. Ibid., 351.

35. Ibid., 346.

36. Ibid., 83–84.

37. Ibid., 88.

38. Whitehead, *Adventures of Ideas,* 259.

39. Whitehead, *Process and Reality*, 105.

40. Ibid., 250.

41. Ibid., 251. In *Adventures of Ideas,* Whitehead terms "Eros" what he refers to as "God" in *Religion in the Making* and *Process and Reality*. I inserted the word "God" where Whitehead used "Eros" for ease of understanding.

42. Whitehead, *Adventures of Ideas,* 268.

43. Ibid., 267.

44. Ibid., 269.

45. Ibid.

46. Ibid., 260–61.

47. Ibid., 258.

48. Ibid.

49. Ibid., 259.

50. Whitehead, *Process and Reality*, 340.

51. Ibid., xiii–xiv.

52. Whitehead, *Adventures of Ideas*, 285.

53. Ibid.

54. Ibid., 286.

55. Whitehead, *Process and Reality*, 4.

56. Process theology leans heavily on the fields of science and philosophy to provide information about the world. Whitehead's background as a physicist and mathematician can be seen as one source of this correlation between process thought and science. In his discussion of the relation between experience and speculative philosophy, Whitehead highlights the relationship between science and religion: "Philosophy frees itself from the taint of ineffectiveness by its close relations with religion and with science, natural and sociological. It attains its chief importance by fusing the two, namely, religion and science, into one rational scheme of thought. . . . Science finds religious experience among its percepta; and religion finds scientific concepts among the conceptual experiences to be fused with particular sensitive reactions" (*Process and Reality*, 15, 16). Many process theologians have taken Whitehead's directive very seriously and continued to connect process theology with religion and science. John Cobb and biologist Charles Birch came together to write *Liberation of Life: From the Cell to the Community* (Denton, Tex.: Environmental Ethics, 1990), a liberative theology for the natural world based on the insights of evolution. Likewise, process theologian David Ray

Griffin has written and edited numerous works dealing with science, philosophy, and process theology, including *The Reenchantment of Science: Postmodern Proposals* (Albany: State University of New York, 1988), *Religion and Scientific Naturalism: Overcoming the Conflicts* (Albany: State University of New York, 2000), and "Science and Religion: A Postmodern Perspective" in William Desmond, John Steffen, Koen Decoster, eds., *Beyond Conflict and Reduction: Between Philosophy, Science and Religion* (Leuven, Belgium: Leuven University Press, 2001). With such emphasis on science and philosophy, process theology has been able to build a rather solid bridge between science and religion, reason and faith. For that same reason, however, it is often accused of an overreliance on philosophy and theory, and of lacking sufficient grounding in the concrete experiences of people. Process theologians have not utilized history, literature, or music to the extent that they have employed the fields of science and philosophy. Notable exceptions are Catherine Keller's *Apocalypse Now and Then: A Feminist Guide to the End of the World* (Boston: Beacon, 1996) and Ann Pederson's *God, Creation, and All that Jazz: A Process of Composition and Improvisation* (St. Louis: Chalice, 2001). With history and music, respectively, these feminist process theologians have incorporated the social and aesthetic sciences into their process constructions.

57. Whitehead, *Process and Reality*, 5.

58. Ibid., 13.

59. William R. Jones, "Process Theology: Guardian of the Oppressor or Goad to the Oppressed: An Interim Assessment," *Process Studies* 18, no. 4 (Winter 1989): 268–81.

60. Thandeka, "I've Known Rivers: Black Theology's Response to Process Theology," *Process Studies* 18, no. 4 (Winter 1989): 282–93.

61. Whitehead, *Process and Reality*, 265.

62. Ibid., 346.

63. Thandeka, "I've Known Rivers," 285.

64. Ibid., 288.

65. Henry James Young, "Process Theology and Black Liberation: Testing the Whiteheadian Metaphysical Foundations" *Process Studies* 18, no. 4 (Winter 1989): 259–67; Henry James Young, *Hope in Process: A Theology of Social Pluralism* (Minneapolis: Fortress Press, 1990).

66. Theodore Walker Jr., *Mothership Connections: A Black Atlantic Synthesis of Neoclassical Metaphysics and Black Theology*, SUNY Series in Constructive Postmodern Thought (Albany: State University of New York Press, 2004).

67. Ibid., chap. 5.

68. Other Whiteheadian theologians have done this as well. For one example, see George Michael Zbaraschuk, "The Purposes of God: Providence as Process-Historical Liberation" (Ph.D. diss., Claremont Graduate University, 2002).

69. Thandeka, "I've Known Rivers," 284.

Chapter 3

1. Sonia Sanchez, "For Sweet Honey in the Rock," in *Shake Loose My Skin: New and Selected Poems* (Boston: Beacon, 2000), 148. The words of this poem form the foreground for a recording of the song "Stay on the Battlefield" by the African American female a capella group Sweet Honey in the Rock (*Sacred Ground*, Earthbeat, 1996). They sing the African American spiritual "I'm Gonna Stay on the Battlefield" in conjunction with the words of Sanchez's poem.

2. Cobb writes about creative transformation in Whiteheadian terms: "The initial aim is at a relevant novelty rather than at reenactment. The novelty that is aimed at is one that allows maximum incorporation of elements from the past in a new synthesis. This novelty must struggle for actualization against habit, anxiety, and defensiveness. To whatever extent the new aim is successful, to that extent there is creative transformation" (John B. Cobb Jr., *Christ in a Pluralistic Age* [Philadelphia: Westminster, 1975], 76). Creative transformation is what happens when the initial aim conforms to a strong degree to the superjective aim of the occasion.

3. Independent of Whitehead, Pierre Teilhard de Chardin describes a process of creative transformation that occurs in the world. See Pierre Teilhard de Chardin, *Christianity and Evolution* (London: Collins, 1971), 21–24. Relying on Whitehead's thought, Henry Nelson Wieman also discusses creative transformation. See Henry N. Wieman, *The Source of Human Good* (Chicago: University of Chicago Press, 1946). Cobb acknowledges his indebtedness and departure from Teilhard and Wieman—see John B. Cobb Jr., *God and the World* (Eugene, Ore.: Wipf and Stock, 1998), 51–57.

4. John Cobb, "Can Christ Become Good News Again?" in *Can Christ Become Good News Again?* (St. Louis: Chalice, 1991), 97.

5. Cobb's goal in this book is to articulate a Christology that will open Christians to religious pluralism: "Christ, as the image of creative transformation, can provide a unity within which the many centers of meaning and existence can be appreciated and encouraged and through which openness to the other great Ways of mankind can lead to a deepening of Christian existence." *Christ in a Pluralistic Age*, 21.

6. John B. Cobb Jr. and David Ray Griffin, *Process Theology: An Introductory Exposition* (Philadelphia: Westminster, 1976), 100.

7. Cobb, *God and the World*, 49–50.

8. Ibid., 45.

9. Cobb's goal in this book is to articulate a Christology that will open Christians to religious pluralism: "Christ, as the image of creative transformation, can provide a unity within which the many centers of meaning and existence can be appreciated and encouraged and through which openness to the other great Ways of mankind can lead to a deepening of Christian existence." *Christ in a Pluralistic Age*, 21.

10. Ibid., 71.

11. Ibid., 59.

12. Ibid., 59–60.

13. Ibid., 183.

14. John B. Cobb, Jr., "Christ beyond Creative Transformation," in *Encountering Jesus: A Debate on Christology*, ed. Stephen T. Davis (Atlanta: John Knox, 1988), 146. Cobb elaborates on this concept in *The Structure of Christian Existence* (Philadelphia: Westminster, 1967), 107–24, and *Christ in a Pluralistic Age*, 111–46. I will not go into detail here, because this section is about creative transformation and not Cobb's Christology proper.

15. Cobb writes, "The center from which [Jesus'] world was organized was co-constituted by his personal past and by God's present agency. There was truly one person, at once fully divine and fully human. These experiences are thus distinguished structurally, but not metaphysically, from the ordinary experiences of Christian believers." John B. Cobb Jr., "Christology in Process-Relational Perspective," *Word and Spirit: A Monastic Review* 8 (1986): 88.

16. Cobb, *Christ in a Pluralistic Age*, 131.

17. John B. Cobb Jr., "Kingdom Come and the Present Church," in *Can Christ Become Good News Again?* 118.

18. Cobb, "Christ Beyond Creative Transformation," 147.

19. I also detail these four characteristics of Cobb's articulation of creative transformation in "An Exchange of Gifts: Process and Womanist Theologies," *Handbook on Process Theology*, ed. Donna Bowman and Jay McDaniel (St. Louis: Chalice, 2006), 162–64.

20. Cobb, *Christ in a Pluralistic Age*, 59.

21. Ibid., 72.

22. Cobb and Griffin, *Process Theology*, 105.

23. Cobb, *Christ in a Pluralistic Age*, 84.

24. Ibid., 85.

25. Cobb and Griffin, *Process Theology*, 103.

26. Cobb, *Christ in a Pluralistic Age*, 59.

27. Ibid., 172.

28. Cobb, "Kingdom Come," 116.

29. Cobb, "Christ in Process-Relational Perspective," 86.

30. Cobb, "Christ beyond Creative Transformation," 144.

31. John B. Cobb Jr., "Christian Universality Revisited," in *Can Christ Become Good News Again?* 85.

32. John B. Cobb Jr., "Theology: From an Enlightenment Discipline to Global Christian Thinking," in *Can Christ Become Good News Again?* 36.

33. Charles Birch and John B. Cobb Jr. *The Liberation of Life: From the Cell to the Community* (Denton, Tex.: Environmental Ethics Books, 1990), 188.

34. Cobb, "Christ beyond Creative Transformation," 144. Cobb's understanding of creative transformation has been influenced by his work with biology, evolution, and ecological justice. He admits that what he has called "Life" in the book *Liberation of Life* is also Christ and creative transformation. In his early work, Cobb identified creative transformation as "the way." In this late work, creative transformation becomes the life and the truth, following the Christological statement in the Gospel of John.

35. Cobb, "Christ beyond Creative Transformation," 143.

36. Birch and Cobb, *Liberation of Life*, 202.

37. Cobb, *Christ in a Pluralistic Age*, 87.

38. Cobb and Griffin, *Process Theology*, 101.

39. Cobb, "Theology: From an Enlightenment Discipline to Global Christian Thinking," 36.

40. In "Christ beyond Creative Transformation," Cobb associates the consequent nature of God as "truth" that experiences humanity. His Logos-Christology becomes a Sophia-Christology whereby Christians can learn and share wisdom with non-Christian religions.

41. See Karen Baker-Fletcher, *Sisters of Dust, Sisters of Spirit: Womanist Wordings of God and Creation* (Minneapolis: Fortress Press, 1995): "Environmental abuse cannot be separated from socioeconomic and racial discrimination" (55); "Care of the land is interrelated with care for our bodies, minds and spirits" (56).

42. Kelly Brown Douglas, *The Black Christ*, no. 9, Bishop Henry McNeal Studies in North American Black Religion (Maryknoll, N.Y.: Orbis, 1994), 108.

43. See Nancy L. Eiesland, *The Disabled God: Toward a Liberatory Theology of Disability* (Nashville: Abingdon, 1994), 69–75.

44. Delores S. Williams, *Sisters in the Wilderness: The Challenge of Womanist God-Talk* (Maryknoll, N.Y.: Orbis, 1993), 167.

45. JoAnne Marie Terrell, *Power in the Blood? The Cross in the African American Experience*, no. 15, Bishop Henry McNeal Turner/Sojourner Truth Series in Black Religion (Maryknoll, N.Y.: Orbis, 1998), 141.

46. Ibid., 142.

47. Kelly Brown Douglas writes, "If womanist theologians continue to maintain silence concerning the oppression of our lesbian sisters, not only do we perpetuate their oppression, but we fall short of our own vision for wholeness." *The Black Christ*, 101–2.

48. Ibid., 103.

49. Baker-Fletcher, *Sisters of Dust*, 20.

50. Martin Luther King Jr., "Letter from a Birmingham Jail," in *A Testament of Hope: The Essential Writings and Speeches of Martin Luther King, Jr.*, ed. James M. Washington (San Francisco: Harper & Row, 1986), 290.

51. Marjorie Hewitt Suchocki, *The End of Evil: Process Eschatology in Historical Context* (Albany: State University of New York Press, 1988), 89.

52. Alfred North Whitehead, *Process and Reality: An Essay in Cosmology*, Corrected Edition, ed. David Ray Griffin and Donald W. Sherburne (New York: Free Press, 1978), 21.

53. See discussion of subjective immortality in chap. 4 for reference.

54. Suchocki, *The End of Evil*, 122–23.

55. Ibid., 130.

Chapter 4

1. Birago Ishmael Diop, "Souffles," in *Birago Diop: Écrivan Sénégalais*, ed. Fernand Nathan, Classiques du Monde, Littérature Africaine 6 (Paris: F. Nathan, 1965), 16. Senegalese poet Diop (1906–1989) of the Negritude movement first became famous with this poem. Written in French, it is titled "Souffles." This is usually translated as "The Invocation of the Dead." Ysaye Maria Barnwell put this poem to music for the female a capella group Sweet Honey in the Rock in the song "Breaths" (*Good News*, Flying Fish Records, 1981). I have used their translation. This line of the poem reads, *"Ceux qui sont morts ne sont jamais partis."* I would have translated it to read, "Those who have died have never departed." I think the original meaning is preserved either way.

2. Alfred North Whitehead, *Process and Reality: An Essay in Cosmology*, Corrected Edition, ed. David Ray Griffin and Donald W. Sherburne (New York: Free Press, 1978), 226-27.

3. Karen Baker-Fletcher and Garth Kasimu Baker-Fletcher, *My Sister, My Brother: Womanist and Xodus God-Talk*, no. 12, Bishop Henry McNeal Turner/Sojourner Truth Series in Black Religion (Maryknoll, N.Y.: Orbis, 1997), 90.

4. Ibid., 155.

5. Moving in a different direction than I do here, Carol P. Christ believes that part of an individual's spirit remains in places where those individuals frequented: "Part of [the ancestors'] spirits or energy fields entered into the places they loved when they were alive and remained there." In those cases, visiting grave sites and favorite locations of the ancestors gives those of us in the present access to the spirit of those who have died. See "We Are Nature: Environmental Ethics in a Different Key" (paper presented at the Sixth International Whitehead Conference, Salzburg, Austria, 5 July 2006).

6. Baker-Fletcher, *My Sister, My Brother*, 187.

7. Ibid., 30.

8. Ibid., 91.

9. In a technical sense, we are never alone because of our relationship with the rest of the world. I am referring to "alone" in the popular use of the word.

10. See anthropologist Melville J. Herskovits's *The Myth of the Negro Past* (Boston: Beacon, 1958), and sociologist E. Franklin Frazier's *The Negro Family in the United States* (Chicago: University of Chicago Press, 1939), for the most famous discussants of this tension.

11. Albert J. Raboteau, *Slave Religion: The "Invisible Institution" in the Antebellum South* (New York: Oxford University Press, 1978), 4.

12. I use the terms *syncretized*, *creolized*, and *blended* interchangeably to indicate the way that two or more religions and cultures encountered one another and created a new religion that bears the markers of its forebears. Indeed, a new religion has come into being, but there are still strong commonalities with the "parent" religion. In anthropology, these terms are hotly debated and connote the preferences of different emphases. In the process of becoming described in the postmodern theological framework, these "new" religions are examples of the process of becoming on a larger cultural and religious scale.

13. Raboteau, *Slave Religion*, 5–7.

14. Leonard Barrett, "African Religion in the Americas: The Islands in Between," in *African Religions: A Symposium*, ed. Newell S. Booth Jr. (New York: NOK, 1977), 193.

15. Frances Henry, *Reclaiming African Religions in Trinidad: The Socio-Political Legitimation of the Orisha and Spiritual Baptist Faiths* (Jamaica: University of the West Indies Press, 2003), 1.

16. Many òrìṣà in Yoruba religion have multiple names, although they signify the same force. This is partly attributable to the distribution of the religion throughout Yorubaland, and the Yoruba-based religions in the New World. Here I may refer to Olódùmarè/Olorun, Obatala/Oriṣa-nla, Orunmila/Ifâ, Èṣù/Elegba/Elegbara. I will also use the "ṣ" to indicate the sound of "sh." There is no consistency in scholarship (usually because of the capability of word processors and attempts to translate into English), so "àṣẹ" is also "ashe" and "òrìṣà" is also "orisha." Note òrìṣà is the same in the plural or singular usage.

17. Barrett, "African Religion," 183.

18. Also written as "Pukkumina."

19. Rudolph Eastman and Maureen Warner-Lewis connect carnival traditions to African traditional religions: "Masquerade occasions have also involved the practice of African spirituality. This is because masquerade groups have grown out of secret societies on the West African model. . . . Some masquerades represent spirits: the *jab molasi* or *jabjab*, based on the Efik *ekpo* ancestor masquerades." Eastman and Warner-Lewis, "Forms of African Spirituality in Trinidad and Tobago," in *African Spirituality: Forms, Meanings and Expressions*, no. 3, World Spirituality: An

Encyclopedic History of the Religious Quest, ed. Jacob K. Olupona (New York: Crossroad, 2000), 404.

20. Dianne M. Stewart, "African Religious Traditions in the Caribbean," in *Encyclopedia of Women and Religion in North America*, ed. Rosemary Keller and Rosemary Radford Reuther (Bloomington: Indiana University Press, forthcoming), 9.

21. Eastman and Warner-Lewis, "Forms of African Spirituality," 404.

22. Margarite Fernandez Olmos and Lizabeth Paravisini-Gebert, *Creole Religions of the Caribbean: An Introduction from Vodou and Santeria to Obeah and Espiritismo* (New York: New York University Press, 2003), 131.

23. Barrett, "African Religion in the Americas," 190.

24. Olmos and Paravisini-Gebert, *Creole Religions of the Caribbean*, 131.

25. One 1787 Jamaican law states, "Any slave who shall pretend to any supernatural power, in order to affect the health or lives of others, or promote the purposes of rebellion shall upon conviction thereof suffer death, or such other punishment as the Court shall think proper to direct." Joseph J. Williams, *Voodoos and Obeahs: Phrases of West Indian Witchcraft* (New York: Dial, 1932), 159–61, quoted in ibid., 132.

26. John Campbell, *Obeah: Yes or No? A Study of Obeah and Spiritualism in Guyana* (1976), 39, quoted in ibid., 133.

27. Daniel Yon, "Identity and Differences in the Caribbean Diaspora: Case Study from Metropolitan Toronto" in *The Reordering of Culture: Latin America, the Caribbean and Canada in the Hood*, ed. Alvina Ruprecht (Canada: Carleton University Press, 1995), 491.

28. Larry G. Murphy, ed., *Down by the Riverside: Readings in African American Religion* (New York: New York University Press, 2000).

29. Raboteau, *Slave Religion*, 55–92.

30. See Yvonne P. Chireau, *Black Magic: Religion and the African American Conjuring Tradition* (Berkeley: University of California Press, 2003).

31. See Margaret Washington Creel, *A Peculiar People: Slave Religion and Community Culture among the Gullahs* (New York: New York University Press, 1988).

32. Mary Cuthrell-Curry, "African-Derived Religion in the African-American Community in the United States," in *African Spirituality*, 450–51.

33. Ibid., 451.

34. Ibid., 453–54.

35. Ibid., 458.

36. Gary Edwards and John Mason, *Black Gods: Orisa Studies in the New World* (Brooklyn: Yoruba Theological Archministry, 1985), 3–4.

37. Jacob K. Olupona, "To Praise and to Reprimand: Ancestors and Spirituality in African Society and Culture," in *Ancestors in Post-Contact Religion: Roots, Ruptures, and Modernity's Memory*, ed. Steven J. Friesen (Cambridge: Harvard University Press, 2001), 51.

38. Ibid.

39. I use "ancestors" as described by Olupona. This reflects the way the term is used within African traditional religions. This "ancestor" will be distinguished from my use of the term.

40. Ibid.

41. Again, Carol P. Christ has a different way of thinking of ancestor veneration in keeping with the previously noted understanding of place and spirit. She writes, "Venerating the ancestors is not simply about connection to human forebears, but also about their connection (and our own) to place. Venerating the ancestors is a way of expanding the boundaries of our skins, horizontally through time, and vertically into the earth. When we feel ourselves connected to places, we are more likely to want to preserve them." See Carol P. Christ, "We Are Nature: Environmental Ethics in a Different Key" (paper presented at the Sixth International Whitehead Conference, Salzburg, Austria, 5 July 2006).

42. Olupona, "To Praise and to Reprimand," 50.

43. Ibid., 57.

44. Ibid., 58.

45. Ibid., 60–61.

46. The concept of spirit possession is widely used by ethnographers and anthropologists to refer to a religious practice that is common to the world's indigenous religions, and sometimes found in Western religious practices as well—most notably those influenced by Christian holiness and Pentecostal traditions.

47. I. M. Lewis, *Ecstatic Religion: A Study of Shamanism and Spirit Possession*, 3rd ed. (New York: Penguin, 1971; New York: Routledge, 2003), 15.

48. Carl B. Becker, *Paranormal Experience and Survival of Death* (Albany: State University of New York Press, 1993), 11, quoted in David Ray Griffin, *Parapsychology, Philosophy and Spirituality: A Postmodern Explanation* (Albany: State University of New York Press, 1997), 169.

49. See Marjorie Hewitt Suchocki, *The End of Evil: Process Eschatology in Historical Context* (Albany: State University of New York Press, 1988), for a full discussion of this concept. I have omitted many details of her description in the interest of using more accessible language than the discipline-specific language of process theology. I have tried to retain the spirit of her argument, highlighting those aspects that contribute to the concept of ancestral immortality outlined here.

50. Ibid., 96.

51. Baker-Fletcher, *My Sister, My Brother*, 91.

52. Anthony B. Pinn, *Varieties of African American Religious Experience* (Minneapolis: Fortress Press, 1998), 33.

53. Baker-Fletcher, *My Sister, My Brother*, 156.

54. See Awo Fá'lokun Fatunmbi, *Ìwà-pèlé: Ifa Quest, The Search for the Source of Santería and Lucumí* (Bronx: Original, 1991).

55. Suchocki does have an active subjective immortality in God, but not in the world.

56. Whitehead, *Process and Reality*, 215.

57. Marjorie Hewitt Suchocki, *The Fall to Violence: Original Sin in Relational Theology* (New York: Continuum, 1994), 41.

58. Griffin, *Parapsychology, Philosophy and Spirituality*, 273.

59. LeRhonda S. Manigault, "Listening to the Dead Speak: Gullah/Geechee Women and the Ethnographic Imagination" (paper presented at the Workshop on Race and Religion: Thought, Practice and Meaning, University of Chicago, 30 October 2007). See Manigault's doctoral dissertation, "'Ah Tulk to de Dead All de Time': An Investigation of Gullah Culture through Womanist Ethnography" (Atlanta: Emory University, 2007).

Chapter 5

1. June Jordan and Bernice Johnson Reagon put this poem to music for the female a capella group Sweet Honey in the Rock's song "Oughta Be a Woman," from *Good News* (Chicago: Flying Fish Records, Songtalk Publishing Company, 1981). Also referenced in Barbara Smith, "Introduction," in *Home Girls: A Black Feminist Anthology* (New York: Kitchen Table—Women of Color Press, 1983), xxix.

2. Octavia Butler, *Parable of the Sower* (New York: Warner, 1993).

3. Emilie M. Townes, *In a Blaze of Glory: Womanist Spirituality as Social Witness* (Nashville: Abingdon, 1995).

4. Katie G. Cannon, *Katie's Canon: Womanism and the Soul of the Black Community* (New York: Continuum, 1995), 61.

5. Joanna Russ, "What Can a Heroine Do? Or Why Women Can't Write," in *Images of Women in Fiction*, ed. Susan Comillon (Bowling Green, Ohio: Bowling Green University Popular Press, 1972), 18.

6. Dingbo Wu, "Understanding Utopian Literature," *Extrapolation* 34, no. 3 (Fall 1993): 242.

7. Peyton E. Richter, ed., *Utopia/Dystopia?* (Cambridge, Mass.: Schenkman, 1975), 17.

8. Joseph H. Wellbank, "Utopia and the Constraints of Justice," in Richter, ed., *Utopia/Dystopia?* 33.

9. Ibid., 33–34.

10. Preston Williams, "Black Perspectives on Utopia," in Richter, ed., *Utopia/Dystopia?* 51.

11. Ibid.

12. Ruby Rohrlich, "Introduction," in *Women in Search of Utopia: Mavericks and Mythmakers*, ed. Ruby Rohrlich and Elaine Hoffman Baruch (New York: Schocken, 1984), xii.

13. Ibid., 3.

14. Marleen Barr, *Alien to Femininity: Speculative Fiction and Feminist Theory* (Westport, Conn.: Greenwood, 1987), xxii, n. 1.

15. Ibid., xvii–xviii.

16. Ibid., 61.

17. Ibid., 63.

18. Ibid., 73.

19. Ibid., 80.

20. Ibid., 81.

21. Wu, "Understanding Utopian Literature," 243.

22. Wole Soyinka, *Myth, Literature and the African World* (Cambridge: Cambridge University Press, 1976).

23. Henry Louis Gates Jr., *The Signifying Monkey: A Theology of African-American Literary Criticism* (New York: Oxford University Press, 1988), 5.

24. Jacob K. Olupona, "To Praise and to Reprimand: Ancestors and Spirituality in African Society and Culture," in *Ancestors in Post-Contact Religion: Roots, Ruptures, and Modernity's Memory*, ed. Steven J. Friesen (Cambridge: Harvard University Press, 2001), 61.

25. Gates, *The Signifying Monkey*, 4.

26. Alexis Brooks DeVita, *Mythatypes: Signatures and Signs of African/Diaspora and Black Goddesses* (Westport, Conn.: Greenwood, 2000), 6. In addition, her concept of mythatypes is not limited to application in Pan-African women's literature. She also asserts the presence of mythatypes in European literature; see pp. 23–27. In those cases, she looks at Egyptian gods and goddesses because of the North African roots of classical Greek and European civilization.

27. Ibid., 1–2.

28. Ibid., 229–30.

29. Ibid., 230.

30. Awo Fá'lokun Fatunmbi, *Oya: Ifa and the Spirit of the Wind* (Bronx: Original Publications, 1993), 12.

31. Akinwumi Isola, "Oya: Inspiration and Empowerment," *Dialogue and Alliance* 12 (Spring-Summer 1998): 61.

32. Judith Gleason, *Oya: In Praise of an African Goddess* (San Francisco: HarperSanFrancisco, 1992), 38.

33. Also spelled "Shango."

34. Gleason, *Oya: In Praise*, 60–61.

35. Ibid., 18.

36. Ibid., 7.

37. Ibid., 1.

38. Ibid., 12.

39. Butler, *Parable of the Sower*, 143.

40. Ibid, 54.

41. Gleason, *Oya: In Praise*, 32.

42. Judith Gleason, "Oya in the Company of the Saints," *Journal of the American Academy of Religion* 68, no. 2 (June 2000): 276.

43. Gleason, *Oya: In Praise*, 31.

44. Butler, *Parable of the Sower*, 143.

45. Ibid., 35.

46. Ibid., 44.

47. Ibid., 15.

48. Ibid., 13.

49. Ibid., 16.

50. Ibid., 173.

51. Ibid., 124.

52. Ibid., 36.

53. Fatunmbi, *Oya*, 3.

54. Butler, *Parable of the Sower*, 301.

55. Ibid., 69.

56. Ibid., 78.

57. Ibid., 79.

58. Ibid., 78.

59. Ibid., 26.

60. Ibid., 22.

61. Fatunmbi, *Oya*, 3.

62. Ibid.

63. Butler, *Parable of the Sower*, 25.

64. Ibid., 295.

65. Ibid., 15.

66. Ibid., 221.

67. Ibid., 247.

68. Ibid., 309.

69. Ibid.

70. Gleason, *Oya: In Praise*, 1.

71. Ibid., 2.

72. Although she was one of three wives in her human relationship with Ṣango, Oya is known as an independent woman who protects the rights of women. In her marriage to a mortal hunter, Oya remained childless for many years. During that time, she experienced the contempt of childless women in Yoruba society. Isola links this passion about the mistreatment of women to the origin of the Egungun cult: "*Oya* decided to do something about the traditional discrimination against women and their poor living conditions. She discovered that men routinely abused and battered women. She decided to found a cult that would protect the rights of women." Isola, "Oya: Inspiration and Empowerment," 68.

73. Ibid., 70.

74. Gleason, *Oya: In Praise*, 2.

75. Butler, *Parable of the Sower*, 291.

76. Ibid., 115.

77. Ibid., 193.

78. Ibid., 84.

79. Ibid., 222.

80. Alfred North Whitehead, *Science and the Modern World: Lowell Lectures, 1925* (New York: Macmillan, 1925; reprint, New York: Free Press, 1967), 51.

81. Butler, *Parable of the Sower*, 79.

82. Ibid., 262.

83. Ibid., 85.

84. Ibid., 179.

85. Ibid., 223.

86. Ibid., 213.

87. Ibid., 269.

88. Ibid., 99.

89. Jenny Jarvie, "Black Clergy Tackle Homophobia: A Summit Put on by a Gay Rights Group Gathers Christian Leaders to Explore Attitudes Toward Homosexuality," *Los Angeles Times*, January 21, 2006, http://www.aegis.org/news/Lt/2006/LT060107.html (accessed December 2, 2007).

90. This information is cited in Herndon L. Davis, "God, Gays and the Black Church: Keeping the Faith within the Black Community, Part II," special to AOL Black Voices, September 2, 2005. http://www.blackvoices.com/black_lifestyle/soul_spirit_headlines_features/canvas/feature_article/_a/god-gays-and-the-black-church-keeping/20050825153809990001 (accessed December 2, 2007). The leading cause for the spread of HIV among black women and men is sexual contact—heterosexual contact for black women and homosexual contact for black men.

91. United Church of Christ, "Statement of Faith of the United Church of Christ," United Church of Christ, http://www.ucc.org/beliefs/statement-of-faith.html (accessed December 2, 2007).

92. Exodus International, "Who We Are," Exodus International, http://exodus.to/content/category/6/24/57/ (accessed December 10, 2007).

93. Melva Wilson Costen, *In Spirit and in Truth: The Music of African American Worship* (Louisville: Westminster John Knox, 2004), 1.

94. Kathi Elaine Martin (GSN Ministries) in discussion with the author, October 2007.

95. Cornel West and Eddie S. Glaude Jr., "Introduction," in *African American Religious Thought: An Anthology* (Louisville: Westminster John Knox, 2003), xxii.

96. Drew Jubera, "Atlanta: A Bug for Black Gays," *Atlanta Journal-Constitution*, February 22, 2004, http://gay_blog.blogspot.com/2004/02/atlanta-hub-for-black-gays.html (accessed December 2, 2007).

97. Trevor Pettiford, quoted in Jubera.

98. Jubera, "Atlanta: A Bug for Black Gays."

99. Ibid.

100. Ibid.

101. Ibid.

102. Ibid.

103. Horace L. Griffin, *Their Own Receive Them Not: African American Lesbians and Gays in Black Churches* (Cleveland: Pilgrim, 2006), 111–12.

104. These three responses—filtering, searching, and abandoning—are identified in Kathi Elaine Martin, "Wounded and Healed in the House of a Friend: The Faith Experience of African American Gay and Lesbian Persons" (D.Min. diss., Columbia Theological Seminary, 2001), 9.

105. Associated Press, "Some Black Ministers Openly Welcome Gays, Lesbians into Their Flocks," *The Oak Ridger Online*, September 20, 2002, http://www.oakridger.com/stories/092002/rel_0920020034.html (accessed December 2, 2007).

106. David Smith (former member, GSN Ministries) in discussion with the author, December 2007.

107. Griffin, *Their Own Receive Them Not*, 187–88.

108. Ibid., 187.

109. Donna Payne, quoted in "Some Black Ministers Openly Welcome."

110. Jubera, "Atlanta: A Bug for Black Gays."

111. Quoted in Martin, "Wounded and Healed," 10.

112. Griffin notes that there are four types of passing in these circumstances: guilty, angry, silent, and opportunistic. *Their Own Receive Them Not*, 140–61.

113. Ibid., 146.

114. Martin, "Wounded and Healed," 14–15.

115. Jubera, "Atlanta: A Bug for Black Gays."

116. Frank M. Reid III, quoted in Davis, "God, Gays and the Black Church."

117. Ibid.

118. Kathi Martin, "Flip the Script," Sermon, *Day 1: A Ministry of the Alliance of Christian Media*, November 16, 2003, http://www.day1.net/print.php5?tid=42 (accessed December 2, 2007).

119. Ray Hammond, quoted in Davis, "God, Gays and the Black Church."

120. Human Rights Campaign, "A GLBT Community Response to 700 Club and Charlene Cothran," *FemmeNoir: the WebPortal for Women of Color*, August 21, 2007, http://www.femmenoir.net/new/content/view/504/9/ (accessed December 2, 2007).

121. Ibid.

122. Jarvie, "Black Clergy Tackle Homophobia." Sharpton is committed to working on this issue. He was referencing the gay rights advocacy group National Black Justice Coalition's first-ever black church summit in January 2006.

123. Jubera, "Atlanta: A Bug for Black Gays."

124. Jarvie, "Black Clergy Tackle Homophobia."

125. Martin, discussion with author.

126. D. L. Foster, "The Question Is . . . : Black Gays and Ex-gays Alike Look to Church Leaders for Answers That May Never Come," *Witness Freedom Ministries: Leading the Way out of Homosexuality and into Holiness*, April 9, 2002, http://www.witnessfortheworld.org/cm27.html (accessed December 2, 2007). This Christian organization encourages and supports women and men of color to abandon their homosexual identities and activities.

127. Other issues include school choice, affordable health care, and "wealth creation." Ellen Barry, "Atlanta 'Legacy' March Troubles Rights Leaders; King's Daughter in Anti-gay Marriage Protest," *San Francisco Chronicle*, December 11, 2004, http://www.sfgate.com/cgi-bin/article.cgi?f=/c/a/2004/12/11/MNGP-DAAEJ01.DTL (accessed December 2, 2007).

128. Charlene Cothran, interview by Charlene Israel, *700 Club*, CBN, July 21, 2007, 10 min., 9 sec.; from Charlene Israel, "A Lesbian's Deliverance," CBNNews.com, http://www.cbn.com/CBNnews/180565.aspx (accessed April 4, 2008).

129. Laura Douglas-Brown, "Ex-gay Tools: After a Summer Filled with Headline-Grabbing 'Former' Homosexuals, Atlanta Activists Take Matters—and Video Cameras—into Their Own Hands," *The Southern Voice*, 31 August 2007, http://www.southernvoice.com/2007/8-31/view/editorial/7402.cfm (accessed December 2, 2007).

130. HRC Media, "A GLBTQ Response to 700 Club and Charlene Cothran," August 15, 2007, 8 min., 21 sec., http://www.youtube.com/watch?v=m4LI0Vm KZrw&feature=related (accessed December 2, 2007).

131. Dyana Bagby, "'We Are the Rest of the Bird': Lesbian Christians Gather in Atlanta to Reinforce Coming Out and Not Ceding Church Leadership to the 'Right Wing,'" *Southern Voice*, July 6, 2007, http://www.sovo.com/2007/7-6/ locallife/feature/7168.cfm (accessed December 2, 2007).

132. Townes, *Blaze of Glory*, 81.

133. Martin, discussion with author.

134. Ibid.

135. Quoted in Jarvie, "Black Clergy Tackle Homophobia."

136. Hammond, quoted in Jarvie.

137. Martin, discussion with author.

138. "Intersex" refers to individuals who, in some way, have both male and female biological criteria.

139. Kathi E. Martin, "I Am Everyday People," *Preach 2 Me*, September 2007, http://www.preach2me.com/p_women.htm (accessed December 2, 2007).

140. Ibid.

141. Martin, "Wounded and Healed," 23.

142. Martin, discussion with author.

143. Martin, "Wounded and Healed," 23.

144. Smith, discussion with author. "God Is Still Speaking" or "The Still Speaking Initiative" is the name of the identity and slogan of the advertising campaign adopted by the United Church of Christ in 2004.

145. Martin, discussion with author.

146. Martin, "Wounded and Healed," 27.

147. Ibid.

148. Martin, discussion with author.

149. Ibid.

150. Ibid.

151. Kathi E. Martin, "Mysterious Visitations," Sermon, *Day 1: A Ministry of the Alliance of Christian Media*, December 21, 2003, http://www.day1.net/print .php5?tid=37 (accessed December 2, 2007).

152. Martin, discussion with author.

153. Ibid.

154. Ibid.

155. Ibid.

156. Ibid.

157. Martin, "Wounded and Healed," 23.

158. Ibid., 28.

159. Ibid., 30.

160. Smith, discussion with author.

161. Ibid.

162. Elliott Sommerville, "A Talk with Rev. Kathi Martin: Body, Soul & Spirit," *Together in Love: Celebrating Committed Same Gender Relationships in the African American Community*, http://www.togetherinlove.org/zine/articles/full/a_talk_with_rev_kathi_martin/ (accessed December 2, 2007).

163. William Warch, *The New Thought Christian* (Marina del Rey, Calif.: Christian Living, 1977), 9; quoted in Martin, "Wounded and Healed," 12.

164. Martin, discussion with author.

165. Ibid.

166. Smith, discussion with author.

167. Sommerville, "A Talk with Rev. Kathi Martin."

168. Martin, "Wounded and Healed," 21.

169. Martin, discussion with author.

170. Ibid.

171. Ibid.

172. Smith, discussion with author.

173. Ibid.

174. Ibid.

175. Ibid.

176. Ibid.

Bibliography

Verse

Nathan, Fermand, ed. *Birago Diop: Écrivain Sénégalais*. Classiques du Monde, Littérature Africaine 6. Paris: F. Nathan, 1965.

Jordan, June, and Bernice Johnson Reagon. "Oughta Be a Woman," *Good News*. Chicago: Flying Fish Records, Songtalk Publishing Company, 1981.

Sanchez, Sonia. "For Sweet Honey in the Rock," *Shake Loose My Skin: New and Selected Poems*. Boston: Beacon Press, 2000.

Womanist and Black Theologies

Anderson, Victor. *Beyond Ontological Blackness: An Essay on African American Religious and Cultural Criticism*. New York: Continuum, 1995.

Baker-Fletcher, Karen. *Sisters of Dust, Sisters of Spirit: Womanist Wordings of God and Creation*. Minneapolis: Fortress Press, 1995.

Baker-Fletcher, Karen and Garth KASIMU Baker-Fletcher. *My Sister, My Brother: Womanist and Xodus God-Talk*. Bishop Henry McNeal Turner/Sojourner Truth Series in Black Religion, no. 12. Maryknoll, N.Y.: Orbis Books, 1997.

_____. *Dancing with God: The Trinity in Womanist Perspective*. St. Louis: Chalice Press, 2006.

_____. "A Womanist Journey." *Deeper Shades of Purple: Womanism in Religion and Society*. Religion, Race, and Ethnicity. Ed. Stacey M. Floyd-Thomas, no. 10. New York: New York University Press, 2006. 158–75.

Beale, Frances. "Double Jeopardy: To Be Black and Female." In *Black Theology: A Documentary History, 1966–1979*, eds. James H. Cone and Gayraud Wilmore, 284–292. Maryknoll, N.Y.: Orbis Books, 1979.

Cannon, Katie G. *Katie's Canon: Womanism and the Soul of the Black Community*. New York: Continuum, 1995.

Cooey, Paula M., William R. Eakin, and Jay B. McDaniel, eds. *After Patriarchy: Feminist Reconstructions of the World Religions*. Maryknoll, N.Y.: Orbis Books, 1991.

Coleman, Monica A. "An Exchange of Gifts: Process and Womanist Theologies," *Handbook on Process Theology*. Ed. Donna Bowman and Jay McDaniel. St. Louis: Chalice Press, 2006. 160–76.

_____. "Must I Be Womanist?" *Journal of Feminist Studies in Religion* 22, no. 1 (Spring 2006): 85–96.

Cone, James H. and Gayraud S. Wilmore, eds. *Black Theology: A Documentary History, 1966–1979*. Maryknoll, N.Y.: Orbis Books, 1979.

_____. *Black Theology: A Documentary History, Volume 2: 1980–1992*. Maryknoll, N.Y.: Orbis Books, 1993.

Crawford, A. Elaine. "Womanist Christology: Where Have We Come From and Where Are We Going?" *Review and Expositor* 95 (1998): 367–82.

Douglas, Kelly Brown. *The Black Christ*. Bishop Henry McNeal Studies in North American Black Religion, no. 9. Maryknoll, N.Y.: Orbis Books, 1994.

_____. "Is Christ a Black Woman?: A Womanist Understanding of Christ Is Rooted in Healing Fractured Communities." *The Other Side* 30 (1994): 8–11, 54.

Eiesland, Nancy L. *The Disabled God: Toward a Liberatory Theology of Disability*. Nashville: Abingdon Press, 1994.

Floyd-Thomas, Stacey M. *Deeper Shades of Purple: Womanism in Religion and Society*, Religion, Race, and Ethnicity, ed. no. 10. New York: New York University Press, 2006.

Grant, Jacquelyn. *White Women's Christ and Black Women's Jesus: Feminist Christology and Womanist Response*. American Academy of Religion Academy Series, no. 64. Atlanta: Scholars Press, 1989.

_____. "Tasks of a Prophetic Church." In *Theology in the Americas: Detroit II Papers*. Probe Third World Studies, ed. Cornel West, Caridad Guidote, and Margaret Coakley, 136–42. Maryknoll, N.Y.: Orbis Books, 1982.

_____. "The Sin of Servanthood and the Deliverance of Discipleship." In *A Troubling in My Soul: Womanist Perspectives on Evil and Suffering*, Bishop Henry McNeal Studies in North American Black Religion, ed. Emilie M. Townes, no. 8, 199–218. Maryknoll, N.Y.: Orbis Books, 1993.

_____. "Servanthood Revisited: Womanist Explorations of Servanthood Theology." In *Black Faith and Public Talk: Critical Essays on James H. Cone's Black Theology and Black Power*, ed., Dwight N. Hopkins, 126–37. Maryknoll, N.Y.: Orbis Books, 1999.

Harris, Melanie L. "Womanist Humanism: A New Hermeneutic," *Deeper Shades of Purple: Womanism in Religion and Society*. Religion, Race, and Ethnicity. Ed. Stacey M. Floyd-Thomas, no. 10. New York: New York University Press, 2006. 211–25.

_____. "Alice Walker's Ethics: An Analysis of Alice Walker's Non-Fiction Work as a Resource for Womanist Ethics." Ph.D. diss., Union Theological Seminary, New York, 2006.

_____. "Loving the Spirit: Expressions of Paganism in Alice Walker's Non-Fiction." Paper presented at the annual meeting of the American Academy of Religion. Washington, D.C., 20 November 2006.

Hill, Renee L. "Disrupted/Disruptive Movements: Black Theology and Black Power 1969/1999." In *Black Theology: A Documentary History, Volume 2: 1980–1992*, ed. James H. Cone and Gayraud S. Wilmore, 138–49. Maryknoll, N.Y.: Orbis Books, 1993.

Holmes, Barbara A. *Race and the Cosmos: An Invitation to View the World Differently*. Harrisburg, Pa.: Trinity Press International, 2002.

Hoover, Theressa. "Black Women and the Churches: Triple Jeopardy." In *Black Theology: A Documentary History, 1966–1979*, eds. James H. Cone and Gayraud Wilmore, 227–88. New York: Orbis Books, 1979.

Hopkins, Dwight N. *Introducing Black Theology of Liberation*. Maryknoll, N.Y.: Orbis Books, 1999.

_____, ed. *Black Faith and Public Talk: Critical Essays on James H. Cone's Black Theology and Black Power*. Maryknoll, N.Y.: Orbis Books, 1999.

Hucks, Tracey E. "Burning with a Flame in America: African American Women in African-Derived Traditions," *Journal of Feminist Studies in Religion* 17, no. 2 (2001): 89–106.

Majeed, Debra Mubashir. "Womanism Encounters Islam: A Muslim Scholar Considers the Efficacy of a Method Rooted in the Academy and the Church," *Deeper Shades of Purple: Womanism in Religion and Society*. Religion, Race, and Ethnicity. Ed. Stacey M. Floyd-Thomas, no. 10. New York: New York University Press, 2006. 38–53.

Medine, Carolyn. "Jan Willis's *Dreaming Me*: Constructing a Baptist-Buddhist Womanist Identity." Paper presented at the annual meeting of the American Academy of Religion. Washington, D.C., 20 November 2006.

Musser, Donald W., and Joseph L. Price. *A New Handbook of Christian Theology*. Nashville: Abingdon, 1992.

Ormerod, Neil. *Introducing Contemporary Theologies: The What and the Who of Theology Today*. Maryknoll, N.Y.: Orbis Books, 1997.

Pinn, Anthony B. *Why Lord? Suffering and Evil in Black Theology*. New York: Continuum, 1995.

Razak, Arisika. "Response to 'Must I Be Womanist?' " *Journal of Feminist Studies in Religion* 22, no. 1 (Spring 2006): 99–107.

Settles, Shani. "The Sweet Fire of Honey: Womanist Visions of Osun as a Methodology of Emancipation." *Deeper Shades of Purple: Womanism in Religion and Society*. Religion, Race, and Ethnicity. Ed. Stacey M. Floyd-Thomas, no. 10. New York: New York University Press, 2006. 191–206.

Skye, Lee Miena. "Response to 'Must I Be Womanist?' " *Journal of Feminist Studies in Religion* 22, no. 1 (Spring 2006): 119–23.

Smith, Barbara, ed. *Home Girls: A Black Feminist Anthology.* New York: Kitchen Table—Women of Color Press, 1983.

Terrell, JoAnne Marie. *Power in the Blood? The Cross in the African American Experience.* Bishop Henry McNeal Turner/Sojourner Truth Series in Black Religion, no. 15. Maryknoll, N.Y.: Orbis Books, 1998.

Thomas, Linda E. "Womanist Theology, Epistemology, and a New Anthropological Paradigm." *Cross Currents* 48 (1998–99): 488–99.

Townes, Emilie M. *In a Blaze of Glory: Womanist Spirituality as Social Witness.* Nashville: Abingdon Press, 1995.

_____, ed. *Embracing the Spirit: Womanist Perspectives on Hope, Salvation and Transformation,* Bishop Henry McNeal Turner/Sojourner Truth Series in Black Religion, no. 13. Maryknoll, N.Y.: Orbis Books, 1997.

_____, ed., *A Troubling in My Soul: Womanist Perspectives on Evil and Suffering,* Bishop Henry McNeal Studies in North American Black Religion, no. 8. Maryknoll, N.Y.: Orbis Books, 1993.

Walker, Alice. *In Search of Our Mothers' Gardens: Womanist Prose.* San Diego: Harcourt Brace Jovanovich, 1983.

Williams, Delores S. *Sisters in the Wilderness: The Challenge of Womanist God-Talk.* Maryknoll, N.Y.: Orbis Books, 1993.

_____. "The Color of Feminism: Or Speaking the Black Woman's Tongue." *Journal of Religious Thought* 43 (Spring–Summer 1986): 164–65.

_____. "Black Women's Surrogacy Experiences and the Christian Notion of Redemption," in *After Patriarchy: Feminist Reconstructions of the World Religions,* ed. Paula M. Cooey, William R. Eakin, and Jay B. McDaniel, 1–14. Maryknoll, N.Y.: Orbis Books, 1991.

_____. "A Womanist Perspective on Sin." In *A Troubling in My Soul: Womanist Perspectives on Evil and Suffering,* Bishop Henry McNeal Studies in North American Black Religion, ed. Emilie M. Townes, no. 8, 130–49. Maryknoll, N.Y.: Orbis Books, 1993.

_____. "Womanist Theology: Black Women's Voices." In *Black Theology, A Documentary History, Volume 2: 1980–1992,* ed., James Cone and Gayraud S. Wilmore, 265–72. Maryknoll, N.Y.: Orbis Books, 1993.

_____. "Re-Imagining Jesus," presented at the international gathering of women participating in the World Council of Churches' Ecumenical Decade in Solidarity with Women. Minneapolis. 5 November 1993.

_____. "Straight Talk, Plain Talk: Womanist Words about Salvation in a Social Context," *Embracing the Spirit: Womanist Perspectives on Hope, Salvation and Transformation,* Bishop Henry McNeal Turner/Sojourner Truth Series in Black Religion, ed. Emilie M. Townes, no. 13, 97–121. Maryknoll, N.Y.: Orbis Books, 1997.

Washington, James M. *A Testament of Hope: The Essential Writings and Speeches of Martin Luther King, Jr.* San Francisco: Harper & Row, 1986.

Process and Postmodern Theologies

Becker, Carl B. *Paranormal Experience and Survival of Death.* Albany: State University of New York Press, 1993.

Birch, Charles, and John B. Cobb, Jr. *The Liberation of Life: From the Cell to the Community.* Denton, Tex: Environmental Ethics Books, 1990.

Bowman, Donna, and Jay McDaniel, eds. *Handbook on Process Theology.* St. Louis: Chalice Press, 2006.

Christ, Carol P. *She Who Changes: Re-imagining the Divine in the World.* New York: Palgrave Macmillan, 2004.

————."We are Nature: Environmental Ethics in a Different Key." Paper presented at the Sixth International Whitehead Conference. Salzburg, Austria. 5 July 2006.

Cobb, John B., Jr. *The Structure of Christian Existence.* Philadelphia: Westminster Press, 1967.

————. *Christ in a Pluralistic Age.* Philadelphia: Westminster Press, 1975.

————. *Process Theology as Political Theology.* Philadelphia: Westminster Press, 1982.

————. *Can Christ Become Good News Again?* St. Louis: Chalice Press, 1991.

————. *God and the World.* Eugene, Ore.: Wipf and Stock Publishers, 1998.

————. "Christ beyond Creative Transformation," in *Encountering Jesus: A Debate on Christology*, ed. Stephen T. Davis, 141–78. Atlanta: John Knox Press, 1988.

————. "Christology in Process-Relational Perspective," *Word and Spirit: A Monastic Review* 8 (1986): 79–94.

Cobb, John B., Jr., and W. Widick Schroeder, eds. *Process Philosophy and Social Thought.* Chicago: Center for the Scientific Study of Religion, 1981.

Cobb, John B., Jr., and David Ray Griffin, *Process Theology: An Introductory Exposition.* Philadelphia: Westminster Press, 1976.

Griffin, David Ray. *The Reenchantment of Science: Postmodern Proposals.* SUNY Series in Constructive Postmodern Thought. Albany: State University of New York Press, 1988.

————. *Parapsychology, Philosophy and Spirituality: A Postmodern Explanation.* SUNY Series in Constructive Postmodern Thought. Albany: State University of New York Press, 1997.

_____. *Religion and Scientific Naturalism: Overcoming the Conflicts.* SUNY Series in Constructive Postmodern Thought. Albany: State University of New York Press, 2000.

_____. "Science and Religion: A Postmodern Perspective." *Beyond Conflict and Reduction: Between Philosophy, Science and Religion.* Louvain Philosophical Studies, 16. Ed. William Desmond, John Steffen, and Koen Decoster. Leuven: Leuven University Press, 2001.

Griffin, David R., William A. Beardslee, and Joe Holland. *Varieties of Postmodern Theology,* SUNY Series in Constructive Postmodern Thought. Albany: State University of New York Press, 1989.

Jones, William R. "Process Theology: Guardian of the Oppressor or Goad to the Oppressed: An Interim Assessment." *Process Studies* 18, no. 4 (Winter 1989): 268–81.

Keller, Catherine E. *Apocalypse Now and Then: A Feminist Guide to the End of the World.* Boston: Beacon Press, 1996.

Ogden, Schubert. *Faith and Freedom: Toward a Theology of Liberation.* Nashville: Abingdon Press, 1979.

Pederson, Ann. *God, Creation and All That Jazz: A Process of Composition and Improvisation.* St. Louis: Chalice Press, 2001.

Potter, Ronald C. "A Comparison of the Conceptions of God in Process and Black Theologies." *The Journal of the Interdenominational Center* 12, nos. 1–2 (Fall 1984–Spring 1985): 50–61.

Reeves, Gene. "Liberation: Process Theology and Black Experience." *Process Studies* 18, no. 4, 225–39.

Rescher, Nicholas. *Process Metaphysics: an Introduction to Process Philosophy.* SUNY Series in Philosophy. Albany: State University of New York Press, 1996.

Suchocki, Marjorie Hewitt. *The End of Evil: Process Eschatology in Historical Context.* Albany: State University of New York Press, 1988.

_____. *Fall to Violence: Original Sin in Relational Theology.* New York: Continuum, 1994.

Thandeka. "I've Known Rivers: Black Theology's Response to Process Theology." *Process Studies* 18, no. 4 (Winter 1989): 282–93.

Walker, Theodore, Jr., *Mothership Connections: A Black Atlantic Synthesis of Neoclassical Metaphysics and Black Theology.* SUNY Series in Constructive Postmodern Thought. Albany: State University of New York Press, 2004.

_____. "Hartshorne's Neoclassical Theism and Black Theology." *Process Studies* 18, no. 4 (Winter 1989): 240–58.

White, Heath. *Postmodernism 101: A First Course for the Curious Christian.* Grand Rapids: Brazos Press, 2006.

Whitehead, Alfred North. *Science and the Modern World: Lowell Lectures, 1925.* New York: Macmillan, 1925; reprint, New York: The Free Press, 1967.

_____. *Religion in the Making: Lowell Lectures, 1926.* New York: Macmillan, 1926; reprint with introduction by Judith A. Jones and glossary by Randall E. Auxier, New York: Fordham University Press, 1996.

_____. *Adventures of Ideas.* New York: Simon and Schuster, 1933; reprint, New York: The Free Press, 1967.

_____. *Process and Reality: An Essay in Cosmology.* Corrected Edition. Ed. David Ray Griffin and Donald W. Sherburne. New York: The Free Press, 1978.

Young, Henry James. *Hope in Process: A Theology of Social Pluralism.* Minneapolis: Fortress Press, 1990.

_____. "Process Theology and Black Liberation: Testing the Whiteheadian Metaphysical Foundations." *Process Studies* 18, no. 4 (Winter 1989): 259–67.

Zbaraschuk, George Michael. "The Purposes of God: Providence as Process-Historical Liberation." Ph.D. diss., Claremont Graduate University, 2002.

Black and African Traditional Religions

Barrett, Leonard. "African Religion in the Americas: The Islands in Between." In *African Religions: A Symposium,* ed. Newell S. Booth Jr., 183–215. New York: NOK Publishers, 1977.

Chevannes, Barry. "Some Notes on African Religious Survivals in the Caribbean." *Caribbean Journal of Religious Studies* 5 (S 1983): 18–28.

Chireau, Yvonne P. *Black Magic: Religion and the African American Conjuring Tradition.* Berkeley: University of California Press, 2003.

Cortez, Julio Garcia. *Pataki: Leyendas y misterios de Orisha Africanos.* Miami: Ediciones Universal, 1980.

Cosentino, Donald. "Who Is That Fellow in the Many-Colored Cap? Transformation of Eshu in Old and New World Mythologies." *The Journal of American Folklore* 100, no. 397 (July–September 1987): 261–75.

Costen, Melva Wilson. *In Spirit and in Truth: The Music of African American Worship.* Louisville: Westminster John Knox, 2004.

Creel, Margaret Washington. *A Peculiar People: Slave Religion and Community Culture among the Gullahs.* New York: New York University Press, 1988.

Cuthrell-Curry, Mary. "African-Derived Religion in the African-American Community in the United States." In *African Spirituality: Forms, Meanings and Symbols,* ed. Jacob K. Olupona, 450–66. New York: Crossroad, 2000.

Deren, Maya. *Divine Horsemen: The Living Gods of Haiti.* New York: Thames and Hudson, 1953; Kingston, N.Y.: McPherson and Company, 1970.

Drewal, Henry, and Margaret Thompson Drewal. *Gelede: Art and Female Power among the Yoruba.* Bloomington: Indiana University Press, 1983.

Eastman, Rudolph, and Maureen Warner-Lewis. "Forms of African Spirituality in Trinidad and Tobago." In *African Spirituality: Forms, Meanings and Expressions,* World Spirituality: An Encyclopedic History of the Religious Quest, ed. Jacob K. Olupona, no. 3, 403–15. New York: Crossroad, 2000.

Edwards, Gary, and John Mason. *Black Gods: Orisa Studies in the New World.* Brooklyn, N.Y.: Yoruba Theological Archministry, 1985.

Fatunmbi, Awo Fá'lokun. *Ìwa-pèlé: Ifa Quest, The Search for the Source of Santería and Lucumí.* Bronx, N.Y.: Original Publications, 1991.

————. *Oya: Ifa and the Spirit of the Wind.* Bronx, N.Y.: Original Publications, 1993.

Frazier, E. Franklin. *The Negro Family in the United States.* Chicago: University of Chicago Press, 1939.

Gleason, Judith. *Oya: In Praise of an African Goddess.* San Francisco: HarperSanFrancisco, 1992.

————. "Oya in the Company of the Saints," *Journal of the American Academy of Religion* 68, no. 2 (June 2000): 265–91.

————, ed. *Leaf and Bone: African Praise-Poems.* New York: Penguin Books, 1980.

Henry, Frances. *Reclaiming African Religions in Trinidad: The Socio-Political Legitimation of the Orisha and Spiritual Baptist Faiths.* Jamaica: University of the West Indies Press, 2003.

Herskovits, Melville J. *The Myth of the Negro Past.* Boston: Beacon Press, 1958.

Isola, Akinwumi. "Oya: Inspiration and Empowerment." *Dialogue and Alliance* 12 (Spring–Summer 1998): 61–70.

Karenga, Maulana. "Black Religion: The African Model." In *Down by the Riverside: Readings in African American Religion,* ed. Larry G. Murphy, 41–47. New York: New York University Press, 2000.

Leach, MacEdward. "Jamaica Duppy Lore." *Journal of American Folklore* 71, no. 293 (July–September 1961): 207–15.

Lewis, I. M. *Ecstatic Religion: A Study of Shamanism and Spirit Possession,* 3rd ed. New York: Penguin, 1971; New York: Routledge, 2003.

Manigault, LeRhonda S. " 'Ah Tulk to de Dead All de Time': An Investigation of Gullah Culture through Womanist Ethnography." Ph.D. diss., Emory University, 2007.

Moore, Joseph G. "Music and Dance as Expressions of Religious Worship in Jamaica." In *African Religious Groups and Beliefs: Papers in Honor of William R. Bascom,* ed. Simon Ottenberg, 265–89. Sadar, India: Archana Publications, 1982.

Murphy, Joseph M. *Santería: An African Religion in America.* Boston: Beacon Press, 1988.

Murphy, Larry G., ed. *Down by the Riverside: Readings in African American Religion.* New York: New York University Press, 2000.

Olmos, Margarite Fernandez, and Lizabeth Paravisini-Gebert. *Creole Religions of the Caribbean: An Introduction from Vodou and Santeria to Obeah and Espiritismo.* New York: New York University Press, 2003.

Olupona, Jacob K., ed. *African Spirituality: Forms, Meanings and Expressions.* World Spirituality: An Encyclopedic History of the Religious Quest. New York: Crossroad, 2000.

————. "To Praise and to Reprimand: Ancestors and Spirituality in African Society and Culture," in *Ancestors in Post-Contact Religion: Roots, Ruptures, and Modernity's Memory,* ed. Steven J. Friesen. Cambridge: Harvard University Press, 2001: 49–71.

Pinn, Anthony B. *Varieties of African American Religious Experience.* Minneapolis: Fortress Press, 1998.

Pradel, Lucie. *African Beliefs in the New World: Popular Literary Traditions of the Caribbean.* Trans. Catherine Bernard. Trenton, N.J.: Africa World Press, 2001.

Raboteau, Albert J. *Slave Religion: The "Invisible Institution" in the Antebellum South.* New York: Oxford University Press, 1978.

Stewart, Dianne M. "African Religious Traditions in the Caribbean." In *Encyclopedia of Women and Religion in North America,* ed. Rosemary Keller and Rosemary Radford Reuther, 1–12. Bloomington: Indiana University Press, forthcoming.

Thompson, Robert Farris. *Flash of the Spirit: African and Afro-American Art and Philosophy.* New York: Vintage, 1983.

West, Cornel, and Eddie S. Glaude Jr., "Introduction," *African American Religious Thought: An Anthology.* Louisville: Westminster John Knox, 2003.

Williams, Joseph J. *Voodoos and Obeahs: Phrases of West Indian Witchcraft.* New York: Dial, 1932.

Wilmore, Gayraud S. *Black Religion and Radicalism: An Interpretation of the Religious History of African Americans,* 3rd. ed. Maryknoll, N.Y.: Orbis Books, 1998.

Yon, Daniel. "Identity and Differences in the Caribbean Diaspora: Case Study from Metropolitan Toronto." In *The Reordering of Culture: Latin America, the Caribbean and Canada in the Hood,* ed. Alvina Ruprecht, 479-498. Canada: Carleton University Press, 1995.

Black Women's Science Fiction and *Parable of the Sower*

Barr, Marleen. *Alien to Femininity: Speculative Fiction and Feminist Theory.* New York: Greenwood Press, 1987.

Butler, Octavia E., *Parable of the Sower*. New York: Warner, 1993.

DeVita, Alexis Brooks. *Mythatypes: Signatures and Signs of African/Diaspora and Black Goddesses*. Westport, Conn.: Greenwood Press, 2000.

Gates, Henry Louis, Jr. *The Signifying Monkey: A Theology of African-American Literary Criticism*. New York: Oxford University Press, 1988.

Lawing, John V. "Sniffing Out Science Fiction." *Christianity Today* 20 (February 27, 1976): 18–20.

May, Stephen. "Salvation, Culture and Science Fiction." *Christ in Our Place: The Humanity of God for the Reconciliation of the World: Essays Presented to Professor James Torrance*. Princeton Theological Monograph Series. Ed. Trevor A. Hart and Daniel Thimell, no. 25, 329–44. Allison Park, Pa.: Pickwick Publications, 1989.

Molnar, Thomas. *Utopia: The Perennial Heresy*. New York: Sheed and Ward, 1967.

Nwazota, Kristina. "Black Writers Bring a Different Perspective to Sci-Fi." *Black Issues Book Review* 4, no. 1 (January–February 2002): 29–30.

Pohl, Frederik. "The Politics of Prophecy," *Extrapolation* 34, no. 3 (Fall 1993): 199–208.

Richter, Peyton E., ed. *Utopia/Dystopia?* Cambridge, Mass.: Schenkman Publishing Co., 1975.

Rohrlich, Ruby, and Elaine Hoffman Baruch, eds. *Women in Search of Utopia: Mavericks and Mythmakers*. New York: Schocken Books, 1984.

Rossman, Parker. "The Theology of Imagination: Science, Science Fiction, and Religion." *Witness* 72 (October 1989): 12–13, 22.

Russ, Joanna. "What Can a Heroine Do? Or Why Women Can't Write." In *Images of Women in Fiction*, ed. Susan Comillon, 3–20. Bowling Green, Ohio: Bowling Green University Popular Press, 1972.

Soyinka, Wole. *Myth, Literature and the African World*. Cambridge: Cambridge University Press, 1976.

Thomas, Sheree, ed. *Dark Matter: A Century of Speculative Fiction from the African Diaspora*. New York: Warner, 2001.

Wellbank, Joseph H. "Utopia and the Constraints of Justice." In *Utopia/Dystopia?* ed. Peyton E. Richter, 31–41. Cambridge, Mass.: Schenkman Publishing Co., 1975.

Williams, Preston N. "Black Perspectives on Utopia." In *Utopia/Dystopia?* ed. Peyton E. Richter, 45–56. Cambridge, Mass.: Schenkman Publishing Co., 1975.

Wu, Dingbo. "Understanding Utopian Literature." *Extrapolation* 34, no. 3 (Fall 1993): 230–44.

GSN Ministries

The Associated Press. "Some Black Ministers Openly Welcome Gays, Lesbians into Their Flocks," *The Oak Ridger Online.* September 20, 2002. http://www.oakridger.com/stories/092002/rel_0920020034.html

Bagby, Dyana. "'We Are the Rest of the Bird': Lesbian Christians Gather in Atlanta to Reinforce Coming Out and Not Ceding Church Leadership to the 'Right Wing,'" *Southern Voice,* July 6, 2007. http://www.sovo.com/2007/7-6/locallife/feature/7168.cfm (accessed December 2, 2007).

Barry, Ellen. "Atlanta 'Legacy' March Troubles Rights Leaders; King's Daughter in Anti-gay Marriage Protest," *San Francisco Chronicle,* December 11, 2004. http://www.sfgate.com/cgi-bin/article.cgi?f=/c/a/2004/12/11/MNGPDAAEJ01.DTL (accessed December 2, 2007).

Davis, Herndon L. "God, Gays and the Black Church: Keeping the Faith within the Black Community, Part II." *Special to AOL Black Voices,* September 2, 2005. http://www.blackvoices.com/black_lifestyle/soul_spirit_headlines_features/canvas/feature_article/_a/god-gays-and-the-black-church-keeping/20050825153809990001 (accessed December 2, 2007).

Douglas-Brown, Laura. "Ex-gay Tools: After a Summer Filled with Headline-Grabbing 'Former' Homosexuals, Atlanta Activists Take Matters—and Video Cameras—into Their Own Hands," *The Southern Voice,* August 31, 2007. http://www.southernvoice.com/2007/8-31/view/editorial/7402.cfm (accessed December 2, 2007).

Exodus International. "Who We Are." Exodus International. http://exodus.to/content/category/6/24/57/ (accessed December 10, 2007).

"Ex-gay Charlene Cothran on 700 Club," http://www.youtube.com/watch?v=yionQDpwTlM (accessed June 19, 2008).

Foster, D. L. "The Question Is . . .: Black gays and Ex-gays alike look to church leaders for answers that may never come." *Witness Freedom Ministries: Leading the Way out of Homosexuality and into Holiness,* April 9, 2002. http://www.witnessfortheworld.org/cm27.html (accessed December 2, 2007).

Griffin, Horace L. *Their Own Receive Them Not: African American Gays and Lesbians in Black Churches.* Cleveland: Pilgrim Press, 2006.

Jarvie, Jenny. "Black Clergy Tackle Homophobia: A Summit Put On by a Gay Rights Group Gathers Christian Leaders to Explore Attitudes Toward Homosexuality," *Los Angeles Times,* January 21, 2006. http://www.aegis.org/news/Lt/2006/LT060107.html (accessed December 2, 2007).

Jubera, Drew. "Atlanta: A Bug for Black Gays," *Atlanta Journal-Constitution,* February 22, 2004. http://gay_blog.blogspot.com/2004/02/atlanta-hub-for-black-gays.html (accessed December 2, 2007).

Martin, Kathi Elaine. "Wounded and Healed in the House of a Friend: The Faith Experience of African American Gay and Lesbian Persons." D. Min. diss., Columbia Theological Seminary, 2001.

_____. "Flip the Script," Sermon. *Day 1: A Ministry of the Alliance of Christian Media*, November 16, 2003. http://www.day1.net/print.php5?tid=42 (accessed December 2, 2007).

_____. "I am Everyday People," *Preach 2 Me*, September 2007. http://www .preach2me.com/p_women.htm (accessed December 2, 2007).

_____. "Mysterious Visitations," Sermon. *Day 1: A Ministry of the Alliance of Christian Media*, December 21 2003. http://www.day1.net/print.php5?tid=37 (accessed December 2, 2007).

HRC Media. "A GLBTQ Response to 700 Club and Charlene Cothran." August 15, 2007. 8 min; 21 sec. http://www.youtube.com/watch?v=m4LI0VmKZrw &feature=related (accessed December 2, 2007).

Human Rights Campaign, "A GLBT Community Response to 700 Club and Charlene Cothran." *FemmeNoir: A WebPortal for Women of Color.* August 21. 2007. http://www.femmenoir.net/new/content/view/504/9/ (accessed December 2, 2007).

Sommerville, Elliott. "A Talk with Rev. Kathi Martin: Body, Soul & Spirit," *Together in Love: Celebrating Committed Same Gender Relationships in the African American Community.* http://www.togetherinlove.org/zine/articles/full/a_talk_ with_rev_kathi_martin/ (accessed December 2, 2007).

United Church of Christ. "Statement of Faith of the United Church of Christ." United Church of Christ. http://www.ucc.org/beliefs/statement-of-faith.html (accessed December 2, 2007).

Warch, William. *The New Thought Christian.* Marina del Rey, Calif.: Christian Living Publishing, 1977.

Index

CPSIA information can be obtained
at www.ICGtesting.com
Printed in the USA
BVHW041852301221
625248BV00013B/905